MACROMEDIA® FIREWORKS® MX

Digital Imaging for the Web

Upper Saddle River, NJ 07458

Library of Congress Cataloging-in-Publication Data

Macromedia Fireworks MX: Digital Imaging for the Web/Against The Clock
   p. cm. — (Against The Clock Series)
Includes Index
ISBN 0-13-112639-3
1. Computer Graphics. 2. Web Sites—Design. 3. Fireworks (Computer File)
I. Against the Clock (Firm) II. Series
T385 M3215 2003
006.6'869—dc21

2002038139

Editor-in-Chief: Stephen Helba
Director of Production and Manufacturing: Bruce Johnson
Executive Editor: Elizabeth Sugg
Managing Editor – Editorial: Judy Casillo
Editorial Assistant: Cyrenne Bolt de Freitas
Managing Editor – Production: Mary Carnis
Production Editor: Denise Brown
Composition: Erika Kendra
Design Director: Cheryl Asherman
Design Coordinator: Christopher Weigand
Cover Design: LaFortezza Design Group, Inc.
Icon Design: James Braun
Prepress: Photoengraving, Inc.
Printer/Binder: Press of Ohio

Pearson Education LTD.
Pearson Education Australia PTY, Limited
Pearson Education Singapore, Pte. Ltd
Pearson Education North Asia Ltd
Pearson Education Canada, Ltd
Pearson Educación de Mexico, S.A. de C.V.
Pearson Education – Japan
Pearson Education Malaysia, Pte. Ltd
Pearson Education, Upper Saddle River, New Jersey

10   9   8   7   6   5   4   3   2   1

Prentice
Hall

ISBN 0-13-112639-3

Contents

GETTING STARTED   1
   Platform...1
   Prerequisites..1
   Resource Files..1
   The Work In Progress Folder 1
   Locating Files...2
   File Naming Conventions 2
   Fonts 3
   Key Commands 3
   System Requirements for Fireworks....................................4

1. IMAGE BASICS   7
   Types of Images...8
      Raster Images 8
      Vector Images 14
   File Formats..15
      The World Wide Web 15
   Creating a New Document 17
   Basic Exporting 19
      Color Palettes 20

2. FIREWORKS BASICS   25
   Exploring the Fireworks Interface......................................26
      Main Pop-Up Menu 27
      Document Window 27
      Panels Property Overview 30
      Properties Panel 34
      Tools Panel Overview 35
      Views 39
   Working with Your Document...41
      Using Rulers 41
      Using Guides 42
      Using Grids 44
      Using the Zoom and Hand Tools..............................48

3. VECTOR SHAPES   53
   Creating Basic Shapes 54
      Rectangle 55
      Rounded Rectangle 55
      Ellipse..56
      Polygon..56
   Creating Complex Shapes 60
      Using the Line Tool 60
      Using the Pen Tool 61
      Using the Vector Path Tool 65
      Using the Redraw Path Tool 66
   GIF Export Options 67
      Color Depth 67
      Transparency..69
      Matte...70
      Interlacing 71

4. Vector Object Properties and Manipulation   73

Vector Object Properties and Manipulation 74
Selecting Vectors...74
    Pointer Tool 74
    Select Behind Tool 74
Subselection Tool 75
Working with Strokes 75
    Stroke Size 75
    Edge 76
    Stroke Categories 76
    Stroke Position 77
    Texture 78
Working with Fills 78
    Solid 79
    Patterns 80
    Textures 81
    Gradients 81
Live Effects and Styles...85
    Bevel and Emboss..87
    Shadow and Glow 87
    Styles 88
Manipulating Shapes 93
    Transforming Shapes...94
    Combining Paths 98
    Altering Paths 102
    Shape Adjustment Tools 105
    Knife Tool 108
Vector Shape Organization 110
    Aligning Shapes 110
    Group/Ungroup..113
    Understanding Stacking Order...114

5. Working with Text   117

Using the Text Tool...118
Setting Text Properties 119
    General 119
    Typographic Settings...122
    Paragraph Settings 126
    Text Block Settings..128
    Anti-Aliasing Levels 129
    Opacity 130
    Blending Modes 130
Spell Checker 133
Converting Text to Paths..135
Attaching Text to Paths 136
    Orientation on a Path 137
    Position of Text..137
    Detaching Text from a Path 138
    Direction of Text...138

Free-Form Project #1   141

Review #1   142

6. WORKING WITH BITMAPS   *143*

Importing Bitmaps...*144*
    Importing to Fireworks...*144*
    Roundtrip Feature with Adobe Photoshop 6 or 7 ....*146*
Making Selections...*148*
    Marquee Tool...*148*
    Oval Marquee Tool...*148*
    Lasso Tool..*148*
    Polygon Lasso Tool...*148*
    Magic Wand Tool...*152*
    Crop Tool...*152*
    Eyedropper Tool..*153*
Adding to/Subtracting from Selections *154*
Drawing Tools *155*
    Brush Tool..*155*
    Pencil Tool...*155*
    Eraser Tool...*155*
    Paint Bucket Tool..*156*
    Gradient Tool..*156*
Optimization Techniques for JPEGs...*160*
    Quality..*161*
    Smoothing...*161*
    Progressive..*161*

7. IMAGE RETOUCHING   *165*

Image Adjustments..*166*
    Adjust Color *166*
    Blur *171*
    Other..*172*
    Eye Candy 4000 LE..*174*
    Alien Skin Splat LE..*176*
Applying Touch-Ups..*176*
    Tools..*177*
Creating a Vignette *189*

8. LAYERS   *193*

Layers Panel Overview..*194*
    Creating Layers *194*
    Duplicating Layers...*194*
    Naming a Layer..*195*
    Selecting a Layer...*195*
    Organizing Layers..*196*
    Viewing/Hiding Layers...*196*
    Collapse/Expand a Layer...*197*
    Locking a Layer..*197*
    Single-Layer Editing *198*
    Deleting a Layer...*198*
Layer Properties...*198*
    Blending Modes...*198*
    Opacity..*200*
Web Layer...*200*

9. ANIMATED GIFS
207

Libraries..*208*
Frame-by-Frame Animation *208*
    Frames Panel...*209*
Onion Skinning..*210*
Animation Using Tweening *213*
    Creating Graphic Symbols...*213*
    Animating Symbols...*214*
    Making an Object Fade In or Fade Out *216*
    Exporting Animated GIFs...*217*
Export Options..*218*
    Options Tab...*218*
    File Tab *218*
    Animation Tab..*219*

10. IMAGE MAPS AND SLICES
221

Creating Hotspots..*222*
Setting Hotspot Properties..*225*
Exporting HTML *226*
Viewing the Web Page...*230*
Exporting to Other Applications..*232*
    Exporting Dreamweaver Library Items. *233*
Understanding Slices..*234*
    Setting Slice Options *238*
    Rollovers in Slices *240*
    Previewing a Web Page and Updating HTML...........*241*

11. NAVIGATION BARS AND POP-UP MENUS
245

Button Editor..*246*
    Creating a Button Symbol *246*
    Understanding Button States..*248*
    Setting Button States and Properties *249*
    Making Use of Button Symbols *252*
    Editing and Updating Buttons *254*
Creating a Disjointed Rollover..*255*
Pop-Up Menus *260*
    Content Tab *260*
    Appearance Tab *261*
    Advanced Tab..*262*
    Position Tab *263*

FREE-FORM PROJECT #2
267

REVIEW #2
268

PROJECTS:

Project A: Globe Illustration (Complete after Chapter 5)..............................*A-1*
Project B: Image Retouching Advertisement (Complete after Chapter 7).....*B-1*
Project C: Animated Banner (Complete after Chapter 9)............................*C-1*
Project D: The Cable Store Web Site (Complete after Chapter 11) *D-1*

GLOSSARY

INDEX

Purpose

The Against The Clock series has been developed specifically for those involved in the field of computer arts, and now — animation, video, and multimedia production. Many of our readers are already involved in the industry in advertising and printing, television production, multimedia, and in the world of Web design. Others are just now preparing for a career within these professions.

This series provides you with the necessary skills to work in these fast-paced, exciting, and rapidly expanding fields. While many people feel that they can simply purchase a computer and the appropriate software, and begin designing and producing high-quality presentations, the real world of high-quality printed and Web communications requires a far more serious commitment.

The Series

The applications presented in the Against The Clock series stand out as the programs of choice in professional computer-arts environments.

We use a modular design for the Against The Clock series, allowing you to mix and match the drawing, imaging, and page-layout applications that exactly suit your specific needs.

Titles available in the Against The Clock series include:

Macintosh: Basic Operations
Windows: Basic Operations
Adobe Illustrator: Introduction and Advanced Digital Illustration
Macromedia FreeHand: Digital Illustration
Adobe InDesign: Introduction and Advanced Electronic Documents
Adobe PageMaker: Creating Electronic Documents
QuarkXPress: Introduction and Advanced Electronic Documents
Microsoft Publisher: Creating Electronic Mechanicals
Microsoft PowerPoint: Presentation Graphics with Impact
Microsoft FrontPage: Creating and Designing Web Pages
HTML & XHTML: Creating Web Pages
Procreate Painter: A Digital Approach to Natural Art Media
Adobe Photoshop: Introduction and Advanced Digital Images
Adobe Premiere: Digital Video Editing
Adobe After Effects: Motion Graphics and Visual Effects
Macromedia Director: Creating Powerful Multimedia
Macromedia Fireworks: Digital Imaging for the Web
Macromedia Flash: Animating for the Web
Macromedia Dreamweaver: Creating Web Pages
Preflight and File Preparation
TrapWise and PressWise: Digital Trapping and Imposition

You will see a number of icons in the sidebars; each has a standard meaning. Pay close attention to the sidebar notes where you will find valuable comments that will help you throughout this book, and in the everyday use of your computer. The standard icons are:

The Hand-on-mouse icon indicates a hands-on activity — either a short exercise or a complete project. The complete projects are located at the back of the book, in sequence from Project A through D.

The Pencil icon indicates a comment from an experienced operator or trainer. Whenever you see this icon, you'll find corresponding sidebar text that augments the subject being discussed at the time.

The Key icon is used to identify keyboard equivalents to menu or dialog box options. Using a key command is often faster than selecting a menu option with the mouse. Experienced operators often mix the use of keyboard equivalents and menu/dialog box selections to arrive at their optimum speed of execution.

The Caution icon indicates a potential problem or difficulty. For instance, a certain technique might lead to pages that prove difficult to output. In other cases, there might be something that a program cannot easily accomplish, so we present a workaround.

If you are a Windows user, be sure to refer to the corresponding text or images whenever you see this Windows icon. Although there isn't a great deal of difference between using these applications on a Macintosh and using them on a Windows-based system, there are certain instances where there's enough of a difference for us to comment.

For the Reader

On the Resource CD-ROM, you will find a complete set of Against The Clock (ATC) fonts, as well as a collection of data files used to construct the various exercises and projects. The ATC fonts are solely for use while you are working through the Against The Clock materials.

A variety of resource files are included. These files, necessary to complete both the exercises and projects, may be found in the RF_Fireworks folder on the Resource CD-ROM.

For the Trainer

The Trainer's materials, available online, includes various testing and presentation materials in addition to the files that are supplied with this book.

- **Overhead presentation materials** are provided and follow along with the book. These presentations are prepared using Microsoft PowerPoint, and are provided in both native PowerPoint format and Acrobat Portable Document Format (PDF).

- **Extra free-form projects** are provided and may be used to extend the training session, or they may be used to test the reader's progress.

- **Test questions and answers** are included on the Trainer's CD-ROM. These questions may be modified and/or reorganized.

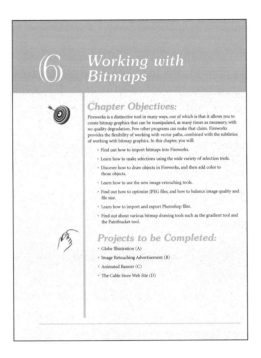

Chapter openers *provide the reader with specific objectives.*

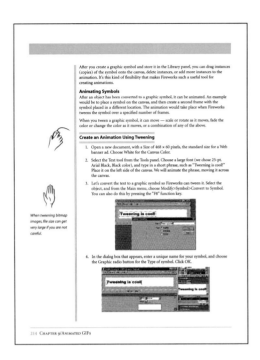

Sidebars and hands-on activities *supplement concepts presented throughout the book.*

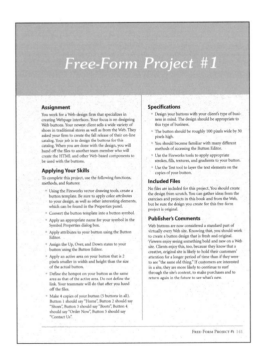

Free-form projects *allow readers to use their imagination and new skills to satisfy a typical client's needs.*

Step-by-step projects *result in finished artwork — with an emphasis on proper file-construction methods.*

Project A: Globe Illustration

One of the most simple — and most important — tasks you will perform using Fireworks is to create vector objects with the Rectangle, Rounded Rectangle, and Ellipse vector tools. Equally important are the abilities to create custom paths with the Pen tool, and to apply various stroke and fill attributes to the objects you create. This project enables you to practice each of these skills as you create a relatively complex vector graphic that could be used for a variety of purposes.

Project B: Image Retouching Advertisement

The ability to manipulate text elements and bitmap images are key elements in every designer's repertoire. In this project, you'll learn to effectively make use of several bitmap-editing tools: the Dodge, Burn, Blur, Sharpen, Smudge, and Rubber Stamp tools. You will find the Rubber Stamp tool to be particularly helpful during development of this image-retouching project. You will also discover a number of advanced design techniques to add to your personal bag of artistic tricks.

Project C: Animated Banner

Animated GIFs can add a sophisticated twist to even the simplest Web site. You'll create a standard-sized animated banner, paying special attention to the limited file size that is allocated for the design. You will also gain valuable experience working with tweening and Live Effects while learning to optimize animated GIF files. The tools you will use in this exercise can be applied to many other design elements — they are not limited to animated banners. Your new skills can ultimately be put to use on a variety of eye-catching animated elements that will entice viewers to remain on your site and browse around for more interesting visual effects.

Project D: The Cable Store Web Site

In this project, you will have the opportunity to make use of a large portion of the information presented in this book. You will create a Web interface for a fictional on-line cable retailer. After creating the site, you will be well versed in everything from button creation, image slicing, interactivity, and exporting, to bitmap and vector manipulation, Live Effects, and the creation of simple and disjointed rollovers. You will also become more aware of general stylistic guidelines for creating Web sites for the average user, as well as how those guidelines can be handled within the Fireworks environment.

I would like to give special thanks to the writers, illustrators, editors, and others who have worked long and hard to complete the Against The Clock series. And special thanks to Gavin Nagatomo, Project Manager, for his hard work and dedication to our team.

Special thanks to Dean Bagley for his invaluable contributions.

A big thank you to the dedicated teaching professionals whose comments and expertise contributed to the success of these products, including Doris Anton of Wichita Area Technical College, Anthony Sheppard of Trident Technical College, Chad Dresbach of Winthrop University, and Carol Buser of Owens Community College.

Thanks to Laurel Nelson-Cucchiara, copy editor, and final link in the chain of production, for her help in making sure that we all said what we meant to say.

A big thanks to Denise Brown and Kerry Reardon for their guidance, patience, and attention to detail.

— *Ellenn Behoriam, November 2002*

Our History

Against The Clock (ATC) was founded in 1990 as a part of Lanman Systems Group, one of the nation's leading systems integration and training firms. The company specialized in developing custom training materials for such clients as L.L. Bean, *The New England Journal of Medicine*, the Smithsonian, the National Education Association, *Air & Space Magazine*, Publishers Clearing House, the National Wildlife Society, Home Shopping Network, and many others. The integration firm was among the most highly respected in the graphic-arts industry.

To a great degree, the success of Lanman Systems Group can be attributed to the thousands of pages of course materials developed at the company's demanding client sites. Throughout the rapid growth of Lanman Systems Group, founder and general manager Ellenn Behoriam developed the expertise necessary to manage technical experts, content providers, writers, editors, illustrators, designers, layout artists, proofreaders, and the rest of the chain of professionals required to develop structured and highly effective training materials.

Following the sale of the Lanman Companies to World Color, one of the nation's largest commercial printers, Ellenn embarked on a project to develop a new library of hands-on training materials engineered specifically for the professional graphic artist. A large part of this effort is finding and working with talented professional artists, authors, and educators from around the country.

The result is the ATC training library.

About the Authors

Caroline Cooper studied anthropology at the University in Florida while honing her skills in Web development, graphic design, video production, and various other technical topics. Caroline is currently working as a project manager for the Florida-based Web development and marketing firm, 352 Media Group.

Michelle Lee is an associate professor of software applications technology at Santa Fe Community College in Gainesville, Florida. She teaches office skills, graphic applications, and multimedia. Michelle has a Master of Arts degree in Educational Technology and a Bachelor of Arts degree in Education.

Chris Collins teaches graphics applications and Web design at the International Academy of Design and Technology in Tampa, Florida. A graduate of the University of Kentucky, Chris also directs an independent studio where he provides database-driven Web design, Flash animation, and Illustrator and Photoshop services to clients around the globe. He is also an accomplished artist, specializing in hyperrealism with an airbrush.

Jamey Weare is a professor at Santa Fe Community College where he has taught courses in Web design and Web development since 1999. He lives and works in Gainesville, Florida. Jamey is working toward a BS/BA degree in computer science at the University of Florida.

Getting Started

Platform

The Against The Clock (ATC) series is designed for both the Macintosh and Windows platforms. On the Macintosh, Fireworks MX requires Mac OS 9.1, 9.2, or Mac OS X 10.1.3. The Windows version runs on Windows 98, Windows NT, Windows 2000, Windows ME, and Windows XP.

Prerequisites

This book is based on the assumption that you have a basic understanding of how to use your computer. This includes standard dialog boxes with OK and Cancel buttons. In the case of many exercises, it is assumed that you will click the OK button to change the values of a dialog box according to the instructions provided.

You should know how to use your mouse to point and click, as well as to drag items around the screen. You should be able to resize and arrange windows on your desktop to maximize your available workspace. You should know how to access pop-up menus, and understand how check boxes and radio buttons work. Lastly, you should know how to create, open, and save files. It is also helpful to have a firm understanding of how your operating system organizes files and folders, and how to navigate your way around them.

The CD-ROM and Initial Setup Considerations

Before you begin using your Against The Clock book, you must set up your system to have access to the various files and tools to complete your lessons.

Resource Files

This book comes complete with a collection of resource files, which are an integral part of the learning experience. They are used throughout the book to help you construct increasingly complex elements. These building blocks should be available for practice and study sessions to allow you to experience and complete the exercises and project assignments smoothly, spending a minimum amount of time looking for the various required components.

All the files that you need to complete the exercises and projects in this book are located on your Resource CD-ROM, and contained in a folder named **RF_Fireworks**. It's best to copy the entire folder onto your hard drive — if you have 100 megabytes or more of available space. If not, you can work directly from the Resource CD-ROM.

The Work In Progress Folder

Before you begin working on the exercises or projects in this book, you should create a folder called **Work_In_Progress**, either on your hard drive or on a removable disk. As you work through the steps in the exercises, you will be directed to save your work in this folder.

If your time is limited, you can stop at a logical point in an exercise or project, save the file, and later return to the point at which you stopped. In some cases, the exercises in this book build upon work that you have already completed. You will need to open a file from your **Work_In_Progress** folder and continue working on the same file.

Locating Files

Files that you need to open are indicated by a different typeface (for example, "Open the file named **clouds.png**."). The location of the file also appears in the special typeface (for example, "Open **chairs.png** from your **Work_In_Progress** folder.").

When you are directed to save a file with a specific name, the name appears in quotation marks (for example, "Save the file as "blends_practice.png" to your **Work_In_Progress** folder.").

In most cases, resource files are located in the **RF_Fireworks** folder, while exercises and projects on which you continue to work are located in your **Work_In_Progress** folder. We repeat these directions frequently in the early chapters, and add reminders in sidebars in the later chapters. If a file is in a location other than these two folders, the path is indicated in the exercise or project (for example, "Open the file from the **Images** folder, found inside your **RF_Fireworks** folder.").

File Naming Conventions

Files on the Resource CD-ROM are named according to the Against The Clock naming convention to facilitate cross-platform compatibility. Words are separated by an underscore, and all file names include a lowercase three-letter extension that you see as part of the file name.

When your Windows system is first configured, the views are normally set to a default that hides these extensions. This means that you might have a dozen different files named "myfile," all of which may have been generated by different applications. This can become very confusing.

On a Windows-based system, you can change this view. Double-click "My Computer" (the icon on your desktop). From the View menu, select Folder Options. From Folder Options, select the View tab. Within the Files and Folders folder is a check box for Hide File Extensions for Known File Types. When this is unchecked, you can see the extensions.

It's easier to know what you're looking at if file extensions are visible. While this is a personal choice, we strongly recommend viewing the file extensions.

Fireworks is unique among programs in the sense that it's capable of opening dozens of different file formats — and equally adept at exporting images in multiple formats. The native Fireworks extension is .png. Other file types include .tif (TIFF), .jpg (JPEG), .gif (GIF), and others, depending on the intended use of your images. You should always add the proper extension to your file names.

Fonts

You must install the ATC fonts from the Resource CD-ROM to ensure that your exercises and projects work as described in the book. These fonts are provided on the Resource CD-ROM in the ATC Fonts folder. Specific instructions for installing fonts are provided in the documentation that came with your computer.

If you choose not to install the fonts, you will receive a warning dialog when you attempt to open a document containing the ATC typefaces.

Key Commands

There are three keys that are generally used as modifier keys — they don't do anything by themselves when pressed, but they either perform some action or type a special character when pressed with another key or keys.

We frequently note keyboard shortcuts that can be used in Firewoks MX. A slash character indicates that the key commands differ for Macintosh and Windows systems; the Macintosh commands are listed first, and then the Windows commands. If you see the command "Command/Control-P", for example, Macintosh users would press the Command key and Windows users would press the Control key; both would then press the "P" key.

The Command/Control key is used with another key to perform a specific function. When combined with the "S" key, it saves your work. When combined with the "O" key, it opens a file; with the "P" key, it prints the file. In addition to these functions, which work with most Macintosh and Windows programs, the Command/Control key can be combined with other keys to control specific Fireworks functions. At times it is also used in combination with the Shift and/or Option/Alt keys.

The Option/Alt key, another modifier key, is often used in conjunction with other keys to access special typographic characters. On a Windows system, the Alt key is used with the number keys on the numeric keypad. For example, Alt-0149 produces a bullet (•) character. The Alt key can be confusing because not only do you use it to type special characters, you can also use it to control program and operating system functions. Pressing Alt-F4, for example, closes programs or windows, depending on which is active. On a Macintosh computer, the Option key is often used with a letter key to type a special character.

The Shift key is the third modifier key. While you're familiar with using this key to type uppercase letters and the symbols on the tops of the number keys, it's also used with Command/Control and Option/Alt in a number of contexts.

System Requirements for Fireworks MX

Macintosh:

- Power Macintosh G3 Processor
- Mac OS 9.1 or higher, or OS X 10.1 and higher
- 64 MB of free available system RAM (128 MB recommended)
- 800 × 600, 8-bit (256 colors) color display or better
- 80 MB of available disk space
- Adobe Type Manager Version 4 or later for use with Type 1 fonts (OS 9.x)
- CD-ROM drive

Windows:

- 300MHz Intel Pentium II Processor
- Windows 98 SE, Windows Me, Windows NT® 4 (Service Pack 6), Windows 2000 or Windows XP
- 64 MB of free available system RAM (128 MB recommended)
- 800 × 600, 8-bit (256 colors) color display or better
- 80 MB of available disk space
- Adobe Type Manager Version 4 or later for use with Type 1 fonts
- CD-ROM drive

Introduction

This Against The Clock book was designed and developed to help you learn how to use Macromedia's Fireworks MX graphics application. Before going further, however, we should take a moment to discuss the "MX" strategy, and what it means to you as a developer, designer, artist, communicator, or information systems professional.

The near-universal adoption by professional designers and developers of Dreamweaver, Flash, Fireworks, and other Macromedia products (such as their server and development tools) underscores the power and effectiveness of the company's products. The MX strategy offers seamless integration of functions and features, providing customized workspaces that are shared between programs. The result is a complete solution for the timely and cost-effective creation of rich user experiences — a dramatic departure from static, non-engaging Web pages.

Fireworks MX is engineered from the ground up to allow you to develop sophisticated navigation graphics — and can automatically generate the requisite JavaScript to make them work on your Web pages. You can even generate graphics automatically, either from XML-compliant data sets or from existing sites. Once you've created your images, Fireworks can export them — in the perfect format — to a wide range of MX and third-party applications.

Another aspect of integration with other applications is the "round-trip" functionality incorporated into both Macromedia's Dreamweaver MX and Microsoft's very popular FrontPage. While developing your sites and individual pages, the round-trip feature allows you to quickly and effectively edit existing graphics and create new ones in Fireworks — without first needing to exit the other application or use the operating system to launch Fireworks MX.

While many other applications only provide editing functions for raster or bitmapped graphics, Fireworks MX's integrated working environment automatically adjusts itself to the type of object you're working on at the time.

For bitmap editing, the program offers the industry-standard functionality you've come to expect from other robust applications, including Dodge, Burn, Blur, Sharpen, and Smudge tools. When working with vector artwork, you can create, cut, copy, paste, intersect, and easily edit shapes. This extends to type elements as well; on-screen, live-text editing allows you to work with type elements from the workspace. Panels and tool sets adjust automatically, so you never have to spend time activating the correct interface element; Fireworks MX does the work for you.

In short, Fireworks MX is one of the industry's most powerful and functional tools for developing interactive and compelling graphic objects for Web sites and interactive applications. Whether you need to create a menu system, a simple navigational object, rollovers, slide shows, splash screens, backgrounds, or informational graphics, you'll find the tools you need in the Fireworks MX environment.

We hope you enjoy this Against The Clock book, and find it useful in your efforts to learn the features and functions of Fireworks MX. As is the case with any powerful application, there's no replacement for practice and experience. The lessons, discussions, hands-on activities, projects, and free-form assignments will certainly provide necessary experience, and help to make Fireworks MX one of your favorite Web-development tools.

1 Image Basics

Chapter Objectives:

In this first chapter of the book, we will explore the basic elements of image development. A solid understanding of images will serve as a guide while you create and modify graphics. It is much easier to understand Fireworks when you know how images are created and can identify their components. We will also examine the two basic types of images — raster and vector — as well as the types of images that are used on the World Wide Web. In this chapter, you will:

- Review the two basic image types.

- Learn the anatomy of a raster image.

- Find out which file formats are used on the Web.

- Explore various color palettes.

- Create a new document.

- Examine the basics of exporting images.

Projects to be Completed:

- Globe Illustration (A)

- Image Retouching Advertisement (B)

- Animated Banner (C)

- The Cable Store Web Site (D)

Image Basics

Computer-based graphics is a relatively new form of art when compared with other types, such as watercolor, oil painting, and charcoal drawing, to name a few. Despite this relative infancy, computer graphics can be fairly complex; this does not mean, however, that graphics programs must be difficult to use. To the contrary, Macromedia's Fireworks MX is intuitive and easy to learn, even for novice graphic designers.

Although Fireworks can be used for a variety of purposes, its strength lies in its versatility, allowing the artist to prepare a wide assortment of graphics for use on the Web. A good foundation in image basics is essential when preparing graphics for the Web or print, which means you must have a working understanding of the file types (vector and raster) used for both of these distribution methods. Most graphic applications allow you to work with either raster or vector images; but Fireworks MX is equally effective with both. Other raster- and vector-editing programs don't provide as much in-depth functionality as Fireworks.

Fireworks combines the strengths of both types of graphics in one application. The program allows you to work with vector tools for one portion of your project, and then seamlessly switch to raster tools for another segment of the piece.

In this chapter of the book, we will cover the basics of working with images; the rest of the book presents techniques you can use with Fireworks to create both raster and vector images.

Types of Images

Digital images can be found in a wide variety of formats, but there are two basic types of images — raster and vector. Most graphics applications focus on one type of image. Typically, applications that work with raster images are referred to as "paint" programs. Popular paint programs include Adobe Photoshop and PaintShop Pro. Applications that primarily focus on vector graphics are labeled "drawing" programs. Adobe Illustrator and Macromedia FreeHand are standard drawing applications. As we said earlier, Fireworks supports both types of images, making it a very versatile program. Each type of image has a particular purpose for which it excels, and each has its drawbacks. Interestingly, the weaknesses of one image type are the strengths of the other. Let's review the basics of each type of graphic.

Raster Images

Raster images, first created in the mid-1970s, are best suited for photographic images because they are capable of showing gradations of color. This type of image is constructed of many tiny squares called *pixels*, a shortened term for "picture element." Pixels provide a very good way to display transition of color. If we put together a series of pixels that range from black to red, we would see a smooth gradient that began as black and gradually changed to red; however, if we looked at the individual pixels of the gradient, each pixel would be a different color. It is helpful to think of raster images as mosaics — up close, you can see the individual pieces, but from a distance, the image appears to be smooth.

Fireworks requires a change of "mode" when you switch from one type of graphic to another. Fireworks MX automatically changes this mode for you, depending on the tool you are using at a given time.

Raster images are what we see when we look at images on the Web.

Raster images are not restricted to photographs; we also use them for static images on the Web.

To avoid pixelation problems, we always create an image in the largest size we'll need and keep an original, unaltered copy at that size.

Raster images are also referred to as "bitmap images."

The strength of raster images lies not only in displaying good transition of color, but in replicating photographic images. All scanned images and pictures from digital cameras are raster images; exact detail and accuracy when reproducing photographs can only be accomplished with the raster image type.

The individual columns of pixels can be seen in the above image due to the high magnification.

The same gradient is viewed at 100% magnification, showing a seamless blend of color from black to red.

The downside of raster images is their inability to scale. The images are made up of a certain number of pixels. When the images are enlarged (scaled up), the pixels appear larger, making them much more noticeable. When we can see the individual pixels in an image, we say it is "pixelated" or that it has the "jaggies." Often, diagonal lines and curves are the first noticeable areas of a pixelated image.

This is an example of a badly pixelated image.

Although not always the case, raster image file sizes can be quite large. Many factors come into play with the file size of an image, such as the file type and compression method used, as well as the attributes of the image itself. In order for a raster image to display accurately, the properties of the image must be set correctly. The four properties that comprise the basic anatomy of raster images include pixels, resolution, bit depth, and a color look-up table. Let's take an in-depth look at the anatomy of raster images.

Pixels

The term pixel is an abbreviation for picture element. A pixel is also referred to as a "dot," even though it is usually presented as a square. Each pixel in an image is a single color. When pixels are organized into rows and columns, they create an identifiable image. Individual pixels are not identifiable in an image until magnified or pixelated.

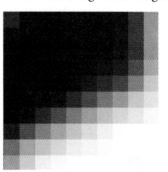

An image was enlarged to 3200% to make the individual pixels visible.

Since pixels are square-shaped, it can be difficult to create smooth curves and diagonal lines. To make curves and diagonals appear smooth, extra pixels are often added in a process called anti-aliasing. *Anti-aliasing* adds pixels to the edges of an image to blend the foreground color with the background color. We will discuss anti-aliasing again in relation to text in Chapter 5 of this book.

The zoomed-in image on the top has no anti-aliasing. The image on the bottom is anti-aliased.

Resolution

The term "resolution" can be used in many ways. Most commonly, resolution simply refers to the size of an image. When we refer to an image's size, we always identify the number of pixels in its width by the number of pixels in its height, or w × h.

When pixel-based images are enlarged, the individual pixels become noticeable, but often times will just become blurry.

Don't get the size of an image confused with its file size. The two are related, but they refer to different properties of the image.

In order to determine the number of pixels needed to construct an image, you must think of the area of the image. An image that is 800 × 600 pixels is made of 480,000 pixels. If the image were reduced to half its size (resolution), it would be 400 × 300 pixels, or 120,000 pixels. Even though half of the original 480,000 pixels is 240,000, only 120,000 pixels are required when the image is halved. Therefore, reducing the image size (resolution) can greatly decrease the image's overall file size.

A computer monitor's resolution refers to the size of the overall image displayed. The more pixels used, the smaller each pixel appears and the smaller the images appear on the screen. We use more pixels in order to fit more images on the screen. A 1024 × 768-screen resolution allows more area to be displayed than a 800 × 600-screen resolution.

If you need to change your Windows-based monitor resolution, you can right-click on the desktop and select Settings from the Properties menu. You can change to any of the available resolutions in the Screen Resolution section of the window. To change the monitor resolution on a Macintosh system, select Monitors from the Control panel in the Apple menu. The resolution is set in the Resolution section of the window. On both systems, you can choose whether or not to keep the new setting.

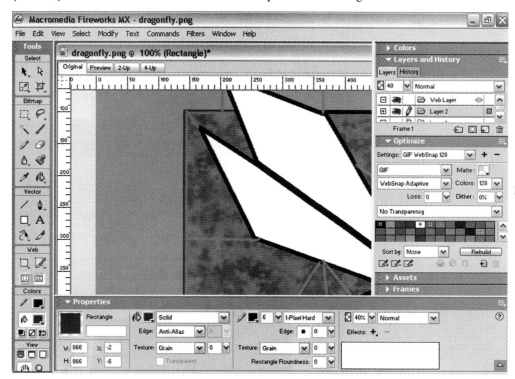

The above image is from an 800 × 600-monitor resolution.

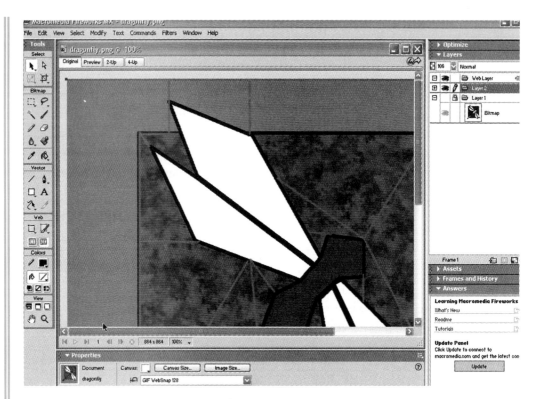

The above image is from a 1024 × 768-monitor resolution.

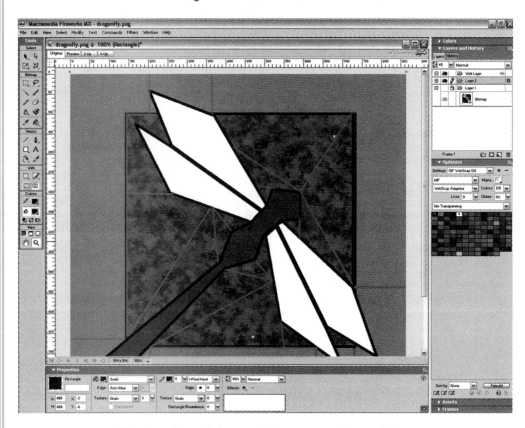

The above image is from a 1280 × 1024-monitor resolution.

Bit Depth

"Bit depth" is also known as "color depth." The *bit depth* of an image defines the number of possible colors that can be stored in each pixel. In a 1-bit image, each pixel can display one of two colors, usually black or white. The chart below shows how bit depth determines the number of colors for a raster image:

1 bit	2^1	2 colors
2 bit	2^2	4 colors
4 bit	2^4	16 colors
8 bit	2^8	256 colors
16 bit	2^{16}	65,536 colors
24 bit	2^{24}	16,777,216 colors

Notice that the number of possible colors in an image is determined by raising the number 2 to the power of the bit depth. Not all raster images have the same bit depths. For example, a GIF image, one of the two basic Web formats, can only store 8 bits of color information, or 256 colors.

The left image has 8-bit depth (256 colors). The right image has 4-bit depth (16 colors).

The human eye can distinguish about 7,000,000 colors. Our eyes cannot see much color difference between a 24-bit image and one with more than 24 bits.

The left image has 2-bit depth (4 colors). The right image has 1-bit depth (2 colors).

Color Look-Up Table

A *color look-up table* (CLUT) is simply the palette of colors used in an image. We often refer to the CLUT as a "palette." If the CLUT of an image is changed, the image might appear totally different from the original. Common color palettes are discussed later in this chapter.

Vector Images

Vector images are the simplest form of computer graphics. They are comprised of points and connecting lines (line segments). Mathematical equations are used to define the points and lines instead of the grid of pixels used for raster images; because of this, vector images can be enlarged and reduced (scaled) with no loss of quality, allowing for multiple image sizes.

Above is a vector image that was enlarged, displaying no degradation in quality.

Most clip art and computer-drawn cartoon images are vector shapes, or at least begin as vector shapes. Sometimes we refer to vector images as cartoon-like since vector images cannot be used to produce a photo-realistic image. Even though vector images are typically comprised of regions of solid color and basic gradients, that doesn't mean they cannot be used to create complex images. Vector lines and shapes can be stacked, and properties can be applied to the stroke (outline) and fill (the interior of a shape) to create very intricate and appealing images.

The above image is an example of a complex vector graphic.

One drawback of using vector images is that they are not as widely supported by software applications or on the Web as raster images. An image is oftentimes drawn as a vector image and then "rasterized." This process converts the vector image into a raster image. Once a vector is rasterized, it no longer possesses the properties of a vector image. Most importantly, it loses the ability to be resized (scaled) without loss of quality.

Since vector images are made from mathematical equations, they do not require as much stored information as raster images; therefore, the file size is typically smaller than a similar pixel-based image. Vector images are sometimes favored because of this factor. For example, Flash files primarily use vector images since file size is an important consideration on the Web (smaller files download faster).

File Formats

File formats are compression schemes. *Lossless* file formats compress the information in an image without losing quality. *Lossy* file formats lose image quality during the compression process. File formats also determine the bit depth available in an image. It is beyond the scope of this book to explore all the different types of graphical file formats, as an entire book could be written on this subject alone.

The World Wide Web

In its infancy, the Internet did not display graphics of any kind; it was strictly a text-based medium. In 1994, the first graphical browser, Mosaic, was introduced; since then, navigating the Internet and the World Wide Web has become an often visually stimulating experience. The two basic image types displayed by Web browsers are the GIF and JPEG file formats. Many other file types can be viewed with helper applications and plug-ins. Certain file types are better for one purpose than another. Let's review the common graphic file formats used on the Web.

PNG

Firework's native file type is the PNG format, which is pronounced "ping," and stands for Portable Network Graphic. This file type was created with the intention that it would replace the GIF file format. PNG files are not yet as widely supported on the Web as the more common GIF and JPEG files, but can be viewed through the use of a helper application, such as the QuickTime Player, depending on the program's settings. Additionally, new versions of several of the most widely-used browsers are capable of displaying the PNG file type within a web page with no helper application. That same capacity can unfortunately not be attributed to all browsers, however. Knowing this, we must convert native Fireworks files to a Web-supported format during the export process.

PNG files are lossless, which means that image quality is not sacrificed when the files are compressed. This file type is an excellent choice for almost any type of image, and can support from 1 to 24 bits of color information. The PNG format supports advanced transparency options, but does not allow for animation.

GIF

The Graphic Interchange Format, or GIF, is also a lossless compression method. The GIF format is a good choice for images that have solid blocks of color and a limited number of colors, found in line art and simple logos. An 8-bit file format, GIFs are only capable of displaying 256 colors, so we would rarely use the GIF file format for a photographic image. Instead, many graphics that begin as vectors end up as GIFs after they are rasterized. When a GIF is created, we can choose between several color palettes, which are described later in this chapter. The GIF format also supports transparency, allowing any color behind the image to show through its transparent portions.

GIF would be an appropriate file format for this image.

In the late 1980s, CompuServe specifically created the GIF file format for use over a network.

Animated GIFs

Animated GIF files are used for simple animations. In Chapter 9, we will learn how to create simple animations in Fireworks and export them as animated GIF files. Animated GIF files store frame information and display the frames in succession at a specified time.

Millions of animated GIFs are available for viewing on the Web. Many are inappropriate for a professional Web site, but are often appropriate for advertisement because of their eye-catching qualities. Over time, animated GIFs have received the reputation of being annoyances; this is mainly due to overuse. If used correctly — and subtly — animated GIFs can be effective for attracting the viewer's attention.

Interlaced GIFs

Interlaced GIFs are not as common as they once were. In the early days of the graphic Web, they were used when dial-up connections were extremely slow — as compared with today's high-speed standards. An *Interlaced GIF* downloads one bit at a time, allowing the viewer to see part of the image before the entire file is downloaded. Typically, images must be completely downloaded before being displayed. Using Interlaced GIFs is still useful today if you have a very large GIF image on the Web. Rather than wait for the image to appear, the viewer gets a sneak preview and can make an educated decision on whether to wait for the download or stop it.

JPEGs

JPEG stands for the Joint Photographic Experts Group. This file format is a lossy compression method with a bit depth of 24. Although lossy, a JPEG can display about 16,777,216 colors, compared to the 256 colors in a GIF. This makes JPEG the format of choice when exporting a photographic image for viewing on the Web.

Most digital cameras take photographs in the JPEG format.

When creating a JPEG image, the compression quality must be selected. The lower the quality, the smaller the file size, and vice versa. We will learn more about these settings when exporting to the JPEG format later in the book.

Photographic images are perfect for the JPEG file format.

Flash

Flash, another Macromedia product, is a multimedia application used primarily for the Web. Flash animates vector images extremely well and quite easily. To view Flash files on the Web, the Flash Player is required. For more information on how to create Flash content, please refer to Macromedia Flash MX: Rich Media for the Web in the Against The Clock Series.

Creating a New Document

To create a new document, a few properties of the document must be identified, including the width, height, resolution, and desired background or canvas color. We suggest you enter the highest possible resolution when creating a new document. All of the options can be changed during development, but decreasing the resolution is always easier than attempting to increase it.

In an earlier discussion, we learned that the word "resolution" has several meanings. Image resolution refers to the image width multiplied by its height. Resolution in pixels per inch (ppi) refers to how many pixels are displayed in one inch. On screen, we typically see either 72 or 96 ppi, depending on the computer system being used. Images meant for viewing only on the computer screen are typically saved at 72 ppi. Images created for print should be saved at a higher ppi, no less than 300 ppi. Printers can print more dots per inch (dpi) than monitors can display pixels per inch.

Selecting the File>New command creates a new Fireworks document. A window appears as shown in the image below. The desired settings can be entered in this window, all of which can be changed at any time using the Modify menu. Even though the settings can be changed, it is always a good idea to begin with the correct settings for the desired output method.

Although it can be done, increasing the resolution of a document often results in poor quality.

We often refer to pixels per inch as dots per inch, or dpi, borrowing the term from the print world.

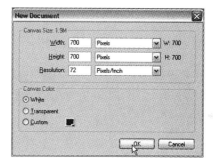

Create a New Web Document

1. Launch Fireworks MX. Once the program is open, select New from the File menu (File>New).

2. In the New Document dialog box, set the canvas Width to 400, and select Pixels in the pop-up menu to the right of the Width field. Set the canvas Height to 500, and select Pixels from the pop-up menu. Set the canvas Resolution to 72, and ensure that Pixels/Inch is selected in the pop-up menu.

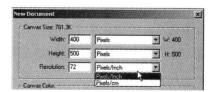

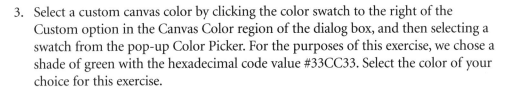

Hexidecimal codes are often used in Web development to denote specific colors, much as RGB values, CMYK values or Pantone colors might be used for graphics in print or other mediums. A "hex code" value is always written as six characters preceded by a pound (#) symbol.

3. Select a custom canvas color by clicking the color swatch to the right of the Custom option in the Canvas Color region of the dialog box, and then selecting a swatch from the pop-up Color Picker. For the purposes of this exercise, we chose a shade of green with the hexadecimal code value #33CC33. Select the color of your choice for this exercise.

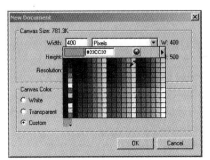

4. Click OK to create the new document.

5. Close the document without saving.

Create a New Print Document

1. From the File menu, select New to create a new Fireworks document.

2. In the New Document dialog box, set the canvas Width to 400, and select Pixels in the pop-up menu to the right of the Width field. Set the canvas Height to 500, and select Pixels from the pop-up menu. Set the canvas Resolution to 300, and ensure that Pixels/Inch is selected in the pop-up menu.

3. Set the Canvas Color to White by clicking the first radio button in the list.

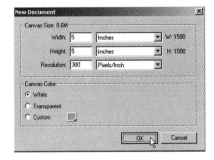

The major differences in creating a document for the Web versus a document for print are the resolution and background color.

If your image is going to be used on the Web, you need a small file size to allow for faster download. GIF and JPEG are the basic file formats for the Web because they do a good job of compressing file size.

4. Click OK to create the new document.

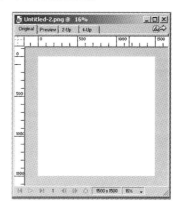

5. Close the document without saving.

Basic Exporting

Many times, you will need a Web-ready document, or you might need to use another file format for a specific image. Knowing which file type is appropriate for each specific purpose is only part of the export process. After selecting the file type for an image, choices specific to each file type must be *optimized* (tweaked) for the perfect balance between decreased file size and acceptable image quality. Once a file has been optimized, it can be exported to the intended file. Let's explore the many ways to export an image.

Quick Export

The Quick Export button in the upper-right corner of the Document window is used when an image is going to be sent to one of the listed applications, including Macromedia Dreamweaver, Flash, FreeHand, or Director, or other applications including Adobe Photoshop, Illustrator, GoLive, or Microsoft FrontPage. Fireworks can export a document with settings specific for the receiving application. For example, when exporting a Web page image to Dreamweaver, Fireworks includes Dreamweaver HTML. Dreamweaver can also utilize library items and other advanced features if the document is exported as a Dreamweaver file. These features are discussed in more depth later in this book.

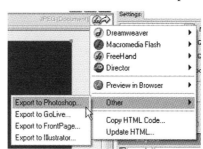

The Optimize Panel

To simply export the image to create a GIF or JPEG, you can optimize the file using the Optimize panel located in the Window menu. You can experiment with the options until the image quality and decreased file size are balanced at the desired level. After the options have been set, exporting is as simple as choosing Export from the File menu. The file should be saved in the original file format for future editing purposes, since an exported file is not as easily edited as the original.

Optimizing a file can be subjective. Practicing the process improves your ability to optimize files.

The Optimize panel.

The Export Window

The two basic file types we will export are the GIF and JPEG formats. As we have already discussed, the GIF format is used for cartoon-like images that contain blocks of solid color, while the JPEG format is used for images that are photo-realistic or have gradation of colors. The GIF options include color palettes, number of colors, dithering, transparency, and animation. The JPEG options include image quality and smoothing. These options aren't the only ones that are available — they are basic options. We will continue to learn more about the export options throughout this book.

Most images require different export options due to differences in image qualities and characteristics.

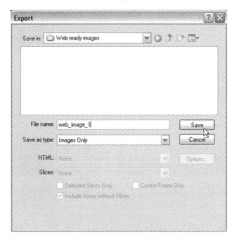

The Export window.

Color Palettes

In computer graphics, a *color palette* can be thought of as an artist's palette. The color palette holds all the colors that can be used in the graphic. The particular colors and number of available colors depends on the file format, bit depth, and type of palette you choose. The color palette is also known as an image's color look-up table. The color palette is chosen during the optimization process.

The color palettes mentioned here are mainly used when exporting an image for use on the Web in the GIF format, which is capable of displaying only 256 colors.

The color chips that first appear when changing stroke and fill colors are the 216 Web-safe colors.

You can choose from a number of color palettes, some more widely used than others. (We mention the more widely used palettes in this chapter.) Not all images use the following palettes. In fact, if an image type can display millions of colors, there is no need for a limited color palette. When you must ensure the colors in an image display exactly the same on every computer — such as in a corporate logo — a limited color palette should be used.

Web 216

On older computers, only 256 colors are used in the display. These 256 colors vary by 40 colors between the Windows and Macintosh platforms; but 216 colors remain constant from one platform to the other. If an image must display the same colors on older Macintosh and Windows machines, the Web 216 color palette ensures the colors are the same on both platforms. Only 216 colors are used to display the image. A limiting color palette such as the Web 216 palette would seriously degrade a photograph, or similar type of image, that could potentially contain thousands of colors or more.

The Web 216 palette is also known as the Web-safe color palette. Many designers do not limit themselves to this palette as they once did. Most computer users now have monitors capable of displaying thousands and often millions of colors. Those who have older machines with a limited color display usually understand that they are sacrificing image quality while using such a display.

The Optimize panel with Web 216 color palette selected.

WebSnap 256

The WebSnap 256 palette is based on 256 colors. If a color occurs in the image that is not in the palette, but is close to a Web-safe color, the color switches or "snaps" to that Web-safe color. After the colors that are close to Web-safe colors have been changed, the other non-Web-safe colors are added to the image. This process creates an image that is primarily Web-safe without having to completely conform to the limited 216 Web-safe color palette.

The Optimize panel with WebSnap and 256 selected. The colors do not display with these settings.

WebSnap 128

This palette works the same as the WebSnap 256 palette, but the colors in the image are limited to 128.

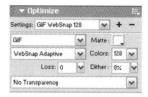

The Optimize panel with WebSnap and 128 selected.

Adaptive 256

The adaptive color palette switches all colors in an image to the closest match of the 256 colors available in the Web browser.

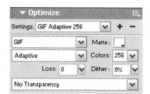

Optimize panel with Adaptive 256 selected.

Custom

The Custom color palette allows you to select the colors you want to include in the image without the constraint of Firework's pre-defined colors. Custom color swatches are saved in files with the extension .act, and are helpful when precise custom colors must be used in a series of images.

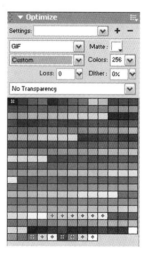

The Optimize panel with Custom selected.

Export a JPEG

1. From the File menu, select Open. In the Open dialog box, navigate to the **RF_Fireworks** folder, and select **cat.png**. Click Open to open the file.

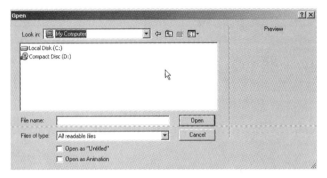

The Open dialog box.

2. If the Optimize panel is not displayed, select Window>Optimize to display it. JPEG – Better Quality should be the default setting in the Optimize panel.

3. With the Preview tab selected at the top of the main Document window, experiment with changing the Optimize format to GIF Web 216, GIF WebSnap 256, GIF WebSnap 128, and GIF Adaptive 256. Note the dramatic difference in image quality and file size when the GIF format is used, rather than the more appropriate JPEG format.

4. After examining the effects of GIF optimization on the photograph, return the Optimize settings to reflect JPEG – Better Quality. Feel free to experiment with other JPEG Optimize options in order to find the best balance between file size and image quality as reflected in the main Document window.

5. Once a satisfactory balance of image characteristics has been reached — we chose JPEG at 67%, which results in a 14K file — select Export from the File menu.

6. In the Export dialog box, navigate to your **Work_In_Progress** folder. After ensuring the Images Only option is selected, click the Save button to export the file.

7. After exporting the file, close the document without saving.

Export a GIF

1. From the File menu, select Open. Locate the **RF_Fireworks** folder, and open the **circles.png** file.

2. In the Optimize panel, GIF WebSnap 256 should be selected by default. Feel free to experiment with all of the options in the Optimize panel to achieve the best balance between file size and image quality. You can monitor these image characteristics by selecting the Preview, 2-Up, and 4-Up tabs at the top of the Document window. Any changes you make in the Optimize panel are reflected in the main Document window.

The 2-up and 4-up views can be very useful in comparing the visual effects of multiple optimization settings. using these views is not necessary for this chapter, but you may find out more about their use at the beginning of Chapter 2 if you wish to experiment.

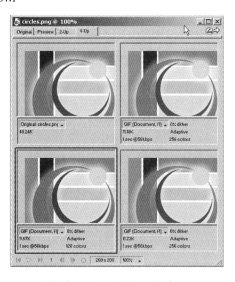

Circles.png Preview window.

3. The image is relatively small, so file size and image quality do not differ very much. The file size and image quality of the GIF WebSnap Adaptive 128 optimization option, however, make this choice slightly better than other standard options. Once you have selected your final GIF optimization setting, select Export from the File menu. In the Export dialog box, navigate to your **Work_In_Progress** folder.

4. Since we are exporting only a simple image, the only available Export options are the File name field and the Save as type pop-up menu. Make sure Save as type is set to Images Only. Click Save to export the file to your **Work_In_Progress** folder.

5. After exporting the GIF file, close the file without saving your changes.

Chapter Summary

In this chapter, you increased your understanding of the basics of images, and you learned about the two basic types of images — raster and vector. The anatomy of raster images was presented, and you learned what file types are used on the Web. You created a new document and learned how to export images to different file formats. You then learned all about the basic color palettes used to develop images destined for the Web.

2 *Fireworks Basics*

Chapter Objectives:

Working in a new program can be a bit intimidating. If you've never used a graphics application before, the interface could look as though it were written in a foreign language — but don't allow that to steer you away from the exciting world of computer graphics. Reviewing what is included in an application is the first step toward understanding the virtually limitless possibilities of what you can produce with it.

In this chapter, we explore Fireworks' interface. Understanding how the interface works, and knowing the location of each tool — as well as its function — is essential to an efficient workflow. We explore the fundamental options that are necessary to create and modify a Fireworks document. In this chapter we will:

- Explore the Fireworks MX interface.

- Learn how to change the view of individual panels.

- Review the function of the available tools.

- Learn which tools are used to lay out an image.

Projects to be Completed:

- Globe Illustration (A)

- Image Retouching Advertisement (B)

- Animated Banner (C)

- The Cable Store Web Site (D)

Fireworks Basics

Fireworks includes a wealth of tools and options that allow for a wide variety of editing possibilities. These tools and options can be daunting, especially if you've never used a graphics application before. If you have used another graphics application, such as Adobe Photoshop, you are probably already familiar with many of the available options you will find in Fireworks.

Fireworks MX has an exciting new look and feel that is consistent with other Macromedia MX products. If you know Macromedia Flash MX and/or Dreamweaver MX, you'll most likely be quite comfortable using Fireworks. The programs are built for different purposes, but the interfaces are similar.

As with all the MX products, the Fireworks interface is well designed. Tools that perform similar functions are grouped together, and options for the tools are easily accessible. The time you spend searching for options will be reduced once you understand the flow of the interface. As with any application, knowing where tools and options are located speeds up your workflow.

Learning the basics of an application while creating a project is a very time-consuming process. In fact, if you don't know where tools and options are located, more time will be spent looking for buttons and menus than developing the project. In this chapter, we will learn the basics of Fireworks MX, including the interface, panels, tools, and options, all of which assist in the image-layout process.

Exploring the Fireworks Interface

The Macromedia MX products have a new look and feel geared toward better accessibility of the options and tools. Learning one of the MX applications makes it much easier to learn any of the other applications in the family of products. If you already know Flash or Dreamweaver, you already know a great deal about how to navigate the Fireworks interface. The work area, Properties panel, and other panels all have a similar setup.

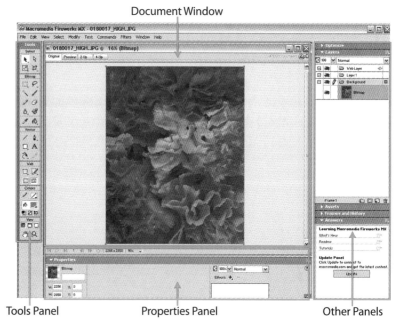

The default Fireworks interface.

The Fireworks interface is similar to the other Macromedia MX products, but it is tailored to the needs of creating and editing graphics, specifically those meant for the Web.

Macromedia uses the term "panel" while other applications often use the term "palette" to describe the small windows within the application that provide options and information.

Main Pop-Up Menu

Pop-up menus are standard in most software programs. Fireworks includes ten pop-up menus that contain many of the options necessary for image editing. Menus aren't as convenient as the easily accessible panels and tools. Below is a review of the basic items included in each menu:

File   Edit   View   Select   Modify   Text   Commands   Filters   Window   Help

- **File**. This menu includes many often-used commands, including Open, Save, Import, Export, Preview in Browser, Print, and more.

- **Edit**. This menu includes Undo, Redo, Cut, Copy, Paste, Find and Replace, Crop, Preferences, and more.

- **View**. A menu that includes Zoom In, Zoom Out, Magnification, Rulers, Grid, Guides, Slice Guides, and more.

- **Select**. Use this menu when you want to Select All, Deselect, Select Inverse, use any of the Marquee selection options, Save Bitmap Selection, and more.

- **Modify**. This menu includes Canvas, Flatten Layers, Transform, Arrange, Align, Combine Paths, Align Paths, and more.

- **Text**. A menu that includes commands for Font, Size, Style, Align, Attach to Path, Convert to Paths, Check Spelling, and more.

- **Commands**. Use this menu when you want to choose Manage Saved Commands, Manage Extensions, Run Script, or examine lists of commands that are grouped by topic.

- **Filters**. This menu includes the Repeat Filter, lists of Fireworks filters, and lists of third-party filters.

- **Window**. A menu that includes New Window, Toolbars, Tools, Properties, all of the available panels, the list of open windows, and more.

- **Help**. Use this menu when you want to access What's New and Using Fireworks, jump to Macromedia Web sites, and more.

Document Window

The Document window conveniently displays a variety of information about your file. The file name and current zoom percentage are displayed at the top left. The Original tab is used during image editing. The Preview, 2-Up, and 4-Up tabs are used for previewing the image with selected export options; we learned in Chapter 1 that these are the options used when converting a file to another file format.

Clicking the Preview tab shows the image as it appears with the current export options. Clicking the 2-Up tab shows the original image with a preview at the current export option setting. Clicking the 4-Up tab shows the original image with three possible export options. Being familiar with the options in the Document window helps you to quickly identify the properties of your documents as well as quickly compare optimization choices.

Top-left portion of the Document window.

The 4-Up view provides an excellent way to learn the differences between export options.

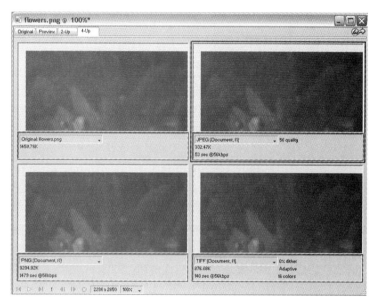

The image is previewed in the 4-Up view. We cover more exporting options in later chapters of this book.

The bottom left of the Document window displays controls that resemble VCR buttons. These controls are used during animation development. In-depth information on these controls and a discussion on animation are presented in Chapter 9.

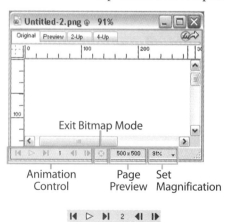

Animation controls.

Many people and applications refer to raster images as "bitmap images." The terms are used interchangeably in this book.

The Exit Bitmap Mode is an option that was used more in previous versions of Fireworks than it is in the MX version of the product. This button is used when you are working in Bitmap mode and you need to switch to Vector mode. You rarely need to use this option because Fireworks MX automatically switches modes to match the tool that is currently selected. If you find you are stuck in Bitmap mode, click this icon to change modes so you can successfully access and use the vector tools.

Exit Bitmap Mode icon.

The image's size is displayed next to the Exit Bitmap Mode icon. If the image size is double-clicked, Page Preview pops up, stating the width, height, and resolution of the image. This tool provides a quick reference of the size and resolution of an image.

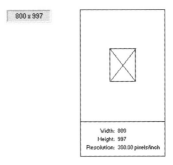

Image size and Page Preview.

In this case, resolution refers not to the width × height, but to the number of pixels per inch in the image.

The Set Magnification option is located to the right of the Page Preview option. This area displays the document's current magnification and allows the zoom to be changed. The zoom can be set anywhere from 6% to 6400%. Smaller magnifications, such as 12% and 25%, allow you to see more of your image because the image displays at a smaller size. The larger the magnification, the larger the image appears. Changing magnification does not actually change the image's size, only the way the image is displayed.

Set Magnification options.

Expand or collapse a panel by clicking the arrow to the left of the panel title.

Panels Property Overview

Panels include controls that help you edit an image, as well as control certain aspects of the image. The interface of the panels is new to the MX version of the product. Each panel can be expanded or contracted in order to manage valuable screen real estate. The panels can be dragged and grouped together to create a custom layout.

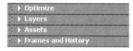
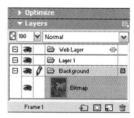

The panels in the left image are contracted. The Layers panel in the right image is expanded.

By default, most of the panels are separate and can be selected from the Window menu. You will find that customizing the panel layout helps you to quickly locate what you need. If you find yourself constantly expanding and contracting panels while you search for an option, you are probably spending too much time looking instead of working on your project. To avoid this problem, panels can be moved and grouped together to save valuable time and enhance your production workflow.

Below is a short description of the uses of some of the most common panels:

Throughout this text, the panels we show may be arranged differently than yours.

- **Color Mixer and Swatches**. This panel allows you to manage the color palette of the image. It also allows for color palette customization. The Color Mixer panel can be accessed by pressing the Shift-F9 keys. The Swatches panel can be accessed by pressing Command/Control-F9.

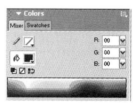

- **Layers**. The Layers panel helps you organize the layer structure of a document and allows for addition, deletion, and changes to the layers. Refer to Chapter 8 of this book for in-depth information on layers. The Layers panel can be accessed by pressing the F2 key. This panel is often grouped with the History panel.

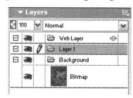

Your panels may be combined. In this section, we individually highlight the panels.

- **Frames**. This panel is used to create and edit frames for animation. The Frames panel can be accessed by pressing the Shift-F2 keys.

- **Info**. The Info panel displays information about the document and objects, as well as the location of the cursor. The Info panel can be accessed by pressing Shift-Option/Alt-F12.

- **Behaviors**. The Behaviors panel sets the controls for mouse movement when creating hotspots and slices for Web content. The Behaviors panel can be accessed by pressing the Shift-F3 keys.

- **History**. The History panel displays the recent steps taken during document development. It allows steps to be quickly undone and redone. It also allows a series of steps to be saved as a command to use again at a later time. The History panel can be accessed by pressing Shift-F10.

- **Optimize**. The Optimize panel contains the options for optimizing the export settings and color palette for the entire image or for individual slices. The Optimize panel can be accessed by pressing the F6 key.

- **Styles**. The Styles panel contains preset and custom combinations of object properties such as fill, stroke, and effects. The Styles panel can be accessed by pressing Shift-F11.

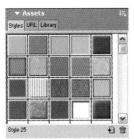

- **URL**. The URL panel contains a library of URLs to use with Web content. The URL panel can be accessed by pressing Shift-Option/Alt-F10.

- **Library**. The Library panel contains Graphic symbols, Button symbols, and Animation symbols. The Library panel can be accessed by pressing the F11 key.

- **Find and Replace**. The Find and Replace panel is used for finding and/or replacing text, font, color, URLs, and non-Web-safe colors. The Find and Replace panel can be accessed by pressing Command/Control-F.

- **Project Log**. The Project Log panel keeps track of changes made in files during Find and Replace or batch processing.

- **Answers**. The Answers panel displays help information. It also connects to Web sites for more information, and provides tutorials. The Answers panel can be accessed by pressing Option/Alt-F1.

Panels often offer the only way to change certain aspects of an image. We suggest you become familiar with the variety of panels and the function of each. Having a firm understanding of the panels saves time as you develop documents. Panels can be docked, undocked, customized, and reset at their defaults, helping you to be as efficient as possible at certain points in your workflow.

Docking/ Floating

Panels can either be docked on the right side of the screen or float around the screen. Docked panels are locked in one location; they do not float around the screen. If you find you are spending a lot of time moving floating panels around the screen in order to access your document, consider docking them to reveal valuable screen real estate.

Example of a floating panel.

Sometimes a floating panel is more easily accessed than a docked panel. If a panel is floating, it can be moved closer to a particular area of the screen where you are working. Clicking on a gripper (the area to the left of the expand/collapse arrow) of a docked panel allows a panel to become undocked and floating. Floating panels are docked when the gripper on the panel is clicked and dragged back to the other docked panels. You will most likely need to frequently dock and undock panels during document development.

Example of a floating panel being docked.

Throughout this book, the panels may have been customized to fit our needs. Do not worry if your panels are laid out in a different way.

Under the Command menu and Panel Layout sets, you see a variety of screen resolutions. These are the default panel layouts for each particular screen resolution.

Default/Customizing

A default layout is perfectly acceptable, but a custom layout can be more effective when certain panels are needed more often than others. Panels can be rearranged to suit any need. You can change the order of panels by clicking to the left of the expand/collapse arrow and dragging the panel to the desired location. It is recommended to group related panels in one location to allow for easier access. You can use the menu on the top right of the panel to select Group With when you want to group one panel with another. Please note that the panel menus change depending on which panel is chosen, but they all include the Group With option.

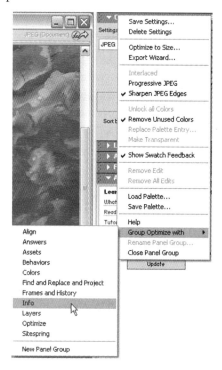

In the above image, the Optimize panel is being grouped with the Info panel.

Properties Panel

The Properties panel is new to Fireworks MX. The panel provides context-sensitive information and options, and is conveniently located at the bottom of the screen. You will undoubtedly find this panel to be an indispensable resource. At almost every point in the editing process, the Properties panel displays exactly what you need to know. If a tool is selected, its options are displayed in the Properties panel. If an object is selected on the canvas, its information and options are displayed in the same Properties panel. The Properties panel can be accessed by pressing Command/Control-F3.

The Properties panel with a new document opened.

The Properties panel can be resized to full size or half size using the triangle at the bottom right of the panel. When the Properties panel is at half size, it uses less screen space, but still displays vital information and options for the selected tools, objects, or the document itself. You can use the triangle at the top left of the panel to collapse it, just as you can with the other Fireworks panels. If a panel takes up too much screen space, consider collapsing it to provide more working space on your monitor. You can expand the panel when needed by clicking the triangle at the bottom of the panel.

The triangle on the left is used to contract the Properties panel.
The triangle on the right is used to expand the Properties panel.

The image on the top displays the triangle used to collapse the Properties panel.
The image on the bottom shows the Properties panel as it appears when contracted.

The Help icon provides context-sensitive help for whatever tool is currently selected. If no tool is selected, the Help icon allows you to quickly access the Fireworks Help files. Rather than becoming frustrated when you don't understand how to use a particular tool or function, we encourage you to take advantage of the Help files, which are very easy to use and understand.

The question mark in the Properties panel is used to quickly access Fireworks Help files.

Tools Panel Overview

Knowing the tools and where they are located can significantly enhance your workflow. Fireworks divides the tools into logical sections, including Select, Bitmap, Vector, Web, Colors, and View tools. Some tools have additional options hidden behind them. You know a tool has options if there is a small triangle at the bottom right of the tool's icon. Clicking and holding on the icon displays the hidden tools.

Below are images and definitions of all the tools in the Tools panel. The keyboard shortcut to access each of the tools is also included.

Select Tools

You can use the following tools to make general selections:

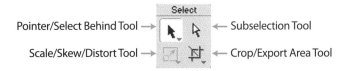

- **Pointer and Select Behind Tools.** Use these keys to make selections and move objects. The Pointer tool, accessed by pressing the "V" or "0" key, is used to select any object on the screen. The Select Behind tool allows you to select objects that are behind other objects.

If a tool has more than one shortcut key, either key can be used to access the tool.

- **Subselection Tool**. Use this tool, accessed by pressing the "A" or "1" (one) key, to select parts and points of an object, mask, or path.

- **Scale, Skew, and Distort Tools**. Use these tools, accessed by pressing the "Q" key, to change the size, proportions, and perspective of objects. The Scale tool sizes objects with the same aspect ratio — the width-to-height ratio is maintained. The Skew tool transforms an object along a plane. The Distort tool warps the perspective of an object from the corners.

- **Crop and Export Area Tools**. The Crop tool is used to eliminate areas of an image, making it smaller. The Export Area tool is used to export a portion of an image. These tools can be accessed by pressing the "C" key.

Bitmap Tools

The following tools are used with bitmaps:

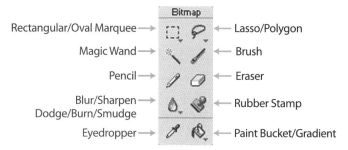

- **Marquee and Oval Marquee Tools**. Use these tools to make rectangular- or oval-shaped selections. Using the Shift key in combination with these tools constrains the selection to perfect squares and circles. Using the Option/Alt key in combination with these tools draws the selection from the middle. You can access these tools by pressing the "M" key.

- **Lasso and Polygon Lasso Tools**. Use these tools to make selections that are neither rectangular nor oval, but are irregular in shape. The Lasso tool allows you to draw a selection according to mouse movement. The Polygon Lasso tool allows you to draw selections according to the location of mouse clicks. You can access these tools by pressing the "L" key.

- **Magic Wand Tool**. Use this tool to make selections based on color. The tolerance, which is set in the Properties panel when this tool is selected, controls the amount of selection. The higher the tolerance, the more colors are selected, and vice versa. You can access this tool by pressing the "W" key.

- **Brush Tool**. Use this tool to paint pixels on an image. You can access this tool by pressing the "B" key.

- **Pencil Tool**. Use this tool to draw one-pixel lines. You can access this tool by pressing the "B" key.

- **Eraser Tool**. Use this tool to erase pixels. You can access this tool by pressing the "E" key.

- **Blur, Sharpen, Dodge, Burn, and Smudge Tools**. Use the Blur tool to make an area of the image appear blurry. Use the Sharpen tool to sharpen an area, making it look crisper. Use the Dodge tool to lighten parts of an image, and the Burn tool to darken areas. The Smudge tool is used to push colors in a particular direction. You can access these tools by pressing the "R" key.

- **Rubber Stamp Tool**. This tool is used to copy pixels from one place on the image to another. It is also known as the Clone tool. You can access this tool by pressing the "S" key.

- **Eyedropper Tool**. Use this tool to take a color in an image and set it as the current fill or stroke color, depending on which color box is selected. You can access this tool by pressing the "I" key.

- **Paint Bucket and Gradient Tools**. Both of these tools are used to fill areas with color. The Paint Bucket tool fills with one color, while the Gradient tool applies a range of colors. You can access these tools by pressing the "G" key.

Vector Tools

The following tools are used to create and edit vector objects:

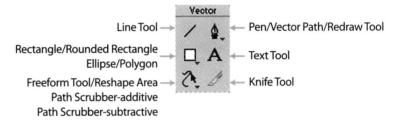

- **Line Tool**. Use the Line tool to draw straight lines in any direction. You can access this tool by pressing the "N" key.

- **Pen, Vector Path, and Redraw Path Tools**. The Pen tool is used to draw straight lines and smooth curves using points. The Vector Path tool is used to draw a vector path. It is similar to using the Brush tool. The Redraw Path tool is used to retain the properties of an existing path while adding to that path. You can access these tools by pressing the "P" key.

- **Rectangle, Rounded Rectangle, Ellipse, and Polygon Tools**. Each of these tools is used to draw its labeled shape. The Polygon tool can create a multi-sided shape, such as a pentagon or a star. Options for the type of polygon you draw, including the number of sides and points, are set in the Properties panel when you select the tool. The Rectangle, Rounded Rectangle, and Ellipse tools combined with the Shift key constrain the objects to perfect squares or circles. Each tool, excluding the Polygon tool, combined with the Option/Alt key, allows you to draw the object from the middle. The Polygon tool automatically draws the object from the middle. You can access these tools by pressing the "U" key.

- **Text Tool**. Use this tool to type text in an image or to edit existing text. You can access this tool by pressing the "T" key.

- **Freeform, Reshape Area, Path Scrubber (Additive), and Path Scrubber (Subtractive) Tools**. All of these tools are used to reshape existing paths. The Freeform tool is used to bend and smooth a selected path without affecting the path points. The Reshape Path tool is used to pull the selected path to a certain area. The Path Scrubber tools change the appearance of the selected path. You can access these tools by pressing the "O" key.

- **Knife Tool**. You can use this tool to cut a path into separate paths. You can access this tool by pressing the "Y" key.

Web Tools

The following tools are used to prepare Fireworks documents and objects for distribution on the Web:

- **Rectangle Hotspot, Circle Hotspot, and Polygon Hotspot Tools.** Each of these tools is used to define an area of an image as a hotspot link in the respective shape. You can access these tools by pressing the "J" key.

- **Slice and Polygon Slice Tools.** Both of these tools are used to slice an image into smaller images for use on the Web. You can access these tools by pressing the "K" key.

- **Show/Hide Slices and Hotspots Tools.** Use these tools to show/hide the slices and hotspots in an image. You can access these tools by pressing the "2" key.

Color Tools

You can use the following tools to define colors:

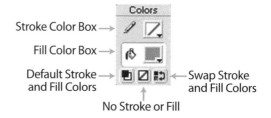

- **Stroke Color Box.** Check this box to change the color of the Pen, Pencil, or Brush tools in use, or of an existing object or path.

- **Fill Color Box.** Check this box to change the fill color used when creating new objects, or to change an existing object's color.

- **Set Default Stroke/Fill Colors.** Use this option to set the stroke to black and the fill to white. You can access this option by pressing the "D" key.

- **No Stroke or Fill.** Use this option to set either the stroke or fill to None, depending on which check box is selected.

- **Swap Stroke/Fill Colors.** Use this option to swap the colors used for the stroke and fill. You can access this option by pressing the "X" key.

Views and Options

You can use the following options to change the view of an image and the interface:

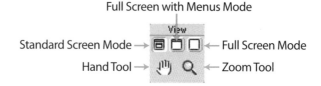

- **Standard Screen Mode.** This is the default view of an image in a window that can be sized. You can access this mode by pressing the "F" key.

- **Full-Screen with Menus Mode**. Use this view with an image in a maximized window with all menus and tools visible. You can access this mode by pressing the "F" key.

- **Full-Screen Mode**. Use this view with an image in a maximized window with a black background and invisible menus. You can access this mode by pressing the "F" key.

- **Hand Tool**. You can use this tool to pan around the document. You can access this tool by pressing the "H" key.

- **Zoom Tool**. Use this tool to zoom in or out of a specific area of an image. You can access this tool by pressing the "Z" key.

Views

Changing the view of a document allows you to isolate what is being created or edited. Fireworks offers three views, each of which is appropriate at a particular time. We suggest you become familiar with each view. Some designers have a strong preference for one view over the others. The icons to change the view are located in the View section of the Tools panel.

Standard Screen Mode

We typically work in this viewing mode. The image is in a separate window that can be resized. All of the tools are visible, as well as the main Menu bar.

Standard Screen mode.

Full-Screen with Menus Mode

In this mode, the image is in a maximized window that cannot be resized. The image fills more of the screen than the Standard Screen mode. All of the tools and panels are visible, but the Title bar of the application is not visible. This view eliminates some unused space, and more efficiently fills your screen.

Full-Screen with Menus mode.

Full-Screen Mode

In Full-Screen mode, the view appears the same as in Full-Screen with Menus mode, except the background of the screen turns to black and the pop-up menus disappear. This mode can be helpful when presenting an image to a client, or when the Menu bar gets in the way of the image and isn't needed.

Full-Screen mode.

Working with Your Document

Similar to most graphics applications, Fireworks provides tools such as rulers, guides, and grids to help you place and align objects relative to other objects and the document. In many applications, rulers, grid lines, and guides act as aids during document layout and development. If you have used these tools in other programs, you are probably already familiar with their usefulness:

- Rulers measure your document, and measure objects that are placed on the document.
- Guides are used for the layout and alignment of objects.
- Grids provide a series of evenly spaced horizontal and vertical lines that aid in a document's arrangement.

You could work with a Fireworks document and never use these tools, just as some traditional artists never use rulers and grids while creating watercolors, charcoals, or mosaics. The value of these tools becomes obvious when working on a particular layout that requires precise measurement or when aligning objects on a document. If you aren't concerned with exact layout or alignment of objects, you probably don't need to use these tools. You will most likely find, however, that they become necessary at some point in your experience with Fireworks.

Using Rulers

Rulers display along the top and left margins of an image and use pixels as their units of measurement. Documents are always measured by default from the top-left corner, but you can change the reference point of the rulers if necessary. Rulers help when placing objects and they allow guides to be added to the document.

Viewing Rulers

Rulers aren't typically visible when a document is created or opened. Rulers are toggled on and off by using the View>Rulers command. By default, the top and side rulers begin with 0 at the top left of the image. Sometimes it can be useful to measure from a point other than the top left. For example, the distance from one point to another may need to be measured. Instead of performing complicated mathematical calculations, you can simply change the ruler position to achieve the same result. To do this, you would click and drag the intersection of the two rulers to the desired position in the image. Double-clicking that intersection resets the rulers at the default position.

The ruler was repositioned in the above image.

Using Guides

Guides are very useful for setting up a document. You'll probably find you'll use guides for a variety of actions. We suggest using guides any time you have a certain order to your design, such as dividing the document into sections. For example, if you want to leave a margin around your document, setting guides can help isolate those margins from the rest of the document. We also use guides when isolating parts of an image into different areas. Guides can be used to slice an image for use on the Web, a technique we discuss later in this book.

Guides are only visible when you are editing a document. They are not exported with an optimized file. There is no need to turn off your guides in order to export an image. We always recommend that you keep a copy of the original .png file with the guides intact so you can edit the image at any time without having to reset the guides.

Creating Guides

Rulers must be visible in order to create guides. You can drag the mouse from the top ruler onto the image to create horizontal guides, and drag from the left ruler onto the image to create vertical guides. Multiple horizontal and vertical guides can be added by simply repeating this process.

Guides are being added to this image.

It is possible to fill up your document with guides, but this is not recommended. We suggest you think about the layout of your document and add guides only where you need them. Guides should not get in the way of image development, but rather they should assist in the layout process.

The images in this chapter were created on a Windows-based computer. A Macintosh computer displays "Windows Gamma" in the View menu instead of "Macintosh Gamma".

Viewing Guides

Guides can be quickly turned on and off without deleting them. The visibility of guides is toggled from the Show Guides option in the View menu. If you find your guides clouding the view of an image, it is best to toggle them off, and turn them on only when needed.

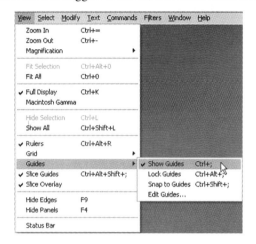

Manipulating Guides

Guides can be rearranged and deleted. You might find when you're working with a document that contains guides that you need to move the guides or delete extra guides. You can move guides by dragging them to a new location. Guides are removed from a document by dragging them off the edge of the document.

Editing Guides Properties

By default, the color of guides is bright green. If a document has the same or similar color in it, the guides could be very difficult to see. To change the color of the guides, you can select Guides>Edit Guides from the View menu. All guides can be cleared at one time by clicking the Clear All button in the Edit Guides dialog box.

The Edit Guides dialog box.

Locking Guides

The guides of a document can be locked so they aren't accidentally moved or changed in any way. Locking guides can also prevent the guides from getting in the way of editing an image. You can lock your guides using the Lock Guides command found in the View>Guides menu.

Objects snap to guides if the Snap to Guides option is selected. When objects snap, they act as though they have a magnetic attraction to the guide. Snapping can assist with exact placement of objects in a document. You can select Snap to Guides in the View>Guides menu to toggle this option. If you no longer want objects to snap to the guides, simply toggle the Snap to Guides option off.

Using Grids

Grids are different from guides, as they display vertical and horizontal lines in a fixed pattern on the document. Grids are similar to guides in that they help in aligning and arranging objects, but the lines on grids are not movable. Grids are intended to aid in the design process, and are not exported with the image.

The size of a grid can be changed, as well as whether or not objects snap to it. Depending on a particular image, you may or may not choose to use grids; not all documents benefit from their use. If you are trying to create an abstract look and feel, using a grid may cause your image to appear too organized and structured. Use your judgement on whether or not grids will enhance your project.

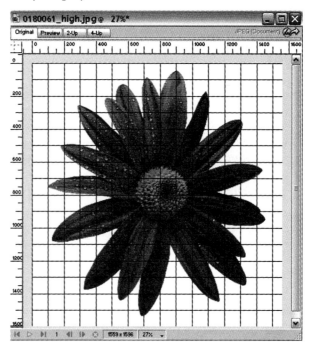

An image with the grid visible.

You can toggle a grid on and off by selecting Grid from the View menu. By default, the grid appears as black lines on the document. Properties such as the color and the size of the grid can be changed.

Editing Grid Properties

Grid properties, such as size and color, may need to be changed according to the requirements of a particular image. Grid properties are modified in the Edit Grid dialog box, accessed from the View menu. You can choose to edit grid properties several times, depending on your design requirements.

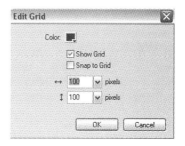

The Edit Grid dialog box.

We recommend that the Snap to Grid option only be used when working with a visible grid. The option can be turned on when the grid is invisible. This becomes an annoyance because it many times won't allow objects to go (and stay) exactly where you place them.

The grid color and the space between the vertical and horizontal lines can be modified. By default, grids are black; but another color may be more suitable for a particular image. Don't be afraid to experiment with grid line color choices.

You may also find that creating a grid that is not perfectly square is helpful for certain projects. The grid can be used in lieu of guides. Instead of spending time setting up guides, you might find it faster and easier to use a grid.

Snapping to Grid

In order to easily place and align objects, the Snap to Grid option can be turned on. When placing an object near a grid line or an intersection of grid lines, the object automatically snaps to the grid line(s). You can toggle this option from the View menu by choosing Grid>Snap to Grid.

Experiment with Guides

1. If it not already running, launch Fireworks. From the File menu, select Open. In the Open dialog box, navigate to the **RF_Fireworks** folder, and select **basic_gradient.png**. Click Open to open the file.

2. From the View menu, select Rulers to display the rulers if they are not already visible.

3. Click on the top ruler and drag your mouse onto the gradient. A green horizontal guide should appear where you release the mouse. Repeat the same procedure, pulling a few guides from the top and left rulers onto the document.

4. From the View menu, select Guides>Edit Guides. In the Guides dialog box, click the green swatch associated with the Color option; select a different color for the guides in the gradient document. Click OK.

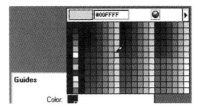

5. From the View menu, select Guides>Snap to Guides if it is not already selected.

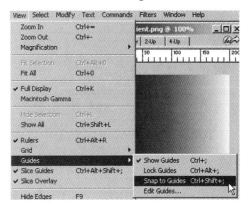

6. Select the Pointer tool from the Tools panel. With the Pointer tool, drag the gradient rectangle around the main document area. Notice how it snaps to the guides you positioned in the window.

7. Release the gradient rectangle. Hover your mouse over a portion of one of the guides on your document. When the cursor changes into two parallel lines with arrows pointing in opposite directions, drag the guide to reposition it.

8. Deselect the Snap to Guides option in the View>Guides menu. With the Pointer tool, drag the gradient rectangle around the document area again. Notice how the gradient no longer snaps to any of the guides you positioned on the main document area.

9. From the View menu, select Guides>Lock Guides. Attempt to hover your cursor over the guides you positioned — which was successful in Step 7. Notice that the guides are now locked, and cannot be moved.

10. After experimenting with the guides in the document, close the file without saving your changes.

Experiment with Grids

1. From the File menu, select Open. Navigate to the **RF_Fireworks** folder and open **checkered_grid.png**.

2. From the View menu, select Grid>Show Grid. Notice that the default black grid lines do not show up very well on the document's black background.

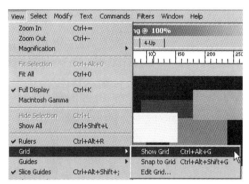

3. From the View menu, select Grid>Edit Grid. Click the Color swatch to display a palette of alternate grid color options. Choose a color that displays well on top of **checkered_grid.png**.

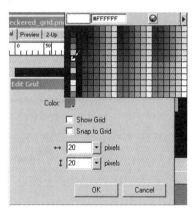

4. In the same dialog box, set the horizontal grid spacing (noted by a horizontal double-headed arrow) to 100. Set the vertical grid spacing (noted by a vertical double-headed arrow) to 50.

5. Still in the Edit Grid window, click the check box next to Snap to Grid. Click OK to apply the new grid options in the main Document window.

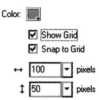

6. Use the overlaid grid and the Snap to Grid feature to arrange the colored rectangles in a checkered fashion.

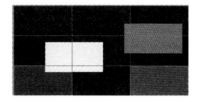

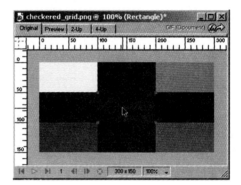

7. After experimenting with the grid and Snap to Grid feature, close the file without saving your changes.

Using the Zoom and Hand Tools

The size of an image can make it difficult to edit. Zooming in or out of the image can aid in getting a better perspective. The Hand tool is used in conjunction with the Zoom tool to navigate around an image.

Many people confuse the Zoom tool with resizing an image. When you use the Zoom tool, you do not change the size of an image, but rather you look at the image at a different magnification level. Using the Zoom tool is analogous to looking at a piece of paper through a magnifying glass. You aren't changing the size of the paper, but simple enlarging your view of the paper.

We recommend you use the Zoom tool often to increase the efficiency of your workflow.

Zooming In

Zooming in on an image is useful when you must edit a section that is very small or difficult to see. To zoom in to a particular section, select the Zoom tool from the Tools panel and click the area that needs to be enlarged. When the Zoom tool is selected, the cursor becomes a magnifying glass with a plus (+) sign symbol. When the Zoom tool is selected, each click of the mouse increases the magnification level. You can click and drag over an area with the Zoom tool to enlarge a specific area of an image. Additionally, you can zoom in to an image by pressing the Command/Control-+/= (plus/equals) keys.

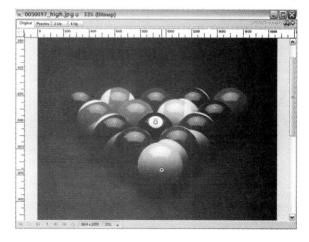

Zooming in with the Zoom tool.

Zooming Out

Zooming out is useful when an area of the image is too large to be fully displayed on the screen, or you have zoomed in too close to the image. The Option/Alt key must be pressed in combination with the Zoom tool to zoom out. The cursor becomes a magnifying glass with a minus (-) sign symbol. You can also zoom out of an image using the Command/Control--/__ (minus/underscore) keys. Zooming out moves an image farther away, so it becomes visibly smaller. Zooming out can sometimes allow the edge of the canvas to become visible. If you zoom in too close to an object, and it falls off the side of the canvas, zooming out is the easiest way to retrieve the object and bring it back into view on the canvas.

To quickly change the zoom of the image to 100%, double-click the Zoom tool.

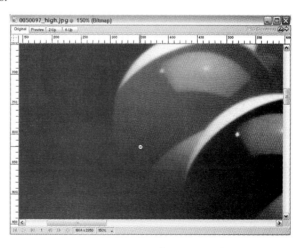

Zooming out with Zoom tool.

Hand Tool

The Hand tool is useful when an image has been enlarged and part of the image needs to be changed. It allows you to reposition the part of the image you need to view and edit. Often, a large image cannot be fully visible on the screen at 100% magnification. The Hand tool allows you to move the image around in order to see the hidden areas.

The Hand tool is also helpful when previewing an optimization setting. When multiple optimization options are visible in the 2-Up and 4-Up viewing modes, chances are the entire image won't be visible. In instances such as these, the Hand tool allows the hidden areas to be seen.

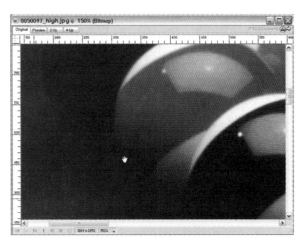

Using the Hand tool.

Use the Zoom and Hand Tools

1. From the File menu, select Open. In the Open dialog box, navigate to the **RF_Fireworks** folder, and select **circles.png**. Click Open to open the file.

2. Select the Zoom tool from the Tools panel. This tool is located near the bottom of the panel in the View section. You may need to turn off the grid if it is still turned on from the previous exercise. From the View menu, select Grid>Show Grid.

3. Click on the center of the document to zoom in.

4. Select the Hand tool from the Tools panel.

5. Click and hold on the main portion of the document to grab the image. Drag your mouse to the right, and then release the mouse button.

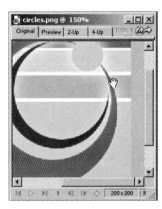

6. Select the Zoom tool again. Hold down the Option/Alt key. The cursor icon should now have a minus sign (-) rather than a plus sign (+) within the magnifying glass. Click on the main portion of the document to zoom out.

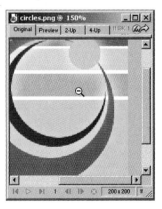

7. Experiment with the Zoom and Hand tools if you prefer, and then close the file without saving when you are done.

Chapter Summary

In this chapter, you explored the Fireworks interface. You created a new document and reviewed the basics of exporting. The Document window, Tools panel, Properties panel, and other panels were presented. The tools that aid in the layout and organization of an image were also discussed. In the next chapter, you will create images using the Fireworks tools and panels.

3 Vector Shapes

Chapter Objectives:

It can be a very easy process to draw vector shapes using Fireworks. Benefits of drawing with vector shapes include the ability to draw perfectly round or square shapes and alter existing shapes. The properties of vector shapes can also be easily changed — which is not quite so easy to do with raster images.

The basic tools for drawing vector shapes are introduced in this chapter. The basic export options for turning vector shapes into raster images for use on the Web are also discussed. In this chapter, you will:

- Learn how to draw basic vector shapes.
- Find out how to develop complex vector shapes.
- Discover how to export vector shapes to Web-ready images.

Projects to be Completed:

- Globe Illustration (A)
- Image Retouching Advertisement (B)
- Animated Banner (C)
- The Cable Store Web Site (D)

Vector Shapes

Fireworks is considered a versatile application because it allows you to simultaneously work with both raster and vector images, whereas most other graphics applications focus on either raster or vector images.

As you recall from Chapter 1, vector images are created from points that are connected by straight or curved lines. A simple vector shape can be made using a rectangular or elliptical shape. A more complex vector shape can be created using a variety of lines and shapes, allowing for more artistic creativity. Before you can attempt to use your creativity to draw a complex vector image, you must start at the beginning, and learn the basics of creating simple vector images.

Raster images are not only difficult to draw, they are also difficult to edit. The beauty of Fireworks is that an image can be created with vector tools and exported as a bitmap (raster) image. Furthermore, the original Fireworks vector file can be saved so the image can be easily edited at any time.

Drawing a perfect circle with vector tools is easy to do. After the shape is drawn, adding a drop shadow and gradient is a simple task. Later, if the shape needs to be altered to appear more oval, the curve of the stroke is easily changed without negatively affecting the drop shadow or gradient.

Vector shapes can also be combined with one another to create more complex graphics. When learning how to draw the basic shapes, think about more complex shapes that can be created by combining shapes. For example, combining several circles and an oval could create a face. The possibilities are virtually endless.

Creating Basic Shapes

Creating basic shapes with the vector drawing tools is a straightforward task. The basic shapes are the rectangle, rounded rectangle, ellipse, and polygon. From these shapes, you can also create squares and circles. Combining several of these shapes can create a wide variety of interesting images.

When drawing any vector shape, the shape appears with the stroke and fill colors that are selected in the Colors section of the Tools panel. If the colors need to be changed after the object is drawn, you can select the object with the Pointer tool and easily modify the colors.

A common mistake that is made when drawing vector shapes is to apply a stroke and fill color of None. If both colors are set to None, the shape cannot be seen on the canvas. The shape is still there, but it is invisible because it lacks all color attributes. It is suggested that you remember this point so you can avoid potential problems during development of Fireworks vector images.

Never set both your fill and stroke color attributes to None. This causes your object to become invisible on the canvas.

If the mouse button is released before the spacebar, the shape sets to its current size.

After a shape is drawn, you can move it around the document by selecting the shape with the Pointer tool and then dragging it. A shape may also be moved during the drawing process. A shape may be moved to a new location while it is being drawn if the spacebar is held down. It is often easier to properly size an object if you move it while you are drawing it. A hand icon appears if the spacebar is held down during the drawing process, signaling that the shape is being moved or can be moved. If the mouse button is still depressed, releasing the spacebar allows you to continue drawing the shape.

Rectangle

The Rectangle tool allows you to draw a rectangular shape. Dragging with the tool creates the shape. The shape can be drawn from any of a rectangle's four corners, depending on where you drag the cursor after placing the initial click.

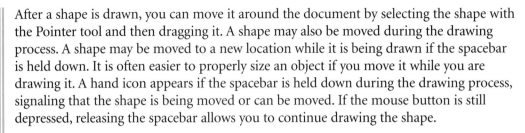

The rectangle on the left is being drawn from the top-left corner.
The rectangle on the right is being drawn from the bottom-right corner.

Holding down the Option/Alt key while drawing with the Rectangle tool creates the shape from the center. Sometimes, it is easier to draw the desired shape when you draw from the center. Drawing a perfect square is a simple task; hold down the Shift key while drawing with the Rectangle tool, and a perfect square is automatically created. Combine the Shift and Option/Alt keys when drawing with the Rectangle tool to draw a perfect square from the center.

Regular Rectangle   Square

Rounded Rectangle

To find the hidden tools under the Rectangle tool, click and hold the tool's icon.

A rectangle can have many uses, and sometimes a rectangle with rounded corners is needed. Many buttons on Web sites consist of rounded-corner rectangles. The Rounded Rectangle tool is located under the Rectangle tool. Use the Rounded Rectangle tool exactly as you would the Rectangle tool.

Example of a rounded rectangle.

A regular rectangle can be converted to a rounded rectangle. A rounded rectangle can be altered to display varying degrees of roundness. To do this, you would select the object, and then change the roundness value in the Rectangle Roundness field in the Properties panel.

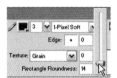

The rectangle roundness is being altered in the Properties panel.

Ellipse

The Ellipse tool allows you to draw many different rounded shapes, including circles. The Ellipse tool operates in a similar manner as the Rectangle tool. Holding the Shift key while drawing with the Ellipse tool creates a perfect circle. Holding the Option/Alt key while drawing with the tool draws the ellipse from the center. Combining the Option/Alt and Shift keys creates a perfect circle drawn from the center.

Example of a variety of ellipses, including a perfect circle on the right.

Polygon

The Polygon tool allows you to draw polygons and stars with anywhere from 3 to 360 sides. The desired shape and number of sides are set in the Properties panel before the shape is created. When drawing a polygon, the shape is always drawn from the center. The shape may be rotated while it is being drawn. Holding down the Shift key while drawing with the Polygon tool constrains the direction of the shape to 45-degree angles.

The slider for the number of sides for a shape created with the Polygon tool only displays 3 to 25 sides, but you can enter any number up to 360.

Examples of polygons drawn with the Polygon tool. The shape on the left is a polygon with nine sides. The right three images are stars with varying numbers of sides.

Use Vector Shape Tools

1. From the File menu, select New to create a new document. In the New dialog box, set the Width to 396 pixels, the Height to 324 pixels, the Resolution to 72, and the Canvas Color to White. Click OK to create the new document.

2. From the File menu, select Save. In the Save dialog box, navigate to your **Work_In_Progress** folder and save the document as **vector_car.png**.

3. From the View menu, select Grid>Edit Grid. Set the Grid Spacing to 36 by 36. You are working with the default colors of black and white, so you may want to select a grid color that will be clearly visible. We chose red. Click the Show Grid and Snap to Grid check boxes in the Edit Grid dialog box. Finally, click OK to apply the grid changes to your document. Throughout the exercise, feel free to deselect and reselect the Show Grid and Snap to Grid options in the File>Grid menu if necessary.

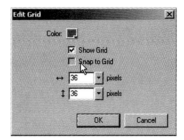

4. Select the Rounded Rectangle tool in the Tools panel. Then select the Default Stroke/Fill button in the Tools panel.

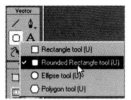

5. Draw a rounded rectangle in the grid squares, starting three horizontal squares from the left and one vertical square down. End the rounded rectangle so it is seven grid squares in width by four grid squares in height. Next, draw a slightly smaller rounded rectangle inside the first, as shown in the following image. Deselect the newly formed rectangle.

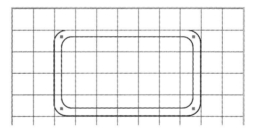

6. Click the Swap Stroke/Fill button. Next, click the pencil icon that is located next to the white color swatch that is used to indicate the stroke color. Now click the No Stroke/Fill button to remove the white stroke value. Deselect this new rounded rectangle after you create it.

Selecting the Swap Stroke/Fill button.

Clicking the pencil icon to select stroke color.

Choosing the No Stroke/Fill button.

7. With the Rounded Rectangle tool still selected, draw a Black rectangle covering the second and third grid squares from the bottom in the third grid column from the left. Next, draw another rounded rectangle in the second and third grid squares from the bottom in the third grid column from the right.

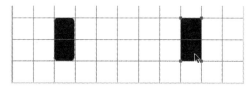

8. Select the Ellipse tool from the Tools panel, and then click the Default Stroke/Fill button to reset the Fill and Stroke colors to Black and White respectively.

9. While holding down the Shift key to keep 1:1 proportions, draw a circle that has a diameter between 1/3 and 1/2 the horizontal width of the larger white rounded rectangle. Select the Pointer tool from the Tools panel. Use the Pointer tool to position the circle on the lower-right half of the smaller rounded rectangle. The circle should overlap the boundaries of both the smaller and the larger rounded rectangles.

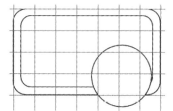

10. Select the Rounded Rectangle tool from the Tools panel. Beginning at the third grid space from the bottom in the second grid column from the left, draw a rounded rectangle that is 3.5 grid squares in height and 9 grid squares in width. Deselect the rounded rectangle.

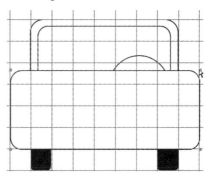

11. Click the Swap Stroke/Fill button to change the Fill color to Black and the Stroke color to White. Click the pencil icon next to the Stroke color swatch and then select the No Fill button to remove the stroke color. Draw a vertical rectangle from the top center of the smallest white rounded rectangle, with a height of approximately 3/4 of a grid square and a width of approximately 1/3 of a grid square.

12. Select the Ellipse tool from the Tools panel. While holding down the Shift key to create a perfect circle, draw a vector shape that is approximately two grid squares in diameter. Use the Pointer tool to select the new black circle. From the Edit menu, select Copy to copy the vector shape, and then select Edit>Paste to paste a copy of the circle onto the canvas. Choose the Pointer tool from the Tools panel, and then center the two black circles, approximately three grid squares apart, within the largest rounded rectangle.

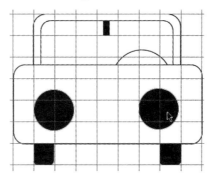

13. Select the Rounded Rectangle tool from the Tools panel, and then click the Default Stroke/Fill button. Draw a rounded rectangle that is approximately 2 grid squares wide by 1/2 grid square high, then use the Pointer tool to center it, slightly overlapping the bottom of the black vertical rectangle.

If you are using Fireworks on a Windows-based computer, you can use Control-C as the keyboard shortcut for the File>Copy command, Control-V for the File>Paste command, and Control-X for the File>Cut command.
On a Macintosh system, the applicable keyboard shortcuts are Command-C to Copy, Command-V to Paste, and Command-X to Cut.

14. Select the Polygon tool from the Tools panel. In the Properties panel, set the Shape to Star, the number of Sides to 17, and the Angle to 25.

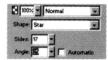

15. Use the Polygon tool to position your cursor over the center of one of the large black circles and draw a star. Repeat the action on the other large black circle.

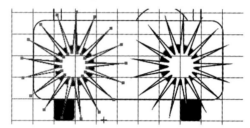

16. Your vector car is complete. Save your changes, and close the document.

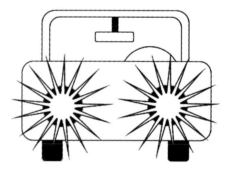

Creating Complex Shapes

Basic shapes are suitable for many purposes; but for complex shapes, the basic tools are quite often insufficient. The Line tool, Pen tool, and their associated optional tools are used to draw more elaborate shapes. Abstract and original shapes can be drawn with the Pen tool. The other vector tools can be used to create shapes or alter existing shapes. As with the basic shapes, the existing stroke and fill properties are applied to any new or modified shapes. These properties may be changed at any time. Chapter 4 provides in-depth information on altering the properties of vector shapes.

Using the Line Tool

The Line tool allows you to draw straight lines in any direction. Lines are drawn with a click and drag of the mouse. The click defines the starting point of the line; dragging and then releasing the mouse button define the direction and length of the line. Lines are constrained to 45-degree angles when the Shift key is depressed while the line is being drawn.

The Line tool only draws line segments, but these segments can be positioned together to form myriad shapes. The Pointer tool allows you to reposition previously drawn lines.

Examples of lines drawn with the Line tool.

Since lines do not contain areas, they only have strokes — no fills. We present in-depth information on strokes and fills in Chapter 4 of this book.

Using the Pen Tool

Learning to use the Pen tool can at times be frustrating; but once learned, the Pen tool can be used to draw virtually any shape. The Pen tool allows you to draw a series of points, which are automatically connected by straight and curved lines (segments).

The basic shape tools restrict you to creating certain types of shapes. The powerful Pen tool, once mastered, places no limits on the variety of shapes you can create. The Pen tool works by creating points and segments called *paths*. Points and connecting segments work together to create original shapes from scratch.

If the last point clicked is on top of the first point created, the path is closed. Not all paths need to be closed; paths that are not closed are called *open paths,* and do not connect at the beginning and end points. The more points created on any path, the less smooth the path typically appears.

When you begin using the Pen tool, it is a good idea to start with basic shapes. The simplest shape to draw with the Pen tool is a straight line; with a straight line, many other shapes can then be created. The Pen tool creates shapes based on mouse clicks and then dragging with the mouse. Simply clicking on the document creates lines much the same as the Line tool. Drawing a triangle requires four clicks of the mouse. The first three clicks define the triangle's points. The last click closes the path as shown in the following series of images. Holding the Shift key while creating points constrains the lines so they are straight.

A step-by-step example of a triangle being drawn with the Pen tool.

The ability to create curves is the fundamental strength of the Pen tool. You can create curves with the Pen tool by clicking the mouse button to add a point. With the mouse button still depressed, you can drag the mouse to curve the line; the more you drag, the more dramatic the curve. If the first point is dragged with the mouse, a curve is created in the direction of the drag when the second point is created. The farther the mouse is dragged from the point, the greater the curve in the line. The line appearing from the point when dragged is called the *point handle.* You can use the Subselection tool to move points after a line shape is created. The point handles can be manipulated to change the curve of a line.

The vertical line is referred to as a "point handle."

Like other vector tools, the Pen tool uses the existing stroke and fill attributes, which may be changed at any time.

The Pen tool can be used to draw lines or shapes. If you're drawing a closed path shape, remember that the first point should be clicked again after the other points are created in order to finish (close) the shape. Adding or deleting points can alter the shape. Clicking with the Pen tool on the existing path adds additional points to the path. The cursor becomes a pen tip with the plus (+) sign. Clicking on an existing point with the Pen tool deletes the point, which in turn reduces the number of points on the path; fewer points on a path results in a smoother path. When points are being removed from a path, the cursor becomes a pen tip with the minus (-) sign.

The image on the left shows a point being added. The image on the right shows a point being deleted. Note the difference in pen tips.

The Pen tool typically creates smooth curved lines or 90-degree angles. Sometimes, a sharp point is needed to create a specific shape. Clicking the last point created produces a sharp point. The cursor turns to an upside-down "v" when a sharp point is created. These sharp points are useful when making shapes that combine curves with sharp points, such as a crescent moon shape.

Clicking twice on the most recent point creates a sharp point.

Use the Line and Pen Tools

1. Create a new document (File>New). Enter 400 pixels as the Width and 300 pixels as the Height. Set the Resolution to 72 and the Canvas Color to White or any custom color that displays black lines and curves. Save this document as **face.png** in your **Work_In_Progress** folder. Take a moment to examine how your final document should look:

Throughout the exercise, use the Pointer tool when necessary to correct the position of the elements of the document.

2. Select the Pen tool from the Tools panel. Click once to place your first point on the document. Using the rulers for rough measurement, create the second point approximately 100 pixels below the first point and slightly to the right of it. Double-click the second point after creating it so the next clicks you make do not create new points on the same curve.

3. Click the second point and pull it up and to the right. Use the point handle to create a line that curls upward near the bottom. To complete the line, use the Pointer tool to deselect the curve, or double-click the final point. This is the nose.

4. Using the Pen tool, create two smaller curves that approximate the arc of the nose, making sure to deselect each curve after creating it. Place one curve immediately below and to the right of the lower point of the nose. Place the next curve below and to the right of the first smaller curve. These curves are the lips of the face.

5. Create a medium-sized arc with approximately the same curvature as the other three curves, and position it just below and to the right of the bottom lip. This curve is the chin.

Be sure to deselect your curves after each one is created. This keeps you from accidentally creating one large curve, which would be much harder to work with during this introductory exercise.

6. Still using the Pen tool, create a U-shaped curve that is higher on the right side than the left. Position this curve next to the nose; it is the right portion of the glasses.

7. Select the Line tool from the Tools panel. Draw a line that loosely connects the U-shaped curve created in Step 6. Also draw a short line that is about 1/3 the length of the first line that projects from the left end of the longer line at a similar angle.

8. Select the Pen tool again. Use it to draw a vertical curve from the left point of the short line drawn in Step 7 so it almost reaches the curve that creates the nose. This curve completes the left lens of the glasses.

9. Draw a vertical curve from the point where the top lines of the glasses meet. It acts as the forehead of the figure.

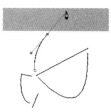

10. Select the Line tool from the Tools panel and use it to draw a straight line at an upward angle, coming from the right lens of the glasses to complete the figure.

11. Save the file and then close it.

The final design.

Using the Vector Path Tool

If you are not comfortable using the Pen tool, the Vector Path tool may be a good alternative while you gain confidence using the Pen tool. As discussed earlier, not all shapes can be drawn with combinations of the basic shapes. The Vector Path tool allows you to use the mouse to draw any shape, similar to how you would use a brush.

The Vector Path tool is easier to use than the Pen tool. Points are automatically created as you draw. Simply moving the cursor around the canvas creates a path. A path drawn with the Vector Path tool is just like a path drawn with the Pen tool, but the shapes drawn with this tool contain many more points. Remember that the more points there are in a shape, the less likely it is that the shape will be smooth.

Since the Vector Path tool creates so many points, it is important to know how to remove redundant points. As with any vector shape, the Pen tool may be used to add and delete points on any path, including those drawn with the Vector Path tool. Another way to delete a point in any vector shape is to use the Subselection tool; you can select the point and press the Delete or Backspace key to remove it. Points that are not selected appear hollow, and points that are selected appear solid.

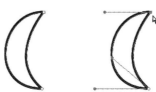

In both images, the Subselection tool was used. The image on the left has no selected points. The image on the right has one selected point.

Using the Redraw Path Tool

The Redraw Path tool is used to redraw or lengthen an existing path. This tool applies the properties (such as stroke and fill color) that are attached to the existing path. To use the tool, you can drag the cursor over an existing path that is currently selected, click where the path should be extended, and then drag. The path is altered according to where the mouse is dragged.

Notice that the path turns red and the cursor changes to a paint brush with the plus (+) sign while it is being altered with the Redraw Path tool. The Redraw Path tool is very useful when you find a path is not what is needed.

The current stroke and fill properties, not the properties of the existing path, are utilized when using the Pen tool or any other vector tool. If you need to add to an existing path, the current settings will not necessarily match. The Redraw Path tool is very useful since it utilizes the existing stroke and fill properties of the path being altered.

The Redraw Path tool is located with the Vector Path tool under the Pen tool.

Example of the Redraw Path tool in use.

Draw with the Vector Path and Redraw Path Tools

1. Create a new document (File>New). Enter 200 pixels as the Width and 200 pixels as the Height, and set the Canvas Color to White. Save this document as **hi.png** in your **Work_In_Progress** folder.

2. Select the Vector Path tool from the Tools panel and set the Stroke color to one that you prefer.

3. Use your mouse to draw a cursive "h" on the left side of the canvas.

4. Select the Redraw Path tool from the Tools panel.

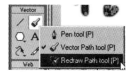

5. Hover your mouse over the tail end of the "h" until you see the points of the line turn red. Click and hold your mouse at this point, drawing a cursive "i" that is attached to the "h". Dot the "i" when you are finished with the main body of the letter.

6. Save the file and then close it.

GIF Export Options

Vector shapes are not photo-realistic, so they are often exported as raster images using the GIF file format. As you learned in Chapter 2, the GIF format works well for images with large blocks of color and/or a limited number of colors. Vector objects can include many gradients and patterns that may require the image to be saved as a JPEG. More often than not, however, the GIF format is more appropriate for vector shapes than the JPEG format.

In this section, you learn to use many optimization options for exporting GIFs so the vector shapes you draw can be viewed on the Web.

In the Optimize panel, you see most of the options for exporting files. A few default export settings can be selected in the Settings pop-up menu. These settings are preset, and are not customized for each particular image. The defaults are often appropriate starting points for optimization. You will create your own settings and concentrate on the options for exporting images to the GIF file format. Other options are available when exporting other image types.

In order to see the result of optimization settings, change the view in the Document window to Preview, 2-Up, and 4-Up in order to see the effects of the optimization settings. The Original tab is the default view you use for editing images. If you have been optimizing images, switch back to the Original tab to further edit the image or to compare the optimization settings to the original version of the image. If you find you cannot edit your image, make sure you are working on the original image or on an export preview. It is not recommended to edit images while in Preview mode.

Color Depth

GIFs are 8-bit images, meaning they can only contain up to 256 colors; this is acceptable for most vector images. The selected color palette may decrease the number of possible colors. The number of colors may also be manually decreased. Let's review the color palettes and find out how to refine the colors in an image.

In the Optimize panel, the file type should be chosen first, followed by your choice of color palette, as these options may affect the number of possible colors that can be used in the image. Then you can choose the desired number of colors. We suggest you use the lowest number of colors that does not noticeably degrade the quality of the image. The file size should decrease as the number of colors is reduced.

When in Preview, 2-Up, and 4-Up views, the file size, estimated download time, and file type are displayed at the top right of the Document window.

When the number of colors in the Optimize panel is reduced to two colors, an image that contains only two colors often appears pixelated on the diagonal and curved lines. Anti-aliasing uses several colors to smooth the diagonals and curves. Although an image appears to have only two colors, it may look better at a higher number of possible colors (to accommodate anti-aliasing) without significantly affecting file size.

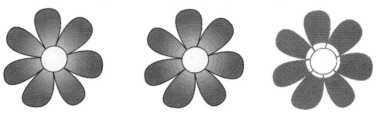

An image shown with 128 colors (left), 32 colors (center), and 2 colors (right).

Individual colors may be edited, snapped to the closest Web-safe color, locked, added, or deleted, depending on the color palette in use. A single color can be changed to another color using the Edit Color option. The Color window appears when a color in the color palette is selected and the Edit Color icon is clicked. The selected color in the color palette is replaced with the color selected in the Color window.

Snapping a color to the nearest Web-safe color changes a non-Web-safe color to a similar Web-safe color. When a color in the color palette is selected, the Snap to Web-Safe Color icon replaces the selected color with the closest Web-safe color.

Locking a color prevents the color from being deleted when the color depth is changed. When a color in the color palette is selected, the Lock Color icon locks the selected color so it won't be replaced if the number of colors in the image is changed.

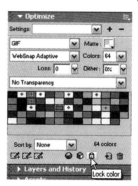

The selected color is being locked.

You may find it necessary to restore a color that was previously deleted from an image. The Add Color icon allows you to choose the color and add it to the image. Notice that if the added color wasn't in the original image, the color does not appear in the exported image.

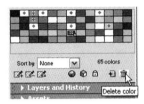

A color is being added to the image's color palette.

A color is deleted from the image if the color is selected and the Delete Color icon is clicked. The color is not exported with the image.

The selected color is being deleted from the image's color palette.

Transparency

All images are rectangular in shape, but you can trick the eye into perceiving an image as a different shape by using transparency. On a Web site, you often see images that don't appear to be rectangular, even though they are. The area between the shape and the outlining bounding box can be transparent, causing the image to appear non-rectangular. GIFs use *index transparency*, which sets a particular color (usually white) to transparent. Transparency is not set by default, so if the image requires transparency, it must be manually set before exporting the image. Although an image may show transparency in Fireworks, unless transparency is selected as an export option, the exported image will not include transparency.

Transparency can only be added to GIF and PNG files. You are working with GIF images, so the image type must be changed to GIF before the transparency settings can be applied. You must select Transparency from the Optimize panel to allow the image to display transparency. The Original tab does not display transparency; you must preview the image to make sure the desired area is transparent. In an image with transparency, a gray-and-white checkerboard appears in the transparent areas of the canvas.

Transparency was selected for this image.

Not all color palettes show the options to control individual colors.

Among the common file types on the Web, only exported .png files use alpha transparency, which is a superior form of transparency.

The Add Color to Transparency icon is used to select the color to become transparent. The transparent color may be selected either from the image itself or from the color palette in the Optimize panel. The Select Transparent Color option allows one color to provide the only transparency in the image. The Remove Color from Transparency icon allows the color set as transparent to be added back to the image by selecting the color.

The left button is Add Color to Transparency, the middle button is Remove Color from Transparency, and the right button is Select Transparent Color.

Matte

If a GIF file includes transparency, the anti-aliasing sometimes produces a white halo effect around foreground objects. These pixels aren't actually white; they are near-white pixels left behind from the anti-aliasing process. To avoid this effect, you can use the color of the intended background as the *matte color*. Anti-aliasing uses the matte color to create the blend from the foreground color to the background color instead of blending to white.

The Matte color chip.

Interlacing

The basic idea behind interlacing was introduced in Chapter 1. Interlacing a GIF image allows parts of the image to display before the entire image is downloaded to the user's system. An image that is not interlaced must be entirely downloaded before the image is displayed. Interlaced GIFs are most useful when the user's Internet connection is slow or the file size is large. Interlacing actually adds a little weight to the file size of an image. To set interlacing, you can select the Interlaced option in the Optimize panel's menu.

A JPEG has a similar option to the interlaced GIF. It is called a Progressive JPEG.

The Optimize panel menu with Interlaced selected.

Use the Interlaced Option

1. Navigate to the **RF_Fireworks** folder and open **gif_optimization.png**. Notice the Optimize panel. The document should be set with defaults of GIF WebSnap Adaptive 128.

2. Select the Preview, 2-Up, or 4-Up tab at the top of the main Document window. Experiment by altering the number of colors included in the document using the Colors pop-up menu. Notice how the lower settings affect the quality of the image, altering colors and making the lines between cells less smooth. As you experiment, make sure Index Transparency is selected in the pop-up menu.

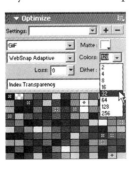

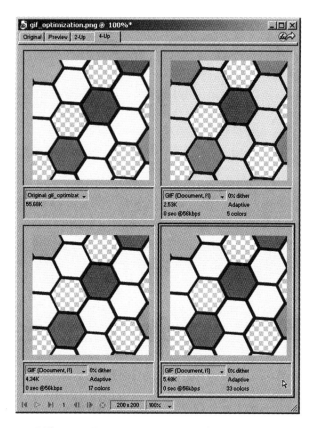

Differences in optimization viewed in 4-Up mode.

3. Select a final Optimization setting that best balances file size and image quality. We recommend a WebSnap Adaptive GIF with 32 colors and Index Transparency.

4. Choose the Interlaced option from the Optimize pop-up menu on the Options panel.

5. Finally, export the document to your **Work_In_Progress** folder by selecting File>Export. Save the file as "gif_optimization.gif" and then close it. Close the file without saving your changes.

Chapter Summary

In this chapter, you learned the basics of creating vector shapes with the vector tools. The basic shape tools and the more complex tools, including the Pen and Vector Path tools, were presented. You also reviewed many options to export vector shapes as Web-ready GIF images.

4 Vector Object Properties and Manipulation

Chapter Objectives:

During development, you may find it necessary to change the properties of a vector object several times in order to create the exact shape you need. To accomplish edits such as these, Fireworks includes many options for changing the appearance of an object's stroke and fill. Using Fireworks, you can create objects that resemble watercolor paintings or those that contain abstract random patterns. The possibilities are virtually endless. In this chapter, you will:

- Learn how to select vector objects.

- Find out how to apply and alter strokes and fills.

- Experiment with applying and changing effects and styles.

- Learn how to transform shapes.

- Find out how to combine and alter paths.

- Explore the shape adjustment tools.

- Discover how to align and arrange vector objects.

- Learn how to group and ungroup objects, and change their stacking order.

Projects to be Completed:

- Globe Illustration (A)

- Image Retouching Advertisement (B)

- Animated Banner (C)

- The Cable Store Web Site (D)

Vector Object Properties and Manipulation

Any object drawn with a vector tool is referred to as a vector object or a vector shape. You can quickly change the appearance of a vector object by editing a few of its properties. It is much easier to change the appearance of a vector image than it is to change a raster image; this is, in fact, one of the major advantages of a vector image. Changing color in a raster image can be a very involved process; the same is true for editing other properties of that type of image.

It is easy to change the shape, color, and overall appearance of a vector image. You can manipulate points to change line curves, and you can add, move, and delete points to change the shape of the object. Vectors can also be moved around the screen and stacked on top of one another — in effect, creating new shapes. Stacked objects can be restacked, and one object can be used to modify the shape of other objects.

Selecting Vectors

Before you can work with vector shapes, you must select them. Shapes react in various ways when different tools are used to select them. By default, a vector object that has been selected has a blue outline. This colored outline provides an easy way to identify which object is selected.

When the cursor of any selection tool is positioned over an object, the shape appears with a red outline by default. The red outline indicates that the particular object will be selected if the mouse button is clicked. If the mouse button is clicked over an object with a red outline, the object becomes selected and the outline turns blue. These selection indicators are crucial to understanding how objects are selected.

Pointer Tool

The Pointer tool selects vector objects that are going to be repositioned on the canvas or modified in some way. The Pointer tool must be used to select a shape; using it does not change the shape of the path. This is probably the tool you will use most often during image development because all objects must first be selected before any manipulation can be applied. The Pointer tool is accessed from the Tools panel or by pressing the "V" or "0" (zero) key.

Select Behind Tool

Vector objects can be stacked one on top of the other (we discuss this in more detail later in this chapter). Sometimes, an object that is stacked underneath another cannot be selected with the Pointer tool. In an instance such as this, the Select Behind tool is invaluable because it selects an object that is underneath another object. The tool is located in the Select section of the Tools panel behind the Pointer tool, and is also accessible by pressing the "V" or "0" (zero) key.

Without having to move the top object, the Select Behind tool allows the object underneath to be selected. After you choose the Select Behind tool, you can move the cursor over the object, and click with the mouse when the outline of the desired object turns red. The object might not be visible, but it can still be selected.

When selecting part of a raster image, "marching ants" define the selected area.

The path is the outline of a vector object and defines the shape.

The "V" or "0" (zero) key pressed multiple times toggles between the Pointer and Select Behind tools.

The stacking order of objects is discussed in-depth later in this chapter.

When a vector object is selected, the Layers panel changes to reflect the selection.

The square behind this rounded shape is selected using the Select Behind tool.

Subselection Tool

The Subselection tool can be very useful in a variety of instances. When a vector object is selected with the Subselection tool, the points that define the shape can be individually selected and manipulated. Once the individual points are selected, they can be moved by dragging, or deleted by pressing the Delete or Backspace key. Although we discuss groups in more detail later in this chapter, the Subselection tool allows individual objects in a group to be selected for modification. This tool is also located in the Tools panel and accessible by pressing the "A" or "1" (number one) key.

The Subselection tool is being used in the above image.

Working with Strokes

The word *stroke* is a fancy term for the outline of a vector object. All vector objects have a stroke property, which can be set to None. The stroke is not visible when set to None. A change in the stroke of an object can have a considerable effect on the overall appearance of a vector object. A stroke can have several different properties including size, edge, category, position, and texture. Experimenting with the stroke of an object can be enlightening as to the available possibilities.

Stroke Size

The size of a stroke determines the thickness of the outline. A thin stroke creates a different effect in the object as compared to a thick stroke. The stroke size can be set by selecting the object with the Pointer tool and increasing or decreasing the size in the Properties panel. The strokes of more than one object can be set at the same time by selecting multiple objects before applying the change.

The stroke size for the square is being set in the Properties panel.

Sometimes a stroke can be so large that the fill is not noticeable.

The size of a stroke is measured in pixels. A stroke size of 10 means the stroke of the object is 10-pixels wide. The Properties panel displays a slider for stroke size, and shows 100 as the maximum size. A larger stroke size can be manually entered in the Size field.

Edge

A stroke's edge determines the softness or hardness of the line. A stroke can range from a hard line to one that is soft and fuzzy. The edge characteristic is determined in the Tip preview area of the Properties panel. The term "tip" is derived from the various writing and drawing tools, and how they produce different edges according to their tip size and shape.

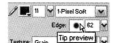

The softness of the edge of an object can be manipulated by moving the slider next to the Tip preview in the Properties panel. The preview of the edge changes as the slider is moved, and the result is also displayed on the canvas. We recommend experimenting with edge properties so you can become familiar with their appearances.

The edge of the star shape is being softened.

Stroke Categories

Stroke categories change the appearance of a stroke. The None category removes the stroke. Some of the other categories represent a different tool that can be used to draw the stroke. These categories include Pencil, Air Brush, Calligraphy, Charcoal, Crayon, Felt Tip, Oil, and Watercolor.

A few of the categories aren't described by a particular tool:

- The Basic category is the most common category, creating a simple line around an object.

- The Random category provides different shapes in scattered locations around an object.

- The Unnatural category provides different futuristic looks that aren't necessarily direct outlines of objects.

The categories become available in the Properties panel when an object is selected.

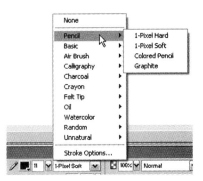

The stroke categories.

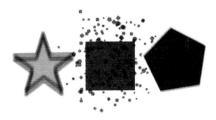

The above image displays objects with several different strokes. The left object shows the Calligraphy Ribbon stroke, the middle object shows the Unnatural Paint Splatter stroke, and the right object shows the Air Brush Textured stroke.

Each stroke category other than None provides a sub-menu that displays options for setting the stroke. Some categories provide more options than others. Experimenting with the many categories and options for each provides you with a solid understanding of the various stroke combinations that are available.

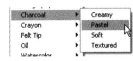

The sub-menu for the Charcoal stroke is displayed.

Stroke Position

The position of the stroke along the path edge provides even more control over the stroke's appearance. A stroke can be applied inside, centered on, or placed outside the path. Changing the stroke position can alter the entire object. From the Stroke category pop-up menu in the Properties panel, selecting Stroke Options allows you to alter the location of the stroke relative to the path. The stroke position can also be set from the Stroke Color pop-up window by selecting Stroke Options. The available options include Inside Path, Centered on Path, and Outside Path. Each option causes the object to appear to change in size.

Even though many different types of strokes are available, you should always choose a stroke that is appropriate for your graphic.

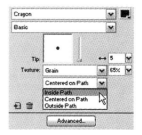

The Location of stroke relative to path menu is displayed from Stroke Options.

Stroke settings can be saved so you can reuse them later. You can do this by setting the stroke and selecting New Style from the Styles panel located in the Assets menu.

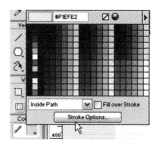

The Stroke Options window is also available from the Stroke Color box.

Click the Advanced button in the Stroke Options window to set advanced stroke options.

In the above image, each object is exactly the same size. The stroke position of the object on the left is Inside Path, in the center it is Centered on Path, and on the right it is Outside Path.

Texture

Texture can be applied to strokes. Not all stroke categories display textures in exactly the same way, allowing for myriad options. You can also change the opacity of the texture. The opacity can display the textures in many different ways, ranging from subtle to very prominent. We suggest taking some time to experiment with the texture options at various opacities.

Working with Fills

The *fill* is the color inside an object. Fills can vary from a solid color to a gradient, or even a pattern or texture. Without a fill, an object looks empty. This is not to say that every object necessarily needs to have a fill; sometimes a fill of None is required to create a particular effect. Let's review the fill options.

If an object is drawn without a stroke or a fill, it is invisible on the canvas.

The object on the left has no fill. The object on the right has a solid-colored fill.

Solid

Similar to setting the stroke color for an object, you must first select the object before you can add a fill color. The Fill Color box is used to set the fill. Any color chip can be selected for a solid-colored fill. A color can also be sampled with the Eyedropper tool by clicking where the desired color is displayed on the image.

You can also use the Color Picker to apply other colors by entering the hexadecimal code for a particular color. The system Color Picker allows any color in the computer system to be used as a fill color. The color cubes appearing in the Fill Color window can be altered if necessary. The window's menu displays different color layouts. The Snap to Web-Safe option can be toggled here, as well.

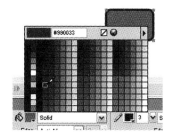

The fill of the selected object is being set in the Properties panel.
The fill color can also be set using the Fill Color box in the Tools panel.

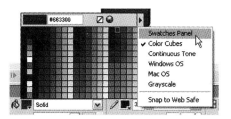

The color display options are shown.

Snap to Web-Safe changes non-Web-safe colors to the closest Web-safe color.

Fill Options can be selected from the Fill Color pop-up menu or the Fill category pop-up menu in the Properties panel. More options are available in the Fill Options dialog box when fills other than solid colors are selected. (We discuss patterns and textures in the next section of this chapter.)

The different types of fills are displayed from the Fill category menu.

Patterns

Patterns are pre-set and can be selected from the Fill category pop-up menu. You can also use the Fill Options window to select the desired pattern. Patterns range from Woods, to Weaves, to Bubbles, and more.

Patterns possess color properties that cannot be changed. Once set, patterns override any current color settings for the fill of a selected object. The size of the pattern, as well as its direction, can be adjusted with the handles that appear when the object is selected with the Pointer tool. The square handles display a smaller pattern when positioned closer to the circle handle.

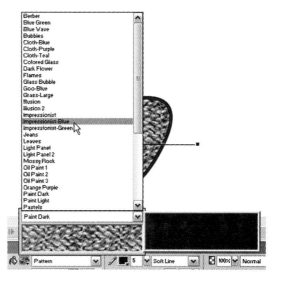

The pattern options are displayed from the Pattern pop-up menu.

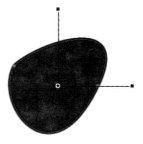

The selected object has the Impressionist-Blue pattern applied.

Textures

A texture can be applied over any type of fill. Textures create the appearance of different types of materials and provide depth of color. When an object is selected, a texture can be chosen in the Properties panel. The opacity of the texture changes the visibility of the texture on the object. The texture can vary from a subtle effect with a lower opacity, to a stronger effect with a higher opacity.

Selecting Transparent in the Fill Options dialog box makes the object semi-transparent to allow objects behind it to show through.

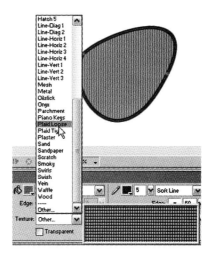

Fill Options was clicked and Texture options are displayed for the selected object.

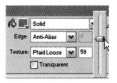

The texture's opacity is being changed.

Gradients

A *gradient* is a combination of colors that blend into one another in a certain pattern over a specified distance. Fireworks doesn't include a Gradients category in the Fill category pop-up menu; instead, it lists the possible gradients, from Linear to Folds. Each gradient pattern displays slightly differently. Different gradients create different effects, depending on the requirements of the object.

The Linear, Cone, and Ripples gradients are applied to the same shape.

By default, a gradient's colors are taken from the stroke and fill colors. You can edit the colors by selecting Fill Options in the Stroke category pop-up menu. Selecting Edit allows you to change the colors and distance between colors in the gradient. You can select the color chips on the bottom of the color display to change the colors of the gradient. Additional colors can be added by clicking in the area of the color chips. You can delete colors by dragging them off the color chip area. If you can imagine a gradient, it can probably be applied with the available editing options.

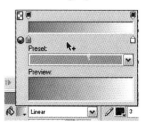

An additional color is being added to the gradient.

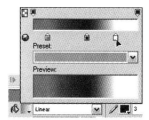

The color chips are being moved to different distances.

The direction of the gradient and the length needed for the gradient to complete a cycle can be changed when the gradient object is selected. The circle handle that appears allows you to set the anchor of the gradient. The square handle(s) that appears allows you to set the direction of the gradient. These same square handles determine the length of the gradient cycle. The closer the square handles are to the circle handle, the shorter the gradient cycle length, and vice versa. The direction of the gradient and cycle length can create various effects.

The gradient can extend beyond the object by dragging the square handles past the object's edge.

The handles of the Starburst gradient applied to the object are being changed.

Change the Stroke and Fill

1. From the File menu, select Open. Navigate to the **RF_Fireworks** folder and open **stroke_and_fill.png**.

2. Select the Pointer tool from the Tools panel, and hold down the Shift key so you can select more than one vector object at a time. Click to select each of the small circles.

3. In the Properties panel, click the Fill category pop-up menu and select Radial from the list of available fills.

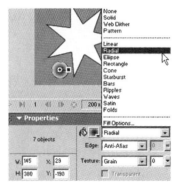

4. With all the circles still selected, click the radial-filled color swatch associated with the Fill icon in the Properties panel. In the dialog box that appears, select the black color chip on the bottom left of the gradient slide. When clicked, a color palette appears. Choose the Red color swatch on the palette.

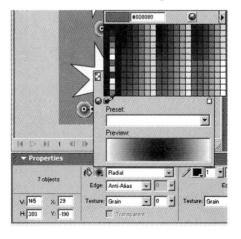

The circles in the document now have a gradient fill that fades from red to white.

5. In the Fill Options area of the Properties panel, change the Texture to Oilslick with a setting of 100%. In the Stroke Options area of the Properties panel, set the Stroke to None.

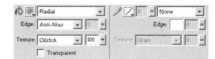

6. Hold down the Shift key, and use the Pointer tool to select each of the star-shaped vector objects. In the Properties panel, click the color swatch associated with the pencil icon (to denote Stroke), and choose a blue color swatch in the color palette that appears.

7. Ensure the star-shaped vector objects are still selected. Click the Stroke Options pop-up menu. Experiment by selecting different stroke types and altering their settings. We chose the Ribbon stroke with an 8-pt. Width, but you can apply any stroke type and settings that you prefer.

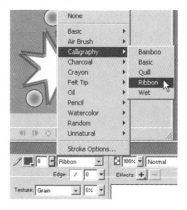

8. Use the Fill Color Picker on the Tools panel to change the color of the stars from White to a light aqua blue. If you cannot find an appropriate shade, enter #CCFFFF in the hexadecimal field at the top of the color palette.

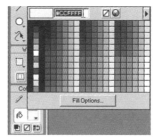

9. In the Fill Options area of the Properties panel, set the Edge characteristic to Feather with a value of 37.

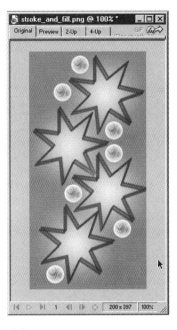

Our final stylized document.

10. You can experiment further by applying various fill and stroke options to the vector forms in the document. You can also create other forms and apply options to them. When you are done experimenting with fills and strokes, close the document without saving your changes.

Live Effects and Styles

Effects, also called Live Effects, can be applied to any vector object, text element, or raster image. The available effects include many options that are only applicable to raster images (these effects will be covered in Chapter 7). The Live Effects that are most commonly used on vector objects are Bevel and Emboss, and Shadow and Glow. These effects have many options, all of which can be edited.

A vector object with the Drop Shadow and Inner Bevel effects applied.

All Live Effects are applied by selecting the object, and then choosing the effect from the Effects pop-up menu in the Properties panel. Multiple effects can be applied to an object; the order in which effects are applied affect the appearance of the object. The stacking order of effects can be changed by dragging and dropping the effects in the Edit and Arrange Effects area, which is simply a list of effects applied to the object.

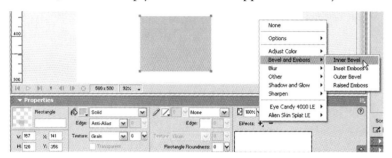

An Inner Bevel effect is being applied to the selected object.

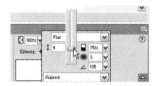

You can enter settings for most Live Effects in pop-up windows such as the one above.

The visibility of the effects can be toggled on and off. In the Properties panel, a check-mark appears to the left of the effect if it is visible. A red "X" appears to the left of the effect if it is not visible. An effect that has been applied but is not visible is not deleted. To delete an effect, you must first select it, and then click the Delete the Current Selected Effect button. All Live Effects can be removed from an object by selecting None in the Add Effects pop-up menu.

The Inner Bevel effect is not visible (red "X"), but the Drop Shadow effect is visible (checkmark).

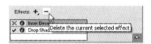

The Inner Bevel is the selected effect, and it is being deleted.

Many third-party effects are available for purchase. Fireworks's standard installation includes samples from some third-party vendors.

Options are available for most Live Effects. The effects we are covering in this chapter all have several adjustment settings. If a Live Effect has settings, they appear as soon as you add the effect. If the settings for the effect need to be changed later, they are made available by double-clicking the effect in the list of effects. Setting options vary according to the effect, but usually encompass the size, color, opacity, and direction of the effect.

The opacity of an applied effect is being altered in the above image.

Bevel and Emboss

Bevel and Emboss effects are often used to create a 3-D effect so your vector objects do not appear to be "flat:"

- The Bevel effect creates an edge that seems to be raised.
- Web buttons often have a bevel to make them appear to be "clickable," while text is often embossed to create the appearance of fine stationary.
- The Inner Bevel effect is applied to the inside of the object.
- The Outer Bevel effect is applied to the outside of the object.
- The Emboss effect makes the object appear as though it were inset into, or raised above, the canvas.
- The Inset Emboss effect makes the object appear as if it were inset into the canvas.
- The Raised Emboss effect makes the object look as though it were popping off the canvas.

Each object has a different Live Effect. From left to right, the effects are Inner Bevel, Inset Emboss, Outer Bevel, and Raised Emboss.

Shadow and Glow

Shadow and Glow effects add a gradient to an object or text element in various ways to provide the object or text element with additional height or emphasis over the rest of the elements in the graphic:

- The Shadow effect adds depth to an object or text element, as if it were casting a shadow from a light source.
- The Drop Shadow effect is one of the most commonly used effects, as it makes an object appear to have a shadow, which can be set in any direction.
- The Glow effect adds a gradient around or inside an object or text element, as if it were glowing with the selected color.
- The Glow effect adds a soft color around the outside of the selected object in the selected color.
- The Inner Glow effect adds a soft color inside the object.
- The Inner Shadow effect adds a shadow inside the object to add depth.

Each object has a different Live Effect. From left to right, the effects are Drop Shadow, Glow, Inner Glow, and Inner Shadow.

Styles

Styles are pre-set effects that can be applied to any object or text element. The available styles appear in the Styles panel and are applied to selected objects by clicking the desired style. Once a style is applied, the effects and colors applied by the style can be changed. Additional styles are easily added for later use in other documents.

Adding your own style might save time if you have a particular set of effects you often add to objects. To add a style, you would select any object that has the desired effect(s), fill, and stroke applied to it. Then you would select Save as Style from the Options menu that appears when a Live Effect is being added to an object. The style must be named, and the desired properties of the object must be selected. The new style is then added to your list of available styles.

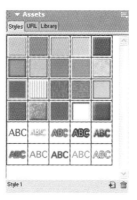

The Styles panel.

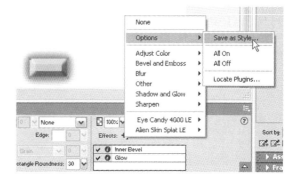

The applied Live Effects and other properties of the selected object are being saved as a style for later use.

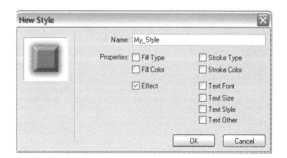

The New Style window.

Since new styles are only available on the computer on which they were created, you need to know how to export and import styles if you need to export your custom styles to another machine, or if you wish to import someone else's custom styles to your system:

- To export a style to another computer, you would select the style, and then choose Export Styles from the Styles panel's menu. The style would be saved as a Fireworks style document.

- To import a style, you would select Import Styles from the Styles panel's menu, and select the desired Fireworks style document. Imported styles appear at the bottom of the Styles panels as new styles.

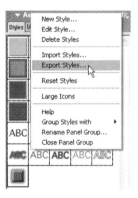

The selected style is being exported.

The exported style is being saved.

Use Styles and Effects

1. Select File>New to open a new Fireworks document. Set the document Width to 300 pixels and Height to 200 pixels. Select White as the Canvas Color. Set the Resolution to 72. Click OK. Immediately select File>Save, and save the document as "flowers.png" in your **Work_In_Progress** folder. Remember to frequently save the document while you work.

2. Select the Ellipse tool from the Tools panel. Set your Stroke to a shade of blue and Fill to yellow; we used #0000FF and #FFFF00 respectively, but you can use any color you prefer. We set our Stroke properties to 4-pt. 1-Pixel Soft, but you can use any characteristics you prefer. With the Ellipse tool selected, draw a horizontal ellipse at the left side of the document.

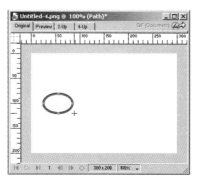

3. With the newly created ellipse still selected, copy the vector object by either selecting File>Copy or by pressing Command/Control-C. Next, paste three copies of the object by selecting File>Paste three times, or press Command/Control-V three times. Once you have pasted the elliptical vector three times, use the Pointer tool to arrange the objects so they are positioned roughly at the top, right, bottom, and left positions and they slightly overlap in the middle.

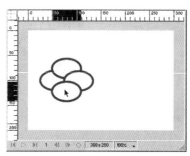

4. Use the Pointer tool to draw a bounding box around the four ellipses; this selects all of the vector shapes. Copy the items (Edit>Copy), and then paste them (Edit>Paste) onto the document to duplicate the arrangement. Position the new cluster of ellipses at the bottom of the canvas, and then set their Fill to Red while they are still selected.

5. Select Edit>Paste or press Command/Control-V to paste another group of the yellow ellipses onto the canvas. Use the Pointer tool to arrange the ellipses at the right of the page, and set the Fill to a shade of pink; we chose #FF99CC. Once arranged, paste another group of ellipses, and reposition the fourth cluster at the top of the page. This time, set the Fill to #9900CC or any other shade of purple you prefer. Deselect the cluster of ellipses.

6. Select the Ellipse tool from the Tools panel and set the Fill to White while keeping the same color and width for the Stroke. Use the Ellipse tool to draw a small white ellipse in the center of each of the four clusters. You can create each of these ellipses with the same shape and dimensions, or, as we have done, you can create the ellipses with different characteristics.

7. Hold down the Shift key while you use the Pointer tool to select each of the yellow ellipses. Click and hold your mouse over the plus (+) sign associated with the Effects portion of the Properties panel. Select Bevel and Emboss>Inner Bevel from the dialog box that appears. Within the dialog box, set the Bevel Edge Shape to Smooth from the topmost pop-up menu. Set the Width to 30, Contrast to 75%, Softness to 3, and Angle to 155. Press the Return/Enter key or click outside the Inner Bevel dialog box to apply the effect.

Locating the Effects portion of the Properties panel.

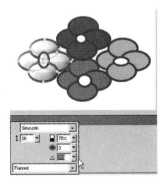

Adjusting the Inner Bevel effect.

8. With the yellow ellipses still selected, click the Effects plus (+) sign again to display the menu options. From this menu, select Shadow and Glow>Drop Shadow to display the Drop Shadow dialog box. Set the Distance to 7, Opacity to 100%, Softness to 4, and Angle to 315. Click the Color swatch to set the glow color to a dark mauve, or enter #996666 in the hexadecimal code field. Press Return/Enter or click outside the dialog box to apply the new Drop Shadow effect.

9. Select the yellow ellipses with the Pointer tool. Click the Add Effects plus (+) sign again to display the menu. Choose Options>Save as Style. In the dialog box that displays, click the Effect check box if it is not turned on by default. Make sure no other check boxes are selected. In the Name field, enter "Bevel_Mauve". Click OK to save the new style.

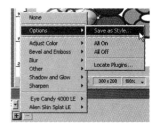

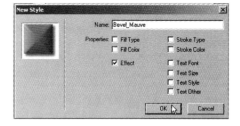

The New Style dialog box displays when you select Options>Save as Style.

10. Deselect the yellow ellipses. Use the Pointer tool to select each of the red, pink, and purple vector shapes. Click the Add Effect plus (+) sign. Notice that Bevel_Mauve, the newly created style, is now a menu option. To apply this style to the red, pink, and purple ellipses, simply click the Bevel_Mauve menu item.

You can also apply the Bevel_Mauve style by clicking the square style swatch in the Assets panel. You can apply, delete, and edit both default and custom styles from this panel; to edit a style, simply double-click the style swatch and make your changes within the resulting dialog box.

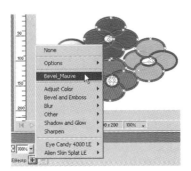

Applying the Bevel_Mauve style after clicking the Add Effect button in the Properties panel.

The Bevel_Mauve style as it appears in the Assets panel.

11. You learned how to apply two commonly used effects, as well as how to create custom styles. If time permits, apply additional effects and some of the pre-set styles. Once you complete your explorations, save the file and close the document.

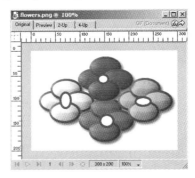

The document after Step 10. If you chose to experiment with other effects and custom styles, your final results may be different than ours.

Manipulating Shapes

You can create many complex shapes by modifying those that are simple to draw. Simple shapes can be distorted, skewed, joined, and altered in many ways to produce original shapes. When you know the options, and you're not afraid to be creative with the tools, you can produce some very unique and interesting shapes. We suggest you become familiar with many of the drawing alternatives so you don't have to repeatedly resort to using the Pen tool or pressing the "Q" key every time you need to create a complex shape.

Transforming Shapes

There are many instances when a shape needs to be modified. For example, distorting a shape can change its perspective. Scaling is often needed when creating multiple objects of various sizes. Simply applying a slight transformation to a shape can turn an object that looks a little out of scale into the perfect shape for your needs. All the transformation options are available from the Modify>Transform menu. The Scale, Skew, and Distort options are available from the Select section of the Tools panel.

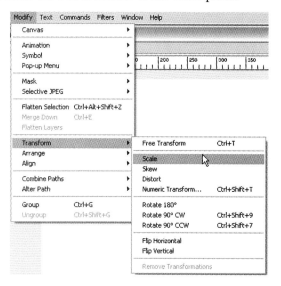

The options available from the Transform section of the Modify menu.

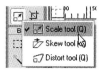

The transform tools, available from the Tools panel.

Free Transform

The Free Transform option allows you to transform an object in almost any way you choose. The option is available from the Modify>Transform menu, or by pressing Command/Control-T. A bounding box appears around the object; it contains six square handles and the anchor point — an almost circular shape in the center of the object. Moving each of the handles changes the shape of the object:

- Drag with the solid arrow cursor to skew and distort the shape.
- Drag with the double-headed arrow cursor to resize the object.
- Drag with the curved arrow cursor to rotate the shape.
- Change the position of the anchor point to change the reference point for all rotations and transformations.

The Free Transform tool allows for many transformation options; it is very useful when you want to change an object in multiple ways at one time.

The four-headed arrow moves the selected object.

The two-headed arrow from a corner handle resizes the object while maintaining aspect ratio.

The two-headed arrow from a top, bottom, or side handle increases or decreases the height or width of the object.

The circular arrow rotates the object.

When an object is selected with a transform tool, a circle appears on the object. The circle is the anchor point around which an object is skewed, distorted, and/or rotated. The circle can be moved, allowing the object to be moved around a new point. When the circle is moved, the transformation effects are applied according to the anchor point's new position.

The anchor point of the object has been moved.

Scale

The Scale option is used to enlarge and reduce the size of the object. If the object is resized from a corner, the proportions of the object are not distorted. If the width or height of an object needs to be changed, the handles on the sides or top and bottom should be used. Any vector object can be enlarged or reduced in size without negatively impacting its quality. If a raster image is scaled, its quality is quickly reduced.

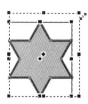

The object is being scaled from the corner to maintain the correct proportions (aspect ratio) of width and height.

Skew

Using the Skew tool horizontally and vertically transforms an object. The corners of an object can be brought together or pushed apart using this tool. Using the Skew tool can change the perspective of an object. You can also move the anchor point to change the skew effect. The Skew tool is useful when you need an object to appear closer on one side than on the other. The larger side of the object appears closer to the viewer than the smaller side.

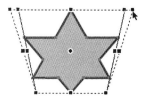

The Skew tool is being used to make the top of the object appear closer to the viewer than the bottom.

Distort

The Distort tool allows an object to be resized from any handle. The handles can be moved independently of one another. This tool is often used to change the perspective of a shape. Use this tool when you need to make one corner of an object appear closer than the rest of the object.

Sometimes transforming a shape makes it unrecognizable. You may want to make a copy of the original shape before transforming, just in case the shape becomes too distorted.

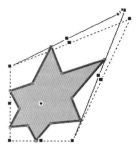

The Distort tool is being used to stretch the top-right corner of the object.

Numeric Transform

An object can also be transformed using percentages. Using Numeric Transform from the Modify>Transform menu, the object can be scaled, resized, and rotated. The options can be toggled to either Scale Attributes or Constrain Proportion. When Scale Attributes is selected, attributes such as Stroke and Pattern are also scaled. When Scale Attributes is not selected, the attributes remain the same size as before the object was altered. Constrain Proportions prevents the width from being changed without changing the height in the same proportional amount. Numeric transformations are useful when you have a precise target size in mind for your object.

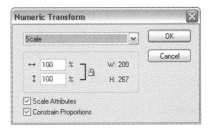

The Numeric Transform window from the Modify>Transform menu.

Objects can also be numerically resized in the Properties panel. When an object is selected, you can enter new width and height measurements in the W and H fields. The X and Y fields can be used to position the object on the canvas according to the horizontal and vertical axes. Both numbers are measured from the top-left corner of the canvas to the top-left corner of the object. The Properties panel doesn't offer you as many options as the Numeric Transform window, but the Properties panel is more readily available to apply numeric transformations.

The Properties panel allows for numeric transformations as well as placement on the canvas.

Rotate

Any of the transform tools can be used to freely rotate an object 180°, 90° clockwise, or 90° counterclockwise. Selecting one of the transform tools and dragging when the cursor is near a corner handle rotates the object in the direction you drag. Holding down the Shift key while freely rotating constrains the rotation to 15° intervals. A constrained rotation is achieved by first selecting an object and then choosing Rotate 180°, Rotate 90° CW, or Rotate 90° CCW from the Modify>Transform menu.

An object is rotated according to its anchor point. An object doesn't have to be rotated around its center. Simply move the anchor point to change the point of reference for any rotation method.

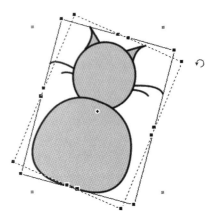

The selected object is being freely rotated.

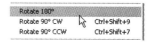

The Rotate options from the Modify>Transform menu.

Flip

Any object can be flipped horizontally or vertically. Flipping objects can create many different effects, including a mirror effect. Objects can be flipped when they are selected, and Flip Horizontal or Flip Vertical can then be chosen. The object is flipped along a horizontal or vertical plane. If you apply Flip Horizontal or Flip Vertical two times, the object returns to its original position. A combination of horizontal and vertical flips is possible, and sometimes required.

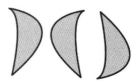

The original shape is on the left. The middle shape was flipped horizontally. The shape on the right was flipped vertically.

Combining Paths

Paths can be combined in several ways to become one new shape. Combining paths is an easy way to make complex shapes. There are many methods you can use to combine shapes, each producing a different result. We recommend becoming familiar with each method so you'll be able to quickly combine shapes without having to search for the desired method. You can apply the Combine Path options by first selecting the paths and then accessing the Modify>Combine Paths sub-menu.

More than one object can be selected, allowing you to transform many objects at one time.

Join

The Join option combines two or more objects into one path. The objects can be overlapping, but this is not required. The fill of two original overlapping paths is deleted. If the path is not closed and the end points of a path are selected, the Join command closes the path. Use this option when several paths are drawn with the intention of making the paths into a single path.

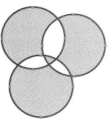

Three overlapping circles are joined.

The original open path is on the left. The path on the right was closed using the Join option.

Split

The Split option is used on paths that were joined, and you then decide to separate the paths into their original state. Open paths that were closed using the Join option cannot be converted back to an open path using the Split option. Use the Split option if the Join command created a path that wasn't the intended result.

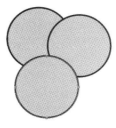

The circles that were previously joined are now split.

Union

The Union option is used to combine two or more overlapping paths into one closed path. This option is similar to the Join option; the difference is that the outside outline of the paths is used as the new path. The properties of the object farthest to the back are used for the new shape. Use this option when you create paths that you want to combine using only the outline paths.

The three circles were combined using the Union option.

Intersect

The Intersect option creates a new shape from the overlapping areas of multiple paths. The new path takes on the attributes of the object farthest to the back. This combined path option is used to create unique shapes from multiple paths.

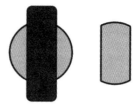

The original objects are displayed on the left. The resulting object after the Intersect command was applied is shown on the right. Notice that the new object takes on the characteristics of the object farthest back.

Punch

The Punch option allows one object to remove portions of another object or objects. The object defining the shape to be removed or "punched" must be the object closest to the front. The top (punch) object alters the objects behind it. This option is similar to using a fancy hole-punch; the top object acts as the shape of the hole-punch.

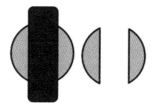

The original objects are displayed on the left. The resulting object after the Punch command was applied is shown on the right. Notice that in this instance, the Punch command created two separate objects.

Crop

The Crop option uses an object to crop and define the shape of another object. The top object is used as the Crop shape and disappears after the Crop option is applied. This option is similar to framing objects. The part of the object that doesn't fit in the frame is eliminated.

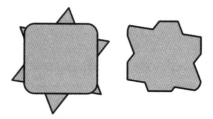

The original objects are displayed on the left. The resulting object after the Crop command was applied is shown on the right.

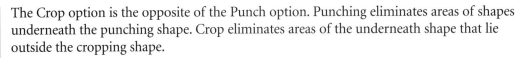

Sometimes the results of the Combine options for the Join and Crop commands are the same.

The Crop option is the opposite of the Punch option. Punching eliminates areas of shapes underneath the punching shape. Crop eliminates areas of the underneath shape that lie outside the cropping shape.

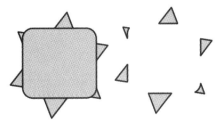

The same objects are shown as above, but the Punch option is used instead of the Crop option.

Combine Options

1. From the File menu, select Open. Navigate to the **RF_Fireworks** folder. Open **combine.png**.

2. Use the Pointer tool and the Shift key in combination to select the three rounded rectangles. From the Modify menu, select Combine Paths>Union.

3. Select the patterned shape in the background and the newly combined blue vector shape. From the Modify menu, select Combine Paths>Intersect.

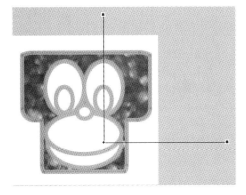

4. Select the large and small ellipses in the upper left of the document. From the Modify menu, choose Combine Paths>Punch. Repeat the process with the large and small ellipses in the upper right.

5. Using the Pointer tool, click the lowest two ellipses. From the Modify menu, select Combine Paths>Punch.

6. When you are finished, close **combine.png** without saving your changes.

Altering Paths

You can alter paths after they have been drawn to achieve a precise look and feel. Sometimes paths need to be simplified, or the edge might need to be changed. Altering paths through experimentation can lead to the perfect appearance you require.

A path has stroke and fill properties that can be altered. Let's explore the three options that allow you to alter the stroke of a path, and the three options that allow you to alter the fill of a path.

Simplify

Quite often, a shape is drawn with too many points. Each additional point in a path adds to the file size; more importantly, too many points detract from the smoothness of the path. The Simplify command eliminates surplus points by the amount specified.

The Simplify window from the Modify>Alter Path command.

You can simplify the path by entering any number, starting with one, into the Amount field on the Simplify dialog box. Larger numbers simplify the path more than smaller numbers. At least one path must be selected before you can apply the Simplify command. Also, there is a certain point where a higher number entered in the Simplify Amount field won't affect the object any more than a smaller number. This command only removes redundant points and does not remove the points that define the object.

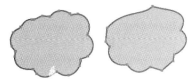

The original shape on the left contains many points.
The Simplify command was applied to the object on the right.

Expand Stroke

The stroke of an object can be turned into a closed path using the Expand Stroke command. This command is useful when the stroke is the defining shape you need. The option expands the stroke into inside and outside strokes with a specified width. The area in between the inside and outside strokes is the fill.

Choosing Expand Stroke from the Modify>Alter Path menu affects selected objects. The Expand Stroke window appears with options for the command. The Width is the space between the inside and outside strokes. The slider displays numbers from 1 to 100, but you can enter a larger number when necessary. The larger the number, the more intricate and unique the object becomes.

The corners created by the Expand Stroke command can be Miter, Round, or Beveled. When Miter is selected, a Miter Limit must be specified. The Miter Limit is a ratio of the corner length to the stroke width. The End Caps option sets the shape of the end of an open path after the Expand Stroke command has been applied. Each option creates a different effect.

The Expand Stroke window.

The Expand Stroke option converts a line into a closed path.

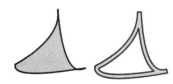

The Expand Stroke option was applied to this object.
The original shape is on the left and the result is on the right.

Inset Path

The Inset Path command expands and contracts a path according to the specified amount. The amount of change can be set using a slider or directly entered from the keyboard. The slider allows the width to be set at a maximum value of 100, but a higher number can be manually entered using the keyboard. The Direction Inside option contracts the path; the Direction Outside option expands the path.

When a path is enlarged or contracted, the corners change. The corners can be set as Miter, Round, or Beveled, similar to when you use the Expand Stroke command. The Miter Limit should be set when using the Miter option. All of the Inset Path options work together to create various effects.

The Inset Path window from the Modify>Alter Path menu.

The original object is on the left. The middle object's path was Inset with the Direction Inside option. The object on the right was Inset with the Direction Outside option.

Hard Fill

The fill of a path is usually anti-aliased. Sometimes, a Hard fill makes an object appear a bit sharper. Hard fills can also create a stair-stepping effect on diagonals and curves. To alter the fill of an object, it must first be selected, and then you can choose an option from the Modify>Alter Path sub-menu.

Rectangular shapes do not allow the fill to be altered because it is not necessary. A rectangular shape doesn't need anti-aliasing because all of the lines on this type of shape are horizontal or vertical, not curved or diagonal. Only curved and diagonal lines require anti-aliasing.

An object with a Hard fill.

An object retains its stroke and fill attributes when the path is altered.

The Hard, Anti-Alias, and Feather fills are only available for non-rectangular objects.

Although the Anti-Alias and Feather fills cannot be applied to rectangular shapes from the Modify>Alter Path menu, these fills can be applied using the Edge of Fills menu found in the Properties panel.

Anti-Alias Fill

The Anti-Alias fill softens the curves and diagonal lines of objects by adding pixels to blend the foreground and background colors along the edges. You can set the Fill option by selecting a shape other than a rectangle and choosing Anti-Alias Fill from the Modify>Alter Path sub-menu.

An object with an Anti-Alias fill.

Feather Fill

A Feather fill creates a gradient blend on the edge of a non-rectangular path. The Feather fill is much more noticeable than an Anti-Alias fill. Once feathering is applied, the amount can be altered in the Properties panel. The larger the number in the Amount of Feather field, the more distance the Feather uses to complete the effect. A large Feather amount might soften the entire fill, depending on the size of the object.

An object with a Feather fill.

Shape Adjustment Tools

A path's shape can be adjusted to form a new shape using the Shape Adjustment tools. These tools can also change the properties of a path. Adjusting points on a path can be a difficult method of altering a path; but adjusting points is not the only way to reshape a path. You can use the Shape Adjustment tools when you need to edit a path without manually adjusting the points on the path.

Freeform Tool

The Freeform tool aids in reshaping or bending a path without touching the individual points on the path. This tool actually adds points to a path. The Freeform tool is used to push the path into a new shape. The cursor changes according to its position. When the Freeform tool is selected, the size of the tool can be adjusted from the Properties panel. The Freeform tool can be accessed from the Vector section of the Tools panel, or by pressing the "O" key.

If the Freeform tool creates too many points on a path, the Simplify command can be used to reduce the number of points.

This cursor indicates that the Freeform tool is selected.

This cursor indicates that a click and drag with the mouse will pull the path according to the direction you drag. The cursor must be directly over a path to pull it.

This cursor indicates that a path is being pulled and reshaped.

The Freeform tool works best when you select the path before you choose the tool.

This cursor indicates that the mouse button is depressed with the Freeform tool selected. Clicking and dragging with the cursor will alter the path around the circle of the cursor.

The Freeform tool is being used to reshape a path.

You can also change the size of the pointer using the Left Arrow and Right Arrow keys.

You can change the size of the Freeform tool in the Properties panel.

Reshape Area Tool

The Reshape Area tool alters a path in the specified area between the two circles in the tool's cursor. The two-circle cursor indicates the Reshape Area tool is selected.

The Reshape Area tool cursor.

When using a graphics tablet rather than a mouse, the pressure used on the tablet corresponds to the strength of the Reshape Area tool without having to change the settings in the Properties panel.

The size of the tool is set in the Properties panel; it indicates the size of the outer circle. The strength of the tool is also set in the Properties panel; it indicates how significantly the tool affects a path. The smaller the distance between the two circles, the greater the strength, and the more the tool affects a path. The entire area of a path can be moved in between the inner and outer circles of the tool. You can access this tool from the Freeform tool in the Tools panel, or press the "O" key.

The size and strength of the tool are set in the Properties panel.

The Reshape Area tool in use.

Path Scrubber Tool (Additive/Subtractive)

The Path Scrubber tools are used to increase or decrease the intensity of a path's stroke properties. The Path Scrubber–Additive tool increases the intensity of the stroke properties when the tool is selected and the cursor is dragged along a path. The properties of the stroke become more intense every time you drag the tool across the path. The tool is only effective on objects that have pressure-sensitive strokes, such as an Air Brush stroke.

The Path Scrubber–Subtractive tool works opposite to the Additive tool — the stroke properties are decreased when you use this tool. The Subtractive tool can be used repeatedly, to the point where the stroke disappears along a path. Both of these tools are available under the Freeform tool in the Tools panel.

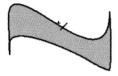

The Path Scrubber–Additive tool in use.

The Path Scrubber–Subtractive tool in use.

The Knife tool is only used on the path; it does not affect the fill of an object.

Knife Tool

The Knife tool slices paths. When you slice a path, the vector object is cut into two or more separate pieces. Cutting an object can produce interesting open paths. The Knife tool cannot create two closed paths from the original closed path; instead, it opens the path.

You can use the Knife tool by dragging it across a path. The path is cut where the cursor is dragged. Once a path is cut, the Pointer tool can be used to select the individual pieces. Once a piece of a path or an entire path is selected, pressing the Delete or Backspace key removes the path. The Knife tool is available from the Vector section of the Tools panel, or by pressing the "Y" key.

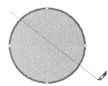

The Knife tool is making two half-circle objects.

Use the Reshape Tool

1. Select File>New to access the New File dialog box. Create a new document with a Width of 300 and Height of 200. Choose a White Canvas Color, and ensure the Resolution is set to 72 Pixels/Inch.

2. Using the Vector Path tool with your own stroke settings, draw one continual line that weaves vertically up and down across the horizontal axis of the document from left to right.

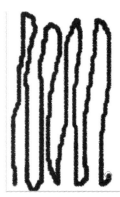

Using the Vector Path tool with a Creamy Charcoal Stroke with a Width of 13 and a 2-pt. Edge.

3. Select the Reshape Area tool from the Tools panel, and use the Properties panel to set the Size to 33 and Strength to 28.

Selecting the Reshape Area tool.

Setting Reshape Area tool properties in the Properties panel.

4. Use the Reshape Area tool to draw an ever-tightening spiral around the edge – and into the center – of the canvas. This creates a chunky, marble-like effect on your document.

5. You can continue to experiment with the Reshape Area tool if you prefer. When finished, close the document without saving.

Drawing a spiral with the Reshape Area tool.

Completing the spiral.

Vector Shape Organization

How shapes are organized and aligned can be important success factors of an image. Oftentimes, a shape is not in the correct position; this decreases the effectiveness of the image. Fireworks provides several tools that help you organize and align vector shapes. Let's discuss shape alignment, grouping shapes, and shape stacking order. Mastering each of these actions will increase your productivity when manipulating vector objects.

Aligning Shapes

After objects are aligned, you should group the objects before repositioning to ensure the alignment is not disturbed.

Many designers have spent countless hours attempting to manually align shapes. Fortunately, Fireworks provides a quick and easy method to automatically align objects. The Align options satisfy any symmetrical alignment requirement, as well as other alignment needs. Objects might only need to be aligned one way, but quite often you must combine multiple alignment options to achieve a desired result.

The Align options are located in the Modify>Align menu, or you can access them from the Align panel. Each Align option is applied only to selected objects. Before aligning objects, we recommend placing them in roughly the correct position. Once the objects are aligned, moving them can shift the proper alignment.

Left Align

Regardless of the size and shape of the objects, a Left alignment places the selected objects in a straight line along the left-most edge of the object that is farthest to the left. You can select this option from the Modify>Align menu, the Align panel, or by pressing the Command/Control-Option/Alt-1 keys in combination.

The three objects are Left aligned.

Keyboard shortcuts for vertical alignments:

Left: Command/ Control-Option/Alt-1

Center Vertical: Command/ Control-Option/Alt-2

Right: Command/ Control-Option/Alt-3

Center Vertical

The Center Vertical alignment places the selected objects along their vertical centers. The objects move to the average vertical center of the objects. You can select this option from the Modify>Align menu, the Align panel, or by pressing the Command/Control-Option/Alt-2 keys in combination.

The three objects are centered vertically.

Right

Regardless of the size and shape of the objects, a Right alignment places the selected objects in a straight line along the right-most edge of the object that is farthest to the right. You can select this option from the Modify>Align menu, the Align panel, or by pressing the Command/Control-Option/Alt-3 keys in combination.

The three objects are Right aligned.

Top

The Top alignment option aligns selected objects according to the top-most edge of the objects. All objects are aligned with the object that is closest to the top of the document. You can select this option from the Modify>Align menu, the Align panel, or by pressing the Command/Control-Option/Alt-4 keys in combination.

The three objects are Top aligned.

Center Horizontal

The Center Horizontal alignment places objects along the horizontal centers of the selected objects. The objects move to the average horizontal center of the objects. You can select this option from the Modify>Align menu, the Align panel, or by pressing the Command/Control-Option/Alt-5 keys in combination.

The three objects are centered horizontally.

Bottom

A Bottom alignment places selected objects along the bottom edge of the object that is farthest to the bottom of the document. Regardless of the size and shape of the objects, they are placed in a straight line along their bottom edges. You can select this option from the Modify>Align menu, the Align panel, or by pressing the Command/Control-Option/Alt-6 keys in combination.

The three objects are Bottom aligned.

Distribute Widths

The Distribute Widths option averages the widths between the selected objects and repositions the objects with the same horizontal width between each object. The Distribute Widths option can only be used when three or more objects are selected. If only two objects are selected, there is only one width between them, which cannot be compared to any other width. This option is useful when you need to evenly space objects, as is often the case with a series of Web buttons. Distribute Widths is available from the Modify>Align menu, the Align panel, or by pressing the Command/Control-Option/Alt-7 keys in combination.

These objects are perfectly aligned and spaced. First the objects were aligned using Bottom align, and then the Distribute Widths option was applied.

A group of objects often has both align and distribute options applied in order to perfectly position them.

Distribute Heights

The Distribute Heights option works the same as the Distribute Widths option, but it distributes the vertical space between three or more selected objects. This option is useful when you need to vertically align many objects. Distribute Heights is available from the Modify>Align menu, the Align panel, or by pressing the Command/Control-Option/Alt-9 keys in combination.

These objects are perfectly aligned and spaced. First, the objects were Left aligned and then the Distribute Heights option was applied.

Group/Ungroup

Objects can be grouped together so you can manipulate all of the objects as if they were one object. Once grouped, the objects can be moved, resized, and otherwise manipulated as a single unit. Grouping is a very common and useful tool. Groups save time, since commands can be applied to all the objects at one time, instead of applying the same command to each of the individual objects. Once a group is created, a gradient can be applied across the entire group, a feature that is not possible without grouping.

The cat is made of several objects that were selected prior to grouping.

The objects in the cat shape are grouped, so the cat can be resized, moved, and further altered as if it were one object.

In most applications that allow objects to be grouped, the individual components of the group cannot be edited. You can use the Fireworks Subselection tool to select and then edit the individual objects in a group. This advanced feature offers the benefits of grouping, combined with the benefits of individual objects.

Although the objects in the cat shape are grouped,
the cat's body is being individually selected with the Subselection tool.

Before you can group objects, first you must select all of the objects and then select Group from the Modify menu. The keyboard shortcut, Command/Control-G, is a helpful timesaver. A grouped object can be grouped with other objects.

Ungrouping returns a group to its individual components. Sometimes, objects are grouped multiple times; in this case, you must use the Ungroup command multiple times to return to the original individual shapes. When you need to ungroup objects, you can select the Ungroup command from the Modify menu, or you can use the Shift-Command/Control-G keyboard shortcut.

Understanding Stacking Order

Objects can be placed one on top of the other and still be editable. The arrangement of layered objects is referred to as the *stacking order*. Just as paper can be placed in a stack, so can objects. Objects can be repositioned in the stack if you want to display the objects in a different way. Objects toward the top of the stacking order cover objects toward the bottom when the objects overlap one another.

Bring to Front

Selecting an object and then choosing Bring to Front from the Modify>Arrange menu repositions the object to the top of the image or in front of all the other objects on the document.

In the image on the left, the shape with points is in front of the oval shape.
In the image on the right, the oval shape is in front of the shape with points.
The image in the front is always higher in the stacking order.

To select multiple objects at one time, hold down the Shift key while selecting the objects.

Stacking order is important when using the Combine Path options.

Bring Forward

A selected object can be repositioned so it is one object closer to the top (front) of the image using the Bring Forward command. You can access this command from the Modify>Arrange sub-menu. Using Bring Forward multiple times brings the selected object one step closer to the top of the image with each command.

In the image on the left, part of the star shape is hidden behind both the square and the oval. In the image on the right, the star shape was brought forward once so it is in between the square and the oval.

Send Backward

A selected object can be repositioned one object closer to the bottom (back) of the image using the Send Backward command. You can access this command from the Modify>Arrange sub-menu. Using Send Backward multiple times sends the selected object one step closer to the bottom of the image with each command.

In the image on the left, the black circle is in front of the other circles. In the image on the right, the black circle was sent backward so it is wedged between the gray and white circles.

Send to Back

Objects can be repositioned using layers, which we discuss in Chapter 8 of this book.

Selecting an object and then choosing Send to Back from the Modify>Arrange sub-menu repositions the object at the back of the image. The object is placed at the bottom of the stacking order.

In the image on the left, the black circle is in front of the other circles. In the image on the right, the black circle was sent to the back, so it is partially hidden by the gray and white circles that are now in front of it.

Chapter Summary

In this chapter, you learned many methods to change vector object properties and manipulate vector objects. The stroke and fill properties were presented. Methods to transform, combine, and alter shapes and paths were discussed in detail. The alignment of objects — top, center, right, left, horizontal, and vertical — was discussed. Finally, we talked about the order of objects as you moved objects to the front and to the back, and learned how the stacking order of images affects how they are viewed in the document.

5 Working with Text

Chapter Objectives:

The Fireworks text tools provide many options for displaying text in an image. You can also convert text elements to graphics to ensure your text looks exactly as you intend, no matter where it is viewed. Text elements are very versatile, and can be used on Web banners and buttons, to create special visual effects, and much more. In this chapter you will:

- Learn how to apply text properties.

- Explore kerning, leading, alignment, and other orientation options.

- Find out how to change text block settings.

- Learn how to use the Spell Checker utility.

- Discover how to convert text to paths, and attach text to paths.

Projects to be Completed:

- Globe Illustration (A)

- Image Retouching Advertisement (B)

- Animated Banner (C)

- The Cable Store Web Site (D)

Working with Text

Images can be greatly enhanced when text elements are included in the design. Some images are entirely text. Fireworks includes many excellent features that make it quick and easy to add text to an image. Editing text properties and converting text to paths can also create some very interesting results.

When you need to create text elements for placement on the Web, Fireworks is an excellent choice. Since not all computers can display all fonts, it is difficult to control how your text will look on various viewers' machines; you might choose to use a certain font that many of your viewers don't have, resulting in very unpredictable (and sometimes very poor) results. To correct this problem, text elements are often converted to images, which are then used on Web pages. This procedure can control the appearance of text elements on your Web pages, regardless of the fonts that are installed on the viewer's machine; the image displays exactly the same on every machine, every time it is viewed.

Web pages often use text on banners, buttons, and links that have been saved as graphics. Text can be edited as long as it is still in the native Fireworks file type — PNG — and hasn't been exported. Once the Fireworks PNG file is exported to a GIF or JPEG, the text cannot be changed, and displays exactly as intended on the Web.

Using the Text Tool

The Fireworks Text tool works in much the same way as the type tools in many other graphics applications. You can select the tool from the Tools panel, click on the canvas, and begin typing. The text is entered directly on the canvas. After text has been added to a document, the Text Editor becomes available. You can use this method — where you can preview what you type before it is placed on the canvas — rather than directly entering text on the canvas. The Text Editor can be useful when text is too small to be seen on the canvas.

Always keep your original PNG file so your text can be edited if necessary.

Previous versions of Fireworks required that text be entered into the Text Editor; you could not type directly on the canvas as you can with Fireworks MX.

Double-clicking in a text block with the Pointer tool switches to the Text tool.

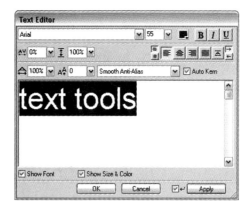

The Text Editor window available from the Text>Editor menu.

The Properties panel is also referred to as the "Properties Inspector."

You can only use fonts that are installed on your computer. If you want to edit a document on a computer that doesn't have the same font, the font can be switched to a default match to the missing font.

Fonts fall into several categories, the most common being "sans serif" or "serif." Serifs are small lines that appear on characters. Sans serif fonts, such as Arial, don't have these small lines. Serif fonts, such as Times New Roman, have the lines.

The font face is the font used for text.

Once text is entered and the Pointer tool is selected, the text can be moved around the canvas. Clicking the text block with the Text tool allows you to edit the text and change its properties. Other tools allow you to further modify the text. We discuss these options throughout this chapter.

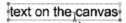

Text being altered on the canvas.

Text can also be imported into Fireworks. If you have a lot of text in another document, such as a Microsoft Word document, it might be easier to import the text rather than re-keying or copying and pasting. Text must be saved in RTF (Rich Text Format) or ASCII (American Standard Code for Information Interchange) format. You can import text from the File>Import menu.

Setting Text Properties

As soon as the Text tool is selected, the Properties panel automatically shows all the options available for editing text. Text has many different properties, including color, font, and size, as well as alignment and orientation options. Paragraph settings can also be applied. Let's discuss these settings and find out how to change them.

General

When creating new text, the general text properties almost always need to be changed. The most basic text properties include the font, size, style, stroke, and fill. These options are used the most because they are the primary controls for the appearance of text. The text properties can be changed before or after text is added to the canvas. Text properties can be changed as long as you are working with the native PNG file.

Font Face

The font applied to text can be set before entering text on the canvas, or changed after the text is in place. To change the font beforehand, you can select the Text tool and set the font in the Properties panel using the Font pop-up menu.

The Font pop-up menu is displayed from the Properties panel.

Once text is added and the cursor is blinking in the text, you can change the font face by highlighting the text and selecting the correct font in the Properties panel. If the cursor is not blinking, you can select the text block with the Pointer tool and change the font in the Properties panel. The Text>Font menu also allows you to change the font. The Properties panel displays a preview of the font before it's applied; the Text>Font menu does not. A preview is an excellent tool when you're not sure how the font looks.

In general, a sans serif font is best for headings, and a serif font is best for large blocks of text in print. A sans serif font is generally easier to read on screen.

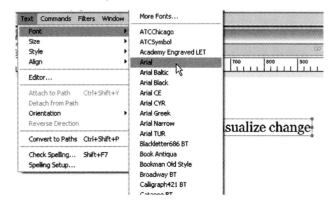

Text is being changed using the Text>Font menu.

Size

The size of text is set much the same as the font. You can set the size before or after the text is on the canvas using the Size pop-up menu. As an alternative, you can manually enter any point size using the keyboard. The size of text can also be changed from the Text>Size menu. Here, the size can be set not only using the point sizes listed, but any number can be entered by clicking Other. The Smaller and Larger options decrease and increase (respectively) the size that is currently applied to the text. If the text needs to be enlarged, it is always best to change the text size instead of scaling the text block with the Transform tool.

Text is measured in points. There are 72 points per inch (ppi).

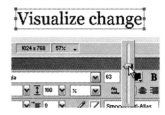

The text block is selected and the text's size is being changed using the slider in the Properties panel.

If text needs to be enlarged, it is always best to change the text size instead of scaling the text block with the Transform tool.

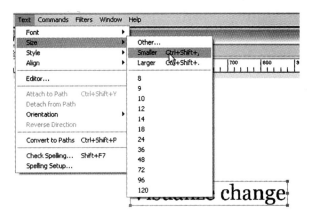

The font size is being changed using the Text>Size menu.

The Text Size window from the Text>Size>Other menu.

Text size is measured from the topmost part of the text to the bottommost part of the text.

Style

Style refers to the Bold, Italic, or Underline properties that are applied to the text. If a font has its own Bold, Italic, or Underline version, it is always best to use those versions instead of applying a style to the text, since they were specifically created for that purpose.

Underlined text many times signifies hyperlinks, so we recommend using underlining only in special circumstances. When creating an image for the Web that will not be linked, avoid the Underline style.

Using underlined text on the Web will confuse the user if it is not linked.

Bold
Italic
<u>Underline</u>

Text with Bold, Italic, and Underline styles applied.

Style can also be set on selected text from the Text>Style menu. Here, you can remove styles by choosing the Plain option.

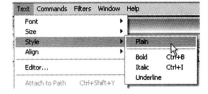

Plain is being selected from the Text>Style menu in order to remove styles from the text.

Stroke and Fill

Similar to vector objects, text elements have stroke and fill properties. When text is added to a document, the current stroke and fill settings are applied to the text. These settings can be changed after the text has been added to an image. To do this, you would select the text and then change the colors in the same way you would change an object's stroke and fill colors.

Imagine

The above text has a stroke and a gradient fill.

Even though the options for stroke and fill (other than color) are not displayed in the Properties panel, the stroke and fill options can still be changed for text elements. To change the stroke properties, you can select Stroke Options from the Stroke Color pop-up window. You can change the fill properties by selecting Fill Options from the Fill Color pop-up window.

If the Properties panel is not visible, expand it so the text properties can be set.

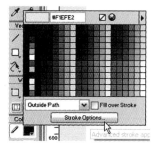

Stroke Options are available from the Stroke Color pop-up window.

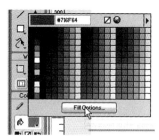

Fill Options are available from the Fill Color pop-up window.

Typographic Settings

Typographic settings allow for precise control over text elements. Settings such as kerning, leading, alignment, orientation, and horizontal scaling can be changed in the Properties panel. All of these settings control how text is displayed. We often change these settings to either make text more visually appealing or easier to read.

Kerning

Kerning refers to the space between pairs of characters. It is sometimes referred to as *tracking*. Sometimes text looks better if pairs of characters are closer together or farther apart. For example, a capital "A" and capital "V" are often spaced far apart, but they would look more appealing if the kerning were reduced to move the characters closer together. Kerning can also be used when you want to change the amount of space that is required to display text. If you use a small text size, the additional space between the characters can make it easier to read the text.

AV AV

The kerning was decreased for the letter pair on the right.

To change kerning, you would place the cursor between two text characters. You can move the slider next to the Kerning or Range Kerning field in the Properties panel to alter the kerning, or you can manually enter a specific number into the value field. Positive numbers increase the space between characters; negative numbers decrease the space. Range Kerning refers to the amount of space between selected characters, not just a character pair.

The Kerning or Range Kerning field in the Properties panel.

You can automatically kern text by selecting Auto Kern in the Properties panel. Auto Kern is an excellent choice for most instances, but sometimes certain letter pairs require "tweaking" — small manual adjustments. The kerning can still be altered even if Auto Kern is turned on.

The Auto Kern toggle option in the Properties panel.

Leading

Leading (pronounced "ledding") refers to the space between lines of text. Leading can be changed to move lines of text closer together or farther apart. Changing the leading can help when you need text to take up more or less space on the page. The amount of leading can affect readability. When lines are too close together or too far a part, our eyes have a difficult time finding the next line. The amount of leading can be set using percentages or absolute pixel values. Leading is set when a block of text is selected and the value is changed in the Properties panel. The Leading Units pop-up menu toggles between percentages and pixels.

Leading settings in the Properties panel.

To change the spacing in a block of text, select the characters and apply kerning to the entire block.

You can select negative pixel leading values; the results are similar to lower leading percentages.

The amount of leading can also be altered using the keyboard. Holding down the Command/Control key while pressing the Up Arrow key increases leading, while pressing the Command/Control and Down Arrow keys decreases the leading.

Fireworks provides many options for altering text in a document. The properties of text can be set in the Properties panel. Text may also be converted to paths and attached to text.
If text is converted to paths it can be edited just like any other path. Some pretty interesting shapes can be created with text that has been converted to paths.

Fireworks provides many options for altering text in a document. The properties of text can be set in the Properties panel. Text may also be converted to paths and attached to text.
If text is converted to paths it can be edited just like any other path. Some pretty interesting shapes can be created with text that has been converted to paths.

The text on the right has increased leading from the original on the left.

Alignment

Text can be aligned using the Left, Center, Right, or Justified options. To apply alignment, you would place the cursor in the text and select the desired alignment button in the Properties panel. Text can also be aligned from the Text>Align menu. The Text>Align menu displays all alignment options for horizontally and vertically oriented text.

Alignment can change the look and feel of your text. Most text is easiest to read with a Left alignment. Center alignment is appropriate for headings; large blocks of text are often difficult to read when they are Center aligned. Sometimes a Right alignment is visually appealing, depending on your design and layout. If you're trying to create the appearance of a newspaper, your best choice is to apply Justified alignment to the text.

Single lines of text usually don't reflect justification — or any alignment for that matter — because they can be positioned anywhere on the screen.

The Alignment buttons in the Properties panel.

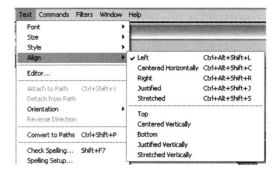

The Text>Align menu.

The Align options change according to the orientation of the text. When text is vertical, the Alignment buttons in the Properties panel change to Top, Center, Bottom, and Justified. Working with vertical text can be challenging. The cursor changes direction, but it works the same as when text is horizontally oriented.

The Alignment buttons change when text is vertically oriented.

Orientation

Text orientation can be set horizontally or vertically. Both options allow text to be displayed left to right, or right to left. The Orientation options allow for a multitude of possibilities and languages. Some languages are written vertically instead of horizontally, and right to left instead of left to right.

Text orientation is set with the Text Orientation buttons located in the Properties panel. The orientation can also be changed using the Text>Align menu. The upper options set the text to a horizontal orientation; the lower options set the text to a vertical orientation.

The Text Orientation options from the Properties panel.

Example of horizontal and vertical orientations.

Stretch alignment stretches text to fill the entire text block.

The Orientation options can be used to create a mirrored text effect by switching a copy of the text to the right-to-left orientation.

The horizontal scale does not affect the height of characters.

Horizontal Scale

Changing the horizontal scale of text alters the width of the text. The higher the percentage of horizontal scale, the wider the character widths appear; the lower the percentage, the narrower the characters appear. The scale is set in percentages using the Horizontal Scale pop-up menu in the Properties panel. A value of 100% is the normal horizontal scale setting. Values smaller than 100% contract the character width, while values greater than 100% expand it.

Horizontal Scale field in the Properties panel.

Horizontal Scale
Horizontal Scale
Horizontal Scale

The middle text is set at a Horizontal scale of 100%. The text on top is contracted. The text on the bottom is expanded.

Paragraph Settings

When typing paragraphs of text, several additional options are available. The Paragraph settings include Indent, Space Preceding, and Space After Paragraphs. Let's discuss these settings in-depth.

Indent

To indent paragraphs, you can use the Paragraph Indent slider in the Properties panel, or manually enter a value using the keyboard. The value in the Paragraph Indent field determines the amount of indent in the first line of a paragraph. Note that most applications define a paragraph by the location of the returns, not by the formal definition of the word "paragraph." A paragraph in Fireworks could be one character, one word, or enough text to fill an entire canvas.

The Paragraph Indent field in the Properties panel.

Fireworks provides many options for altering text in a document. The properties of text can be set in the Properties panel. Text may also be converted to paths and attached to text.

If text is converted to paths it can be edited just like any other path. Some pretty interesting shapes can be created with text that has been converted to paths.

These paragraphs have Indent settings.

Space Preceding Paragraphs

To increase the space before a paragraph, you can use the Space Preceding Paragraph slider in the Properties panel. Values can also be manually entered using the keyboard. The space before a paragraph is measured in points.

The Space Preceding Paragraph field in the Properties panel.

Fireworks and Text

Fireworks provides many options for altering text in a document. The properties of text can be set in the Properties panel. Text may also be converted to paths and attached to text.

If text is converted to paths it can be edited just like any other path. Some pretty interesting shapes can be created with text that has been converted to paths.

The paragraph beginning with "Fireworks provides" has a Space Preceding Paragraph setting.

Space After Paragraphs

Space after a paragraph can be set from the Space After Paragraph slider, or manually entered using the keyboard. The larger the point size you set, the more space is added after a paragraph (before the next paragraph begins). If one paragraph has a "space after" setting and the next paragraph has a "space preceding" setting, the two settings are combined.

The Space After Paragraph field in the Properties panel.

Fireworks and Text

Fireworks provides many options for altering text in a document. The properties of text can be set in the Properties panel. Text may also be converted to paths and attached to text.

If text is converted to paths it can be edited just like any other path. Some pretty interesting shapes can be created with text that has been converted to paths.

The paragraph beginning with "Fireworks provides" has a Space After Paragraph setting.

Live Effects and styles were discussed at length in Chapter 4.

Text often needs to be "set off" from the rest of the image so it doesn't blend into the background. This is especially true when you add text over an image. We often use Live Effects and styles to make text appear to have bevels, shadows, and glow. Text is often embossed to create the appearance of fine stationary. You can apply these settings to text exactly as you would apply them to any vector object.

The text in the above image has the Drop Shadow and Inner Bevel effects applied to give the text depth and separate it from the busy background.

Text Block Settings

Text blocks can be a specified size or can automatically size as text is entered. By default, text blocks are automatically sized. Automatically sized text blocks do not allow the text wrapping to be controlled, which is a feature of fixed-width text blocks. To determine if a text block is auto-sizing or fixed-width, click the Text tool inside the text block. The upper-right corner of the text block displays a hollow circle if the block is auto-sizing, or a hollow square if it is fixed-width.

When the Text tool is selected, you can click and drag to draw a text block of the desired size; by default, the text block is fixed-width when it is drawn with the Text tool. If the Text tool is simply clicked on the canvas, the result is an auto-sized text block that adjusts its size according to the content of the text block. A text block can be changed to the other setting by double-clicking the upper-right corner of the text block. The cursor must turn to a white arrow in order to change the type of text block.

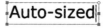

This is an auto-sized text block. Note the small circle in the upper-right corner.

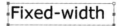

This is a fixed-width text block. Note the small square in the upper-right corner.

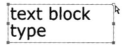

The text block type is being changed. Note the white arrow cursor.

Width

You can change the width of a text block by selecting it and entering the desired width in the W field of the Properties panel. The Transform tools can also be used to resize a text block. Both auto-sized and fixed-width text blocks can be changed in width.

The width of the selected text block is altered using the W field in the Properties panel.

Height

Changing the height of a text block is similar to changing the width. When a text block is selected, the desired height can be entered in the H field of the Properties panel. The Transform tools can also be used to adjust the height. Both auto-sized and fixed-width text blocks can be changed in height.

The height of the selected text block is altered using the H field in the Properties panel.

Location

The location of a text block can be changed using the X and Y fields in the Properties panel. The X and Y values are in pixel units. The location is measured from the top-left corner of the canvas to the top-left corner of the text block.

The location of the selected text block is altered using the X and Y fields in the Properties panel.

Anti-Aliasing Levels

Fireworks provides four levels of anti-aliasing for text:

- The No Anti-Alias option removes all anti-aliasing from the text. Text that is 10 pt. or smaller usually looks best with the No Anti-Alias option applied because the font is crisper when small. The stair-stepping effect is not as noticeable in smaller text characters.

No Ar

We zoomed in on text with a setting of No Anti-Alias to see the effect of the setting.

- The Crisp Anti-Alias option provides a crisp edge; it is the least noticeable of the anti-aliasing options. This anti-aliasing does not add as many blending pixels as some of the other anti-aliasing options. Sans serif text with point sizes between 12 and 18, and serif text with point sizes between 24 and 32 tend to look best with the Crisp Anti-Alias option.

Crisp

We zoomed in on text with a setting of Crisp Anti-Alias to see the effect of the setting.

Changing the text size usually produces better results than resizing a text block.

The effects of numeric positioning and resizing are not viewable until either the Return/Enter key is pressed or the cursor is clicked outside the field.

- The Strong Anti-Alias option is used when the edge needs to be softer than the edge produced with the Crisp Anti-Alias option. Strong Anti-Alias looks best when point sizes range from around 20 to 40 points, depending on the font.

Strong

We zoomed in on text with a setting of Strong Anti-Alias to see the effect of the setting.

- The Smooth Anti-Alias option adds more blending pixels than the other anti-alias options to blend the edge of text with the background. Larger text with sizes of 40 points or more look best with the Smooth Anti-Alias setting.

Smooth

We zoomed in on text with a setting of Smooth Anti-Alias to see the effect of the setting.

Opacity

Opacity can be set for any object on the canvas. There are other tools besides the Text tool that have opacity settings.

The Opacity can be set prior to typing or changed after text has been added.

Opacity refers to how opaque or transparent an object appears. If the opacity of text is set at 100%, it is totally opaque. If the opacity is set at 0%, the text cannot be seen because it is totally transparent. Opacity settings between 0% and 100% render varying degrees of opacity. The opacity can be set in the Layers panel, which we will discuss in Chapter 8. The Properties panel also contains an Opacity field. The Opacity slider allows the selected text's opacity to be adjusted.

Opaque
Less Opaque
Nearly Transparent

Each line actually has a fill property of black. The varying opacities make the bottom two lines appear gray.

The opacity of the selected text block is altered using the Opacity field in the Properties panel.

Blending Modes

Blending modes control the appearance of colors and how they interact with other overlapping colors. The *blend color* is the color that has a blending mode applied to it. The *base color* is the color underneath the blend color. The blend and base colors combine to produce the *result color*. The blending modes control how the result color appears. Blending modes are applied to selected text when the Blending Mode pop-up menu is selected from the Properties panel. We recommend experimenting with the different blending modes to better understand how they affect the colors in the image.

Hue refers to the property of color. We usually refer to hue as color.

The blending modes can be applied to layers, as discussed in Chapter 8.

The various blending modes are as follows:

- **Normal**. No blending mode is applied.
- **Multiply**. This setting multiplies the blend and base colors to result in darker colors. White is discarded, black remains.
- **Screen**. This setting results in lighter colors by multiplying the inverse of the blend color by the base color.
- **Darken**. This setting replaces the lighter of the blend and base colors with the darker of the colors.
- **Lighten**. This setting replaces the darker of the blend and base colors with the lighter of the colors.
- **Difference**. When this setting is used, the blend or base color with less brightness is subtracted from the blend or base color with more brightness.
- **Hue**. With this setting, the blend color's hue is combined with the base color's luminance and saturation.
- **Saturation**. With this setting, the blend color's saturation is combined with the base color's luminance and hue.
- **Color**. When you use this setting, the hue and saturation of the blend color are combined with the base color's luminance.
- **Luminosity**. With this setting, the blend color's luminance is combined with the base color's hue and saturation.
- **Invert**. When you choose this setting, the base color is inverted.
- **Tint**. With this setting, gray is added to the base color.
- **Erase**. With this setting, all the color pixels in the base color are removed.

The blending mode of the selected text block is altered using the Blending Mode pop-up menu, found in the Properties panel.

Apply and Edit Text

1. Select File>Open, and navigate to the **RF_Fireworks** folder. Select **text.png** and click Open.

2. Select the Text tool from the Tools panel. In the Properties panel, set the Text Color to Red. Click somewhere on the **text.png** canvas and type, "Hello, world! I'll soon be an expert at Macromedia Fireworks!"

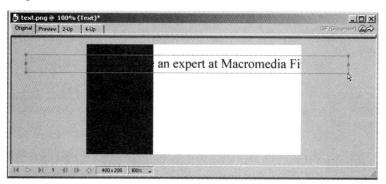

3. The text block is too wide for your canvas, so you need to manually set its width. The easiest method of altering the text block's width is to use the Pointer tool to click and drag the midpoint handles or corner points of the text block.

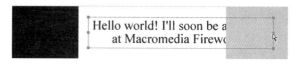

4. Highlight the text inside the text block with your cursor. In the Properties panel, set the Font to Times New Roman, and click the "B" and "I" buttons to apply Bold and Italic styles to the characters. Select the Left Align button if your text is not already aligned on the left side. Next, use the unlabeled Size field to set the Font Size to 34 pt.

The unlabeled Size field, currently set to 34 pt.

There are several ways to apply the characteristics in Step 4. In addition to the specified methods, you can also select the appropriate characteristics prior to typing the text. As a third option, you could apply the specified style by simply clicking once with the Pointer tool to select the entire text box – rather than highlighting the individual words – and then choosing the desired settings.

5. Click once on the text block using the Pointer tool to deselect the text. In the Properties panel, set the Blending Mode to Difference, and note how the text color changes. Scroll through the other options in the Blending Mode pop-up menu and note how each affects the text color; feel free to change the Fill properties to better examine the effects of the blending mode.

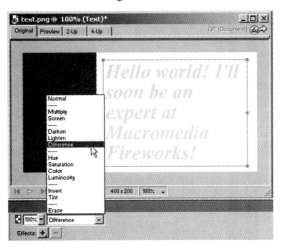

6. Take a few minutes to experiment with the various text attributes. When you're done, close the file without saving your changes.

Spell Checker

New to this version of Fireworks is the Spell Checker utility. The *Spell Checker* looks for potentially misspelled words in selected text blocks or throughout the entire document. If one or more text blocks are selected, using the Text>Check Spelling command checks only the selected blocks. If no blocks are selected, Text>Check Spelling checks all the text blocks in the document. Fireworks prompts you to select a spelling language dictionary.

This window appears the first time the Spell Checker is used, and when a spelling language dictionary is not selected.

The Spelling Setup window appears. Select the desired dictionary or dictionaries. A personal dictionary can also be added. The Edit Personal Dictionary button allows you to add, delete, and edit words. Other options in the Spelling Setup dialog box include toggles for Find Duplicate Words, Ignore Words with Numbers, Ignore Internet and File Addresses, and Ignore Words in UPPERCASE. These options allow you to choose whether or not you want certain categories of text to be ignored; this can be a big timesaver. (Imagine how much time you would waste if you had to click Ignore every time the Spell Checker found an Internet address.) Always be aware of the options that are available to help save valuable time.

If no words have been added to your personal dictionary, selecting Edit Personal Dictionary reveals an empty window.

If a dictionary other than Macromedia.tlx is not selected, the Spelling Setup window appears each time the Check Spelling command is invoked.

The Spelling Setup window.

Once the Spelling Setup options have been selected, the Spelling Setup window no longer appears each time Check Spelling is selected. The Text>Spelling Setup command and the Setup button in the Check Spelling window allow Spell Checker options to be changed.

If a potentially misspelled word is found in the document, the Check Spelling window appears. Suggested words are provided. You have the following options:

- Click the Add to Personal button to add a word to the personal dictionary so Fireworks will not suggest the word again as a potential misspelling.
- Click the Ignore button to ignore the word once.
- Click the Ignore All button to ignore the word throughout the entire document.
- Click the Change button to replace the word in the Word Found field with the word in the Change To field.
- Click the Change All button to replace the word in the Word Found field with the word in the Change To field throughout the entire document.
- Click the Delete button to remove the word from the document.

Once the spelling has been checked for the entire document or for the selected text blocks, a window appears to confirm that the spelling check is complete.

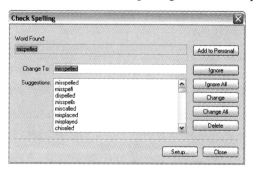

The Check Spelling window.

The Spelling check completed window.

Converting Text to Paths

Refer to Chapter 4 for in-depth information on manipulating paths.

Converting text to paths can be the beginning of unique new fonts.

Text can be converted to paths and further manipulated, just as you can with any vector object. When a text block is converted to a path, all of the text characters are grouped. Ungrouping the path allows you to modify the individual characters of the original text block. Options such as Stroke, Fill, Alter Path, Combine Path, and more can be applied to the newly converted paths.

Text as paths

Text converted to paths.

To convert text to paths, you would select one or more text blocks, and then choose Convert to Paths from the Text menu. Once text has been converted to paths, it is no longer editable as text. Always make sure that the font face and other options are correct before converting to paths, since they cannot be changed afterward.

Convert Text to Paths

1. Select File>Open and navigate to the **RF_Fireworks** folder. Select **text_2.png** and click Open.

2. Use the Pointer tool to select the text block on the canvas.

3. From the Text menu, select Convert to Paths.

4. Use the Pointer tool to click directly onto one of the letters on the canvas. Notice that doing so no longer causes the Properties panel to display Text options; once text is converted to paths, the text properties no longer apply.

5. Close the file without saving your changes.

Attaching Text to Paths

When adding text to a document with the Text tool, the text can only be displayed in a straight line, even if the text block is rotated. The Attach Text to Path command allows text to be attached to any shape so the text can take on a different shape. The path is no longer visible after text has been attached. The text can still be edited.

The shape of the path is the only attribute used for the Attach Text to Path command; it is displayed when the object is selected. The text can also be moved and repositioned along the path. Text is attached to a path when both the text block and the path are selected and Attach to Path is selected from the Text menu.

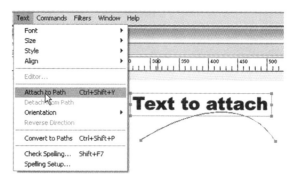

Text being attached to a path.

Text attached to a path.

Text blocks containing returns can produce unexpected results.

Orientation on a Path

Text can be oriented along a path in several ways:

- Text can be rotated around the path. By default, text is oriented with the Rotate Around Path option.

- Text can also be oriented vertically on the path so each character is straight up and down, regardless of the arc of the path. You would select Text>Orientation>Vertical to switch to this orientation.

- Text can also be skewed vertically or horizontally using the Skew Vertical or Skew Horizontal options from the Text>Orientation menu.

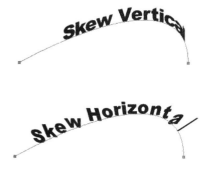

Position of Text

Text is positioned along the path according to the text block properties. Alignments are retained. If the text block is centered, the text is centered along the path. If the text has the Stretch alignment applied, the text stretches along the entire path. If text is longer than the path to which it is applied, the text repeats the shape of the path.

The text can be repositioned along a path by changing the value in the Text Offset field, located in the Properties panel. Text Offset moves the starting position of the text along the path. A positive number moves the text to the right along the path; a negative number moves the text to the left along the path.

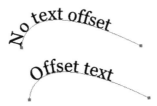

The offset of the text along the path is altered by changing the value in the Text Offset field in the Properties panel.

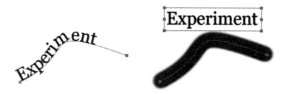

Detaching Text from a Path

Text can be detached from a path. When the text and path are separated, they can be edited as if they had never been attached. The properties of the path again become visible. Text is detached from a path using the Detach from Path command found in the Text menu.

The text on the left is attached to the path. The text on the right is detached from the path.

Direction of Text

The direction of the text depends on a few factors. The direction of the path when it was drawn determines how the text attaches to the path. When the path is drawn right to left, the text appears backward and upside-down.

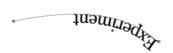

The path was drawn from right to left, and the attached text appears backward and upside-down.

Use the Text Orientation button in the Properties panel to set text orientation.

Settings, such as kerning and indenting, that are applied to text still affect the text when it is attached to a path.

The orientation of the text before being attached to a path also determines the direction of the text after it is attached to a path. If the text orientation is Vertical right to left, the text retains that direction when it is attached to a path. The text orientation settings can be altered even after the text and path are attached. Text can be reversed along a path by selecting Reverse Direction from the Text menu.

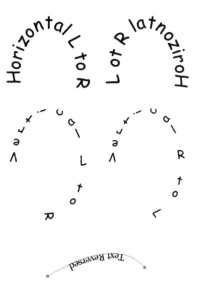

Attach Text to Paths

1. Select File>New to create a new document. Set the Width to 300 pixels, Height to 300 pixels, and Canvas Color to White. Make sure the Resolution is 72 Pixels/Inch. Immediately navigate to your **Work_In_Progress** folder and save the file as "text_path.png."

2. It is easiest to create your initial path with a stroke color. This colored line will be removed after your text has been attached to the path. Choose an easily visible Stroke Color and use the Pen tool to create a curved line in the center of your document. If you prefer, you can create a path with more than one point and different curvatures.

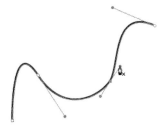

A path created with four points and three different curvatures.

3. Select the Text tool from the Tools panel, and click somewhere on your canvas. Enter your name in the text block that appears.

Even though our exercise covered some very important basics of using text in conjunction with a custom path, we urge you to experiment with text manipulation as much as possible. Try working with the orientation, position, and direction of text. The greater your ability to manipulate the text used in your images, the greater your freedom when creating original documents and graphics.

4. While holding down the Shift key, use the Pointer tool to select both the text block and the original path. From the Text menu, choose Attach to Path. Notice that the stroke color of the path is removed.

5. Highlight the text on the canvas by double-clicking the characters with the Pointer or Text tool and dragging to select the desired text. Use the text options on the Properties panel to appropriately format your name. Experiment with altering the alignment, tracking, font size, font attributes, and any other characteristics you prefer.

6. Close the document without saving your changes.

The text attached to our path is centered 50-pt. Times New Roman with 157% tracking.

Chapter Summary

In this chapter, you reviewed the Fireworks options for adding and editing text in a document. The text properties were discussed, including general, typographic, and paragraph settings. Other properties such as anti-aliasing, blending modes, opacity, and other settings were also presented. Finally, you reviewed the options to convert text to paths and how to attach text to paths.

Complete Project A: Globe Illustration

Free-Form Project #1

Assignment

You work for a Web-design firm that specializes in creating Webpage interfaces. Your focus is on designing Web buttons. Your newest client sells a wide variety of shoes in traditional stores as well as from the Web. They asked your firm to create the fall release of their on-line catalog. Your job is to design the buttons for this catalog. When you are done with the design, you will hand off the files to another team member who will create the HTML and other Web-based components to be used with the buttons.

Applying Your Skills

To complete this project, use the following functions, methods, and features:

- Using the Fireworks vector drawing tools, create a button template. Be sure to apply color attributes to your design, as well as other interesting elements, which can be found in the Properties panel.

- Convert the button template into a button symbol.

- Apply an appropriate name for your symbol in the Symbol Properties dialog box.

- Apply attributes to your button using the Button Editor.

- Assign the Up, Over, and Down states to your button using the Button Editor.

- Apply an active area on your button that is 2 pixels smaller in width and height than the size of the actual button.

- Define the hotspot on your button as the same area as that of the active area. Do not define the link. Your teammate will do that after you hand off the files.

- Make 4 copies of your button (5 buttons in all). Button 1 should say "Home", Button 2 should say "Shoes", Button 3 should say "Boots", Button 4 should say "Order Now", Button 5 should say "Contact Us".

Specifications

- Design your buttons with your client's type of business in mind. The design should be appropriate to this type of business.

- The button should be roughly 100 pixels wide by 30 pixels high.

- You should become familiar with many different methods of accessing the Button Editor.

- Use the Fireworks tools to apply appropriate strokes, fills, textures, and gradients to your button.

- Use the Text tool to layer the text elements on the copies of your button.

Included Files

No files are included for this project. You should create the design from scratch. You can gather ideas from the exercises and projects in this book and from the Web, but be sure the design you create for this free-form project is original.

Publisher's Comments

Web buttons are now considered a standard part of virtually every Web site. Knowing that, you should work to create a button design that is fresh and original. Viewers enjoy seeing something bold and new on a Web site. Clients enjoy this, too, because they know that a creative, original site is likely to hold their customers' attention for a longer period of time than if they were to see "the same old thing." If customers are interested in a site, they are more likely to continue to surf through the site's content, to make purchases and to return again in the future to see what's new.

Review #1

Chapters 1 through 5

In the first five chapters of the book, you developed a solid understanding of how to develop images using Fireworks MX, as well as how to modify images after they have been created. You also explored the Fireworks interface, becoming familiar with the panels, windows, tools, and options it offers you. You found out how easy it is to draw vector shapes using the vector shape tools, and that you can turn vector shapes into raster images for placement on the Web. You took existing vector objects and manipulated them in many ways to create all-new objects, complete with interesting fills, strokes, and other attributes. Then, you explored the use of text elements, and saw how versatile text can be when used in objects that are bound for the Web. Through this series of discussions, exercises, and projects you should:

- Be familiar with vector objects as well as raster images, and understand the properties of both.

- Be able to create a new document using Fireworks MX, and open existing documents.

- Know how to navigate the Fireworks interface, knowing where to find the necessary panels, windows, and tools for image development and manipulation.

- Understand how to create vector objects using the variety of vector shape tools, and know how to turn vector shapes into raster images by exporting.

- Be comfortable using the Pen tool and working with individual paths.

- Be capable of selecting and editing vector objects, and altering their properties to create new and unique shapes and characteristics.

- Be comfortable arranging and aligning objects on the canvas, grouping and ungrouping objects, and changing their stacking order.

- Know how to create text elements, and apply those elements to Web objects, such as banners and buttons.

- Be comfortable converting text to paths, and attaching text to paths.

6 Working with Bitmaps

Chapter Objectives:

Fireworks is a distinctive tool in many ways, one of which is that it allows you to create bitmap graphics that can be manipulated, as many times as necessary, with no quality degradation. Few other programs can make that claim. Fireworks provides the flexibility of working with vector paths, combined with the subtleties of working with bitmap graphics. In this chapter, you will:

- Find out how to import bitmaps into Fireworks.

- Learn how to make selections using the wide variety of selection tools.

- Discover how to draw objects in Fireworks, and then add color to those objects.

- Learn how to use the new image-retouching tools.

- Find out how to optimize JPEG files, and how to balance image quality and file size.

- Learn how to import and export Photoshop files.

- Find out about various bitmap drawing tools such as the gradient tool and the Paintbucket tool.

Projects to be Completed:

- Globe Illustration (A)

- Image Retouching Advertisement (B)

- Animated Banner (C)

- The Cable Store Web Site (D)

Working with Bitmaps

While files created in Fireworks quite often include vector images, fireworks is unique in that the graphics you create are often destined for the Web — usually as JPEG or GIF graphics. If you create a shape with the Fireworks vector tools, apply a fill color, and then zoom in on an edge of the graphic, you will see the properly anti-aliased pixels. If you select the object, you will see the path itself, which can be regarded as the pixels' controller.

Fireworks offers the best of both worlds. You are in fact creating bitmap graphics, but they are vector–driven, so you can manipulate them however you choose, as many times as necessary, with no quality degradation during the process. Fireworks provides the flexibility of working with vector paths, coupled with the subtleties of working with bitmap graphics.

There may be times when you want to edit an image in a purely bitmap fashion, permanently altering the pixels. Fireworks is ready for that task, too, providing a powerful set of bitmap drawing and painting tools. You can open or import images and edit them with these tools, which include a new set of image-retouching tools — Blur, Sharpen, Dodge, Burn, and Smudge.

Importing Bitmaps

Using Fireworks, you can open files that were created in other graphics applications, including most of the popular file formats such as JPEG, GIF (including animated GIF), PNG, and WBMP.

Importing to Fireworks

Let's review the methods for importing files into Fireworks:

- **Drag and Drop.** You can drag and drop any image files residing on your computer, or from any application that supports Fireworks.
- **Import.** You can import image files into a Fireworks document.
- **Copy and Paste.** You can copy and paste into Fireworks from any application that supports it.
- **Scan.** Fireworks can import from any scanner that is Twain-compliant (Windows), or supports Photoshop Acquire plug-ins (Macintosh).

Drag and Drop an Image Into Fireworks

1. Create a new Fireworks document. The exact Canvas size is not important. You can set the Size to whatever you prefer.

2. Open a browser window. Position it to one side of the Fireworks document so you can see the browser and the Fireworks canvas at the same time. In the browser, surf to any page that contains an image.

3. With both applications open side-by-side, click on the image in the browser window, and without releasing the mouse button, drag the image into the open Fireworks document. The image is now an object on the Fireworks canvas.

4. Delete the object and leave Fireworks open for the next exercise.

Import a Bitmap

1. From the open file, select Import. Navigate to the **RF_Fireworks** folder, and choose **dendrobium.tif**. The cursor becomes an inverted "L" (see below), which is your cue that the image is ready to be placed on the canvas.

$$\ulcorner$$

2. On the open document's canvas, click where you want the upper-left corner of your image to be placed. The image imports. Notice that it is now an object on the canvas.

3. Select the image, and then delete it by pressing the Delete/Backspace key, or choosing Edit>Cut.

4. Choose File>Import again, and navigate to the **dendrobium.tif** file again. The cursor changes to the inverted "L".

5. With the inverted "L" cursor, click and drag a marquee over part of your open document. The image imports, resized to the dimensions of the marquee you drew. This method allows you to import and resize an image in one step.

6. Keep the file open for the next exercise. Do not save your changes.

Copy and Paste an Image

1. Select **dendrobium.tif** on your canvas.

2. Copy it by selecting Command/Control-C, or selecting Copy from the Edit menu.

3. Create a new Fireworks document, the same size as the one we created earlier. Paste the copy of **dendrobium.tif** into the new document by selecting Command/Control-V, or by selecting Paste from the Edit menu. Notice how the bitmap image is pasted onto the new document, and it is the same size as it was in the original document.

4. Close both Fireworks documents without saving your changes.

Scan an Image

1. If you have a functioning scanner, open a new Fireworks document and choose File>Scan>Twain Acquire from the Fireworks Main menu. If your scanner is properly installed, the Select Source dialog box appears. Fireworks prompts you to verify the source. Select your scanner from the list of sources and click Select. If you do not see your scanner in the list, consult your scanner's documentation to make sure it is properly installed with the correct driver software.

2. Follow the instructions for your scanning software, and scan any photo or small object. Once scanned, the image appears in a new Fireworks document. The process is the same as if you were scanning an image without the benefit of Fireworks. The advantage of using Fireworks is that the scanned image opens as a new Fireworks document, all in one step.

3. Close the document without saving.

Roundtrip Feature with Adobe Photoshop 6 or 7

At one point or another, you will probably find yourself working with Photoshop files that you've imported to Fireworks. Perhaps you created the files before you saw how effective Fireworks can be when creating a Web page mock-up. It's helpful to know a bit about how these two applications interact with one another.

Importing Photoshop Files

Fireworks provides excellent support for importing Photoshop files, and can also export directly to Photoshop's PSD format. Given that there are some limitations, it's a good idea to respect each application's inherent strengths. For example, Fireworks can only support the first alpha channel in a Photoshop file, and it does not support Photoshop adjustment layers.

Fireworks can preserve the layers in a Photoshop file, including layer masks, layer effects (which convert to Fireworks Live Effects) and blending modes whenever possible.

Exporting to the Photoshop PSD Format

You can export Fireworks files as Photoshop .psd files, which allows you to edit the document's layers from Photoshop.

Maintaining the Photoshop PSD format allows you to work between the two applications whenever necessary. It is recommended that you finish your tasks in Fireworks before exporting to Photoshop. Since neither application supports all of the features of the other, it can be difficult to maintain the appearance of your image by toggling back and forth between the two applications.

Although Fireworks can save a document in PSD format, do so only if you need to edit the document in Photoshop.

Export as a Photoshop Document

1. Open a new Fireworks document. Choose any Size you prefer for the Canvas. Select a drawing tool, such as the Brush tool, and scribble something on the canvas. The drawing tools will be covered in-depth later in the chapter. For now, all you need to do is place some pixels on the canvas so we have some content in our file.

2. Select File>Export, and under Save as type/Save as field, choose Photoshop PSD. Save the file as "fw_to_ps.psd" in your **Work_In_Progress** folder, and click Save.

3. You can also accomplish this by clicking the Quick Export button and selecting Other>Export to Photoshop from the pop-up menu.

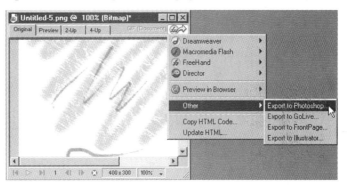

4. Close the Fireworks file without saving your changes.

Import a Photoshop File

1. Choose File>Open, and navigate to any Photoshop document, or the Photoshop document you just exported from Fireworks.

2. Open the file. You can edit the document as if it had been created in Fireworks.

3. Close the file without saving.

Making Selections

Before you can edit a bitmap image in Fireworks, you must first select all or part of it. You can make selections with any of the pixel-selection tools. Once a selection has been made, you can apply any number of edits, and use a wide variety of filters. The first step, however, is to make a selection.

All of the pixel-selection tools allow you to make multiple selections by holding down the Shift key after making your first selection. In this way, subsequent selections will be added to the first selection. Conversely, you can subtract from your selections by holding down the Option/Alt key while you make selections.

Marquee Tool

The Marquee tool selects a rectangular area of pixels in an image. It's the most basic of the selection tools. All you have to do is drag out an area you want to select. This tool is useful for making selections that need to be square or rectangular. To make a perfect square, hold down the Shift key while you drag.

Oval Marquee Tool

The Oval Marquee tool selects an elliptical area of pixels in an image. It is useful for those times when you need to create an oval- or circular-shaped vignette on an image. To make a perfect circle, hold down the Shift key while you drag.

Lasso Tool

The Lasso tool allows you to make irregular-shaped selections by drawing around the desired area. This tool allows for much more precision than what can be accomplished with the marquee tools. When you need to isolate a specific part of an image, this is an excellent tool for the job.

Polygon Lasso Tool

The Polygon Lasso tool makes straight-edged selections. It allows you to get around tight areas where accuracy is critical. Holding down the Shift key as you make your selection constrains the Polygon Lasso tool to increments of 45 and 90 degrees.

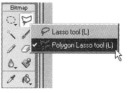

The Polygon Lasso tool can achieve very accurate selections when you need to get into tight areas and avoid selecting neighboring pixels.

Make a Marquee Selection

1. Open **dendrobium.tif** from the **RF_Fireworks** folder.

2. Choose the Marquee tool from the Tools panel and drag around the desired area to make a selection. You see the "marching ants" around your selection. Hold down the Shift key while you drag to constrain your marquee to a perfect square.

3. Look at the Properties panel. You can choose a Hard (not anti-aliased) or a Feathered edge of any Amount your prefer. If Anti-alias is not selected by default, select it from the pop-up menu as shown below.

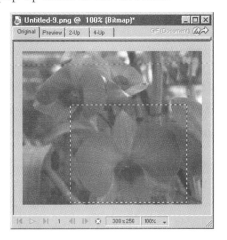

4. The Properties panel also allows you to select options from the Style field. Normal is the default setting, but you can choose a Fixed Ratio or a Fixed Size if you need a specific-sized marquee.

5. If you want to replace this selection with another, simply drag out a new marquee. It replaces the existing marquee

6. After you have created a marquee and see the marching ants, you can drag it around your image to fine-tune your selection. You don't need to select another tool to do this. When you have a selection, just click and drag. Or you can use the Up, Down, Left, and Right Arrow keys to move it in 1-pixel increments. Holding down the Shift key as you press the Arrow keys moves the marquee in 10-pixel increments.

7. To deselect the marquee, choose Select>Deselect, or press Command/Control-D.

8. Leave the file open for the next exercise. Do not save your changes.

Once you have made a selection, you can move it in 1-pixel increments with the Arrow keys.

Make an Oval Marquee Selection

1. With the same file open, make a selection by choosing the Oval Marquee tool from the Tools panel (located behind the Marquee tool) and dragging around the area you want to select. As with the (regular) Marquee tool, you can specify Fixed Size, Fixed Ratio, Hard Edge, or Feather from the Properties panel.

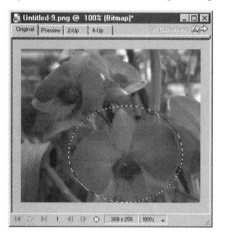

2. Hold down the Shift key while you drag to constrain your marquee to a perfect circle.

3. If your selection was not the right size, drag out another marquee. It replaces the previous marquee with new marching ants.

4. Press Command/Control-D to deselect. Leave the file open for the next exercise. Do not save your changes.

Make a Lasso Selection

1. With the same file open, make a selection with the Lasso tool. Choose the Lasso tool from the Tools panel and drag it around the area you want to select. The dangling rope from the Lasso tool produces a selection as you draw. You can choose Hard Edge, Anti-alias, or Feather from the Properties panel.

2. If you make a mistake, start over again. Your new selection replaces the previous one.

3. After you have made your selection, you can move it with the Arrow keys or drag it. You don't have to select another tool to do this. Just click and drag with the Lasso tool.

4. Press Command/Control-D to deselect. Leave the file open for the next exercise. Do not save your changes.

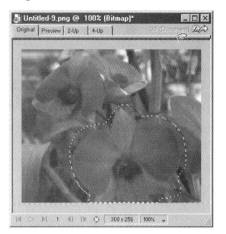

Make a Polygon Lasso Selection

1. With the same file still open, make a selection with the Polygon Lasso tool. Choose the Polygon Lasso tool from the Tools panel (located under the Lasso tool) and click along the edge of the desired selection area. The selection line connects the points as you click along the path. Work your way around until you arrive back at your starting point. Click on top of (or very close to) the starting point to complete your selection and you see the marching ants, the same as with the (regular) Lasso tool.

2. When making your selection, you can click as many times as you prefer, allowing for more accuracy in your selection. It does not take as steady a hand to work with the Polygon Lasso tool as it does the regular (free-form) Lasso tool.

3. Choose Command/Control-D to deselect, and keep the document open for the next exercise. Do not save your changes.

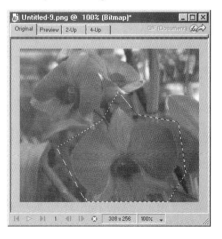

Magic Wand Tool

The Magic Wand tool allows you to select an area of similarly colored pixels in an image. This, in effect, allows Fireworks to make its own selections, based on the color tolerances you specify.

Make a Selection with the Magic Wand

1. Begin with the open file from the previous exercise, or if it is not open, open **dendrobium.tif** from your **RF_Fireworks** folder.

2. Select the Magic Wand tool from the Tools panel. In the Properties panel, choose a Tolerance of 50; the higher the Tolerance, the more inclusive your selection. In the Edge field, select Anti-alias.

3. Click anywhere on the large orchid in the foreground. You see the marching ants selection that corresponds to the color of the pixels in the area where you clicked.

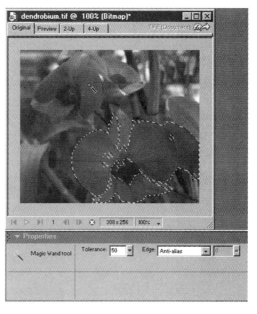

The Magic Wand tool makes the most accurate selections when the object is a different color than its surroundings.

4. You can add to your selection by holding down the Shift key as you click the Magic Wand around other areas.

5. Press Command/Control-D to deselect. Leave the file open for the next exercise. Do not save your changes.

Crop Tool

The Crop tool allows you to remove portions of your image. You can adjust how much of the top, bottom, right side, or left side you want to remove from your image. After the crop is complete, the canvas is resized to the size of the cropped image.

Make a Crop

1. Continue working in the open file. Select the Crop tool from the Tools panel and drag a selection over the large orchid.

2. Double-click inside the selection, or press Return/Enter. The cropped area (inside the marquee) is retained, and everything else (outside the marquee) is discarded.

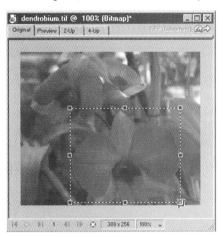

3. Press Command/Control-Z once to undo the crop. Leave the document open for the next exercise. Do not save your changes.

Eyedropper Tool

The Eyedropper tool allows you to select a color by taking a sample from any part of your bitmap image. You can take a 1-pixel sample, 3×3-pixel average, or 5×5-pixel average.

Use the Eyedropper Tool

1. Continue working in the open file. Select the Eyedropper tool from the Tools panel (if it is not already selected). In the Properties panel, choose 5×5 Average from the Sample pop-up menu. Adjacent pixels can vary greatly in color, so when you choose an average, you get a more accurate sample of the main color.

2. From the Tools panel, choose the Eyedropper tool and drag it over the document. Notice how the Fill or Stroke color, depending upon which is selected (both are visible in the Tools panel) changes in real time to match the color of the area under the Eyedropper cursor. This allows you to get accurate color samples that would otherwise be difficult to manually mix.

3. Leave the document open for the next exercise. Do not save your changes.

Adding to/Subtracting from Selections

You can use any of the marquee and lasso tools in conjunction with the Magic Wand tool to make selections. Sometimes a combination of these tools is what it takes to get the selection you need.

To make things easier, you can add to and subtract from a selection, as many times as necessary, to achieve the desired result.

Add to a Selection

1. Continue working in the open document. Select the Magic Wand tool from the Tools panel. Set the Tolerance to 60. Click one of the large petals in the foreground orchid.

2. Hold down the Shift key and click the Magic Wand tool on one of the background orchids. This adds to your selection.

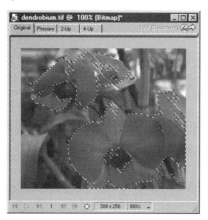

3. Your results may vary, but in the above screen shot, most of the orchid areas were selected with just two clicks of the Magic Wand. The small inner areas of marching ants are surrounding islands of color that were missed. If you want to add more to the selection with the Magic Wand tool, try lowering the Tolerance to 32 (default setting) or even less. This keeps you from choosing too much of the image.

4. Hold down the Shift key (to add to the selection) and experiment with the Marquee and Lasso tools to select these islands of color. If you inadvertently choose an area you don't want, press Command/Control-Z to undo the step.

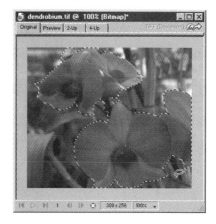

It's often easier to make a selection by first choosing too much, and then subtracting to arrive at the final selection.

With time and practice, you will instinctively toggle between the Shift and Option/Alt keys while you make selections. Do this, and you'll be making selections with ease.

5. To make a very accurate selection, it helps to zoom in on the image at a high magnification. When you are satisfied with your selection, leave the file open with the marching ants in place for the next exercise.

Subtract from a Selection

1. Continue working in the open file. Let's add more to the selection than we need so we can practice subtracting from it. With the Magic Wand tool, hold down the Shift key and select some of the green area.

2. Using any of the tools you feel would be most effective, hold down the Option/Alt key while selecting some of the excess green area. Instead of adding to the selection, doing this will subtract from the selection. You will often find that when making a selection, it's easier to first select too much, and then trim away some of the excess.

3. When finished, close the file without saving.

Drawing Tools

Fireworks provides a powerful set of bitmap drawing tools. With vector tools, you create bitmap images controlled by vector paths. With the bitmap drawing tools, you draw pixels directly, without any editable vector paths. Although this might seem limiting at first, the vector tools are often too cumbersome for certain purposes. This is when the bitmap drawing tools become very useful.

The bitmap objects you make with these tools can be edited in any number of ways, most of which we will cover in the next chapter of the book. For now, let's get acquainted with the bitmap drawing tools.

Brush Tool

The Brush tool allows you to paint a brush stroke that can be customized from the Properties panel. You can adjust the size, color, softness, and even the texture of the brush. This tool allows you to create freehand drawings, which is especially useful when you are using a graphics tablet.

Pencil Tool

The Pencil tool can be used to draw 1-pixel lines, similar to those created with a traditional pencil on paper. You can choose from a Hard or Anti-alias edge from the Properties panel. This tool works similar to the Brush tool, the only difference being that you are restricted to drawing 1-pixel lines.

Eraser Tool

The Eraser tool allows you to remove pixels from an image. You can change the size, shape, and edge softness of the eraser to suit your needs. Regardless of what tool you used to create the pixels, the Eraser tool can remove them.

Paint Bucket Tool

The Paint Bucket tool is used to change the fill color of pixels already on the canvas. You can choose any color, edge softness, and texture for the tool's attributes. In addition, the Tolerance setting determines the sensitivity of the Paint Bucket tool. This tool is useful when you need to fill large areas. It's much easier to make a selection and apply a fill, rather than to laboriously draw it with the Brush tool and then wonder if you missed a spot. With the Paint Bucket tool, you are certain to fill the entire object.

Gradient Tool

The Gradient tool allows you to fill any selection with the standard linear and radial gradients. You can use (and customize) any of the many gradients that are provided with Fireworks, or mix your own complex gradients. The Gradient tool can be found under the Paint Bucket tool. You can click and hold on the Paint Bucket tool, then move the pointer down to select the Gradient tool from the pop-up menu.

With the Gradient tool selected, you can choose the gradient by clicking the swatch next to the Paint Bucket icon on the Properties panel. A Color Picker well pops up, allowing you to change the color.

With the Gradient tool selected, you can also edit a gradient by clicking the fill color on the Tools panel, then clicking Fill Options. Then you can click the Edit button to view the gradient with its sliders. The fastest way to edit a gradient, however, is from the Properties panel (with the Gradient tool selected), as shown below.

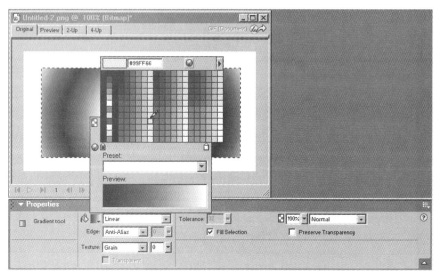

*If you have experience
with Photoshop, you'll feel
right at home with the
Fireworks bitmap drawing
tools.*

Practice with the Bitmap Drawing Tools

1. Create a new Fireworks document with a White Canvas Color and Size of 400-pixels wide by 200-pixels high.

2. Select the Brush tool from the Tools panel and experiment with some of the many textures and available stroke options. You can access all of the parameters of the Brush tool from the Properties panel. This is also true for the rest of the bitmap drawing tools.

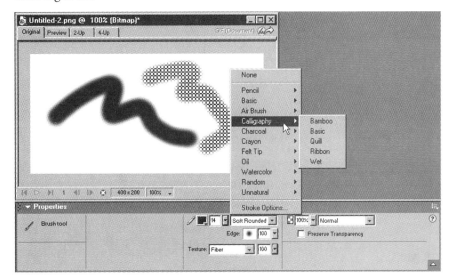

3. Select the Eraser tool from the Tools panel and experiment with different sizes and shapes from the Properties panel, and erase what you just painted with the Brush tool. Then, select a large square eraser shape from the Properties panel and erase the rest of the brush strokes.

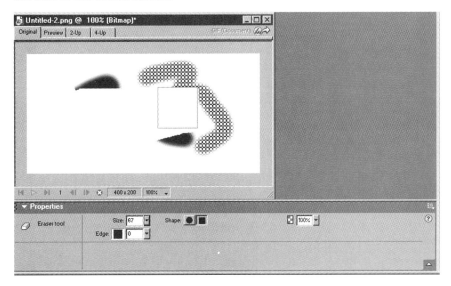

4. Select the Pencil tool from the Tools panel and experiment with it. Notice the smooth appearance of the lines when you select Anti-aliased from the Properties panel.

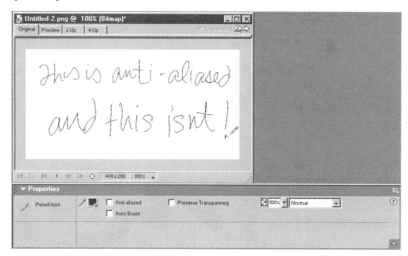

5. Use the Eraser tool to remove the marks you made with the Pencil tool. Select the Brush tool and make a large shape on the right side of the document. Choose any color you prefer.

6. Select the Marquee tool from the Tools panel and drag out a marquee on the left side of the document.

7. Choose a new Fill color in the Tools panel. Select the Paint Bucket tool and click within the confines of your marquee. Deselect by pressing Command/Control-D. The marching ants vanish, leaving your new fill in place.

8. Make sure the Fill Selection check box in the Properties panel is deselected. Set the Tolerance to 32 for the Paint Bucket tool and click the shape you made with the Brush tool. If your shape had a smooth edge, similar to the one pictured here, you might notice a halo of pixels around the edges that was not included at this tolerance. Experiment with different tolerances and notice how the Paint Bucket tool behaves. More pixels are included by the Paint Bucket tool as you raise the Tolerance setting.

For simple shapes, vector tools offer more editing flexibility than bitmap tools.

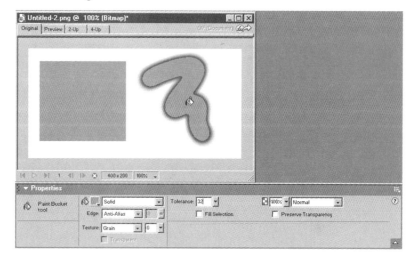

9. Use the Eraser tool to remove everything on the document. Select the Marquee tool from the Tools panel. Drag a marquee almost as large as the canvas.

10. Select the Gradient tool from the Tools panel. In the Properties panel, choose Linear Gradient, set the Edge to Anti-alias, set the Amount of Texture to 0, and make sure the Fill Selection check box is checked.

11. Drag the Gradient tool across the marquee as shown.

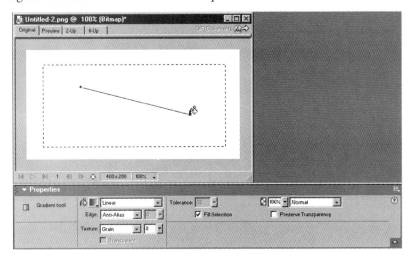

12. As soon as you finish the drag, the gradient fills your selection in the direction you drew. The longer the drag, the more expanded the gradient; the shorter the drag, the more compressed the gradient. If you want the gradient to be perfectly horizontal or vertical, hold down the Shift key while you drag. This constrains the direction of the gradient to 45-degree increments.

13. Starting at Step 10, using the same settings, try the process again; but this time, choose a Radial gradient.

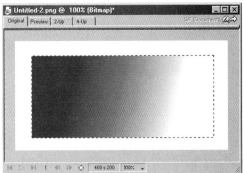 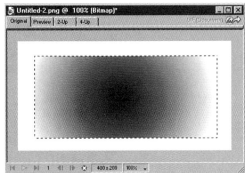

14. Experiment with some of the other gradients. To change the color scheme of a gradient from the Properties panel, choose a gradient from the list of gradients, click the gradient slider tabs to edit the component colors of the gradient, then choose a color from the Color Picker, as shown below.

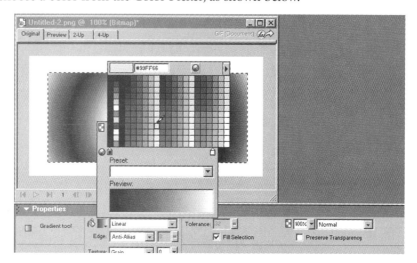

15. Close the document without saving.

Optimization Techniques for JPEGs

JPEG is the preferred compression method for images that contain gradients, as opposed to the GIF format, which is better suited for images with solid blocks of color. Most realistic photographs are well suited for JPEG compression.

Following are the main parameters of JPEG compression that you must understand in order to produce high-quality images for the Web at the lowest possible file sizes. You can choose JPEG compression settings from the Optimize panel. To view the Optimize panel, you can choose Window>Optimize from the Main menu, or press the F6 key on your keyboard.

On the Optimize panel, there is a Settings field. In the example below, the setting is at JPEG-Better Quality. You can also choose JPEG-Smaller File. These two settings are provided for users who are in a hurry, and don't want to take the time to adjust all of the other settings.

The plus (+) and minus (-) signs are for the presets. If you repeatedly use a compression scheme, you can go to the Optimize panel's Options menu (top-right corner icon) and store the setting by choosing Save Settings. As each image's optimization is unique, it's recommended that you make proper settings for each image, if high-quality results are what you hope to achieve.

Never compress a JPEG from a JPEG of the same size. Your image would be needlessly degraded, due to the lossy nature of JPEG compression.

Quality

JPEG is a *lossy* format, meaning that the more an image is compressed, the more image data is discarded (or lost). This data can't be recovered, so it's recommended that you export to JPEG as the final step in making your Web graphic. If you might use the image in the future, we recommended you save the uncompressed version of the file.

JPEG compression can be considered an art. You must continually walk a fine line between image quality and file size, finding a suitable compromise for the job at hand. If many of the users in your Web audience have broadband connections, you can err on the side of too much quality. The majority of users, however, still have slower dial-up Internet connections, and would become very frustrated when downloading very high-quality images.

Smoothing

Besides the Quality setting of your JPEG compression, you can also add a certain amount of Smoothing. This setting lowers the file size, but blurs the image. A greater percentage of file-size savings can be realized with the Quality setting. You would need to add a considerable amount of Smoothing to significantly lower the file size, so we recommend that you add Smoothing in moderation — if at all — and rely more on the Quality settings instead. An exception would be if an image requires a hazy, atmospheric mood. In a situation such as that, Smoothing would be very effective.

Progressive

Years ago, if you were surfing the Web and noticed an image slowly increasing in quality while it downloaded, chances are you were looking at an Interlaced GIF. Progressive JPEG compression was introduced after Interlaced GIF, but it is based on a very similar concept. If you select Progressive JPEG as your compression method, instead of forcing your audience to wait for the entire image to load before they can view it, they will first see a low-quality version of the file. The image quality continues to improve until it's completely downloaded.

If an image is particularly large in file size— larger than 100K — a Progressive JPEG might entice your audience to wait for the image to download in entirety. Studies have shown that the "carrot" of a Progressive JPEG arouses a certain amount of curiosity as to what the image will eventually look like. The drawback is that a Progressive JPEG is higher in file size than its non-Progressive counterpart. This is part of the quality vs. download speed trade-off, something all Web designers must be aware of, and pay attention to.

Compress with the JPEG Format

1. Open **oranges.tif** from the **RF_Fireworks** folder. In the Document window, select the Preview tab. This allows you to see how your compression setting affects the compressed JPEG. Locate the Optimize panel. If it is not visible, choose Window>Optimize from the Main menu.

2. Now you can experiment with the JPEG Optimize settings, noting the relationship of file size vs. quality. First, try the presets under the Settings pop-up menu. JPEG-Better Quality provides a Quality of 80 with 0 (zero) Smoothing. You can see the resultant file size and download time in the top-right area of the Document window. In this case, our file size is 38.21K. This isn't bad, but we can do better.

3. In the Optimize window, select JPEG-Smaller File. This preset shortcut applies a Quality setting of 80 and a Smoothing value of 2, yielding a file size of 14.24K.

4. Try these settings. First, set Smoothing to 0 (zero). The file increases to 15.34K, but notice how much crisper it is. That is 1K well spent.

5. Similar to how you would focus a slide projector, swing back and forth between a low and high Quality setting until you find the perfect compromise for this job. Try a Quality setting of 20. This reduces the file size to 3.24K, but the result is miserable. The trick is to find a happy medium, which in this case would be a Quality setting of around 60 and a Smoothing value of 0 (zero).

6. To use Progressive JPEG, select it from the pop-up menu in the top-right corner of the Optimize panel. The file size increased to 15.62K — not much of an increase, but Progressive JPEG is hardly necessary for a small file like this. As stated in the Document window, it would take about 2 seconds to load.

Progressive JPEG compression creates a larger file size than regular JPEG compression.

7. Click on the 2-Up tab at the top of the Document window. This side-by-side view allows you to compare different compressions. By default, the left view shows the uncompressed version. Select Export Preview from the pop-up menu at the bottom of the left view, as shown. Now you can set that view to a different compression and compare the results.

8. Select the 4-Up tab. It works the same way as 2-Up, but provides 2 additional views. Click in any of the views and compare the different compression settings. The 2-Up and 4-Up views are particularly helpful in those instances when the choice between GIF and JPEG is not clear. Viewing them side by side usually settles the matter.

9. Close the file without saving.

Chapter Summary

In this chapter, you had the opportunity to learn how to work with bitmap graphics. Fireworks allows you to import bitmap graphics in a variety of ways. From there, you can make selections using the Marquee, Lasso, and Magic Wand tools. No matter how skilled you become with the various editing tools, you must first be able to make accurate selections.

You also learned about the bitmap drawing tools. These tools allow you to draw and paint in a wide variety of ways. The Paint Bucket and Gradient tools allow you to quickly fill large areas with solid colors or gradients of many types. Finally, you learned about JPEG compression, and the relationship that exists between image quality and file size.

7 *Image Retouching*

Chapter Objectives:

It would be wonderful if every image were perfect in its original state; but this is very seldom the case. To turn otherwise unsuitable images into images that are perfect for the job, Fireworks provides an extensive collection of image-retouching filters and tools. You can quickly and easily apply brightness/contrast and hue/saturation adjustments. When you need to make more advanced adjustments, the Levels and Curves filters offer high levels of control over the colors in your images. Touch-up tools that were previously only available in Photoshop are now included with Fireworks, making it a very robust image-editing program. In this chapter, you will:

- Find out how to adjust your images using the full range of Fireworks adjustment filters.

- Learn how to blur and sharpen an image to create interesting effects.

- Explore popular third-party plug-ins that expand Fireworks capabilities.

- Find out how to retouch images using the new retouching tools.

- Learn how to create a vignette, and how this effect can be used.

Projects to be Completed:

- Globe Illustration (A)

- Image Retouching Advertisement (B)

- Animated Banner (C)

- The Cable Store Web Site (D)

Image Retouching

Fireworks ships with a comprehensive set of color and tone adjustment filters for editing bitmap images. You can apply any number of adjustments to an image's brightness, contrast, hue, and/or saturation. The Levels adjustment allows you to edit the tonal range of an image, while the sophisticated Curves adjustment allows you to perform many types of edits — from the subtle to the surreal. Fireworks also ships with preview editions of Alien Skin Eye Candy 4000 and Alien Skin Splat, which are third-party plug-ins we explore later in this chapter.

Image Adjustments

You can permanently apply image adjustments to any layer of a Fireworks document (more on layers in the next chapter). When you apply adjustments as Live Effects from the Properties panel, however, the changes are temporary and can be removed or edited at any time. An example of applying a Live Effect from the Properties panel is shown below.

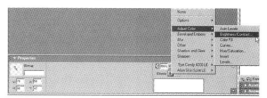

Adjust Color

Image adjustments can be broken down into different categories, such as Bevel and Emboss, or Shadow and Glow. When editing an image, you use the Adjust Color effect, which is also a Live Effect, available from the Properties panel.

The Adjust Color effect has many options, as you can see in the above illustration. Following is an explanation of each of these options.

Brightness/Contrast

The Brightness/Contrast filter adjusts the brightness of colors and the contrast between colors. It affects the entire tonal range of an image (or selected portion of an image), from highlight to shadow. As shown below, you are presented with two sliders for making these adjustments. You can also enter numeric values directly into the appropriate fields.

The Brightness/Contrast filter is best used in situations that require only minor adjustments. When making substantial changes, the Curves and Levels filters offer much more control than Brightness/Contrast. You may even discover that as you gain proficiency with the Curves and Levels filters, you may not need to use the Brightness/Contrast filter at all.

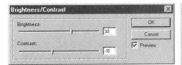

Example of an exaggerated Brightness/Contrast adjustment.

Curves

The Curves filter offers the most precise adjustment of any of the Fireworks bitmap filters.

The Curves filter is similar to the Levels filter, with two distinct differences:

- Curves allows you to adjust any color along the entire color range.
- Curves offers more control than Levels. It features an editable grid with horizontal and vertical axes. The horizontal axis shows the original brightness of the image (also shown in the Input field). The vertical axis shows the new brightness values (also shown in the Output field).

There is a vertical line running from the bottom left to the top right of the graph. When you first open the Curves filter, the line is straight. As you adjust the curve of the line in the dialog box, the image is adjusted according to the sweep of the curve.

Curves adjustments offer the most control of all the color adjustment filters.

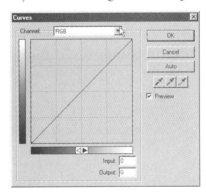

For added control, you can select not only the RGB channel, but the component channels — Red, Green, and Blue — and individually edit them in the same way. (Images you see on a computer monitor or television screen are really just collections of Red, Green, and Blue light. They mix optically to produce the gamut of colors.)

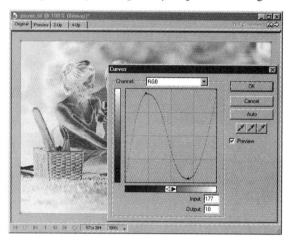

Example of an exaggerated Curves adjustment.

Hue/Saturation

The Hue/Saturation filter adjusts an image's hue (color) and its saturation (intensity). It can also adjust the lightness and darkness of an image.

The Hue component of the filter allows you to shift the color spectrum toward either warmer (the red side of the spectrum) or cooler colors (the blue side of the spectrum), and can also colorize black-and-white images.

The Saturation component of the filter is used to increase or decrease the intensity of the colors in an image. This is especially helpful in nature photography, where brilliant colors are desired. In portrait photography, it is sometimes necessary to tone down the colors in images to maintain realistic skin tones. An image with over-saturated skin tones can cause the model to appear sunburned.

Example of an exaggerated Hue/Saturation adjustment.

Invert

The Invert filter is used to produce the inverse of the colors in an image: reds become greens, and yellows become violets. Colors invert to their opposites (in color theory, also known as their "complements") on the color wheel. The values are also switched around, so black becomes white, and so forth.

The Invert filter is anything but subtle. It is used for a dramatic, surrealistic effect. If realism is your goal, this filter is of little use.

The Invert filter applied from the Main menu.

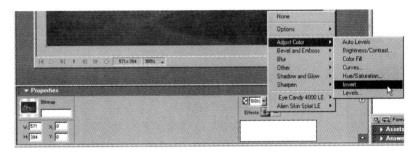

The Invert filter when applied from the Properties panel as a Live Effect.

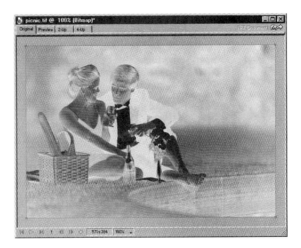

Example of an Invert adjustment.

Levels

The Levels filter is an excellent feature that allows you to adjust the tonal range of an image with none of the drawbacks of the Brightness/Contrast filter. With this filter, you can set the value of the highlights and shadows (an image's tonal range) without "throwing away" information, which can happen with the Brightness/Contrast filter. Use the Levels filter to deepen the darkest shadows, and lighten the brightest highlights. In other words, you can reset the black and white references in an image. Once these two extremes are set, you can adjust the midtones (more on midtones later in this chapter).

A simple Levels adjustment can significantly improve the quality of an image. A scanned or digital photo almost always benefits from the effects of this filter, even if you make only minor adjustments with it.

The following illustration shows a typical *histogram*. A histogram displays the distribution of the color values in an image, ranging from black (on the left side) to white (on the right side).

Levels offer more control than the Brightness/Contrast filter.

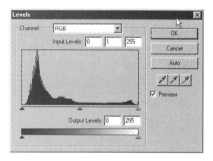

The histogram shows the distribution of color values in an image.

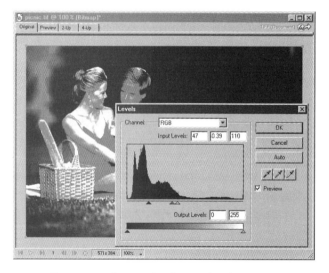

Exaggerated example of a Levels adjustment.

Auto Levels

Auto Levels is an option of the Levels filter. When you choose Auto Levels, you allow Fireworks to make the Levels adjustment decisions for you. While this might be good for beginners, those with an eye for color usually prefer to manually adjust the Levels. You can always run an Auto Levels adjustment, and if you are satisfied with the result, some time was saved. If not, you can return to the image and manually make the adjustments.

Example of an Auto Levels adjustment.

Blur

The Blur filter does just what its name implies — it blurs the image, making it appear out of focus. You can use it to create a softer appearance in your bitmap images. The Blur filter has three options. Let's examine them in turn.

Blur

Running the Blur option slightly blurs the selected area of an image. It does not offer you control over the amount of blur. This is the least effective of the Blur filters.

Blur More

The Blur More filter works similar to the Blur option, but it applies about three times as much blur to an image as the basic Blur option. Again, you cannot control the amount of blur when you use the Blur More filter.

Gaussian Blur

The Gaussian Blur filter uses a more sophisticated algorithm to produce the blur in an image. Of even more importance, this option allows you to control the amount of blur you apply. You can use the Blur Radius slider bar or you can manually enter a numeric amount in the value field. When applied as a Live Effect, you can adjust the amount of blur at any time — it is non-destructive to the pixels you select for blurring.

The Gaussian Blur filter offers the most control of the Blur filters, so it is recommended to use Gaussian Blur whenever possible, rather than the Blur or Blur More filters.

Example of an exaggerated application of the Gaussian Blur filter.

Other

There are two other Live Effects that don't fall so neatly under categories such as Blur or Sharpen. These two effects are Convert to Alpha and Find Edges. You can find them in both the Main menu and the Properties panel (as Live Effects) under the "Other" category.

Convert to Alpha

The Convert to Alpha filter converts an object or bitmap image into a grayscale version. The lighter the pixels, the more transparent they appear. The darker the pixels, the less transparent they appear. Pure white would be 100% transparent, and pure black would be 0% transparent (totally opaque).

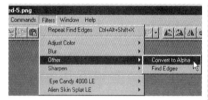

Example of a Convert to Alpha adjustment.

Find Edges

The Find Edges effect alters a bitmap image so it resembles a line drawing. When you apply this filter, lines are substituted for areas of color transition. This is an all-or-none effect (you can't adjust the amount applied — it's either on or off), but it can be used in conjunction with other effects so it does not look as though it came "out of the box."

Example of a Find Edges adjustment.

Sharpen

It is impossible to put detail into an image where none existed before, but the Sharpen filter does a good job at producing the illusion of detail. It accomplishes this by increasing the contrast between adjacent pixels. Keep in mind that although images appear sharper, data is actually lost during the sharpening process. As with other filters, it's suggested that you use the Sharpen filter as a Live Effect; that way, you are free to adjust the amount of sharpening at any time in a non-destructive way.

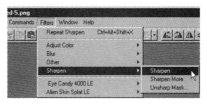

The Sharpen filter accessed from the Main menu.

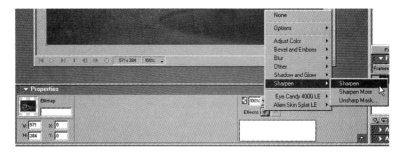

The Sharpen filter accessed from the Properties panel as a Live Effect.

The Sharpen filter has three options. They are Sharpen, Sharpen More, and Unsharp Mask:

- **Sharpen**. The Sharpen option sharpens an image by a small amount. It's often the correct amount you need to add that "little extra something" for a particular image. Since images are displayed on a computer monitor at only 72 ppi, the Sharpen option makes an image appear crisper. This is an "all-or-none" filter. For control over the amount of sharpening, you can use the Unsharp Mask option.

- **Sharpen More**. The Sharpen More filter works the same as the Sharpen option, but it is about three times stronger than Sharpen. In most circumstances, you will find the Sharpen More option is too strong. Use it sparingly, and only when needed.

- **Unsharp Mask**. The Unsharp Mask filter provides precise control over the sharpening of images. This is accomplished by allowing you to control not only the amount of sharpening, but the threshold at which you want the sharpening to occur. This is the most effective of the Sharpen filters.

Using the Sharpen filter is a quick way to sharpen smaller images when you don't need the precision that the Unsharp Mask offers.

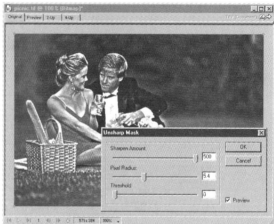

Exaggerated example an Unsharp Mask adjustment.

As you gain proficiency using the Sharpen filters, you will discover that most Web images displayed at 72 ppi can benefit from at least a slight bit of sharpening to give them extra "snap." The trick is to use it in moderation so your Web audience can't discern what was done to the image. A trained eye can instantly spot an over-sharpened image, so use these filters with care.

Eye Candy 4000 LE

Alien Skin Eye Candy 4000 is one of the most popular third-party plug-ins for Fireworks and Photoshop. It enables you to create a wide variety of unusual effects for bitmap images.

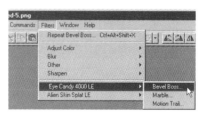

For more information on the Alien Skin product set, visit their Web site at www.alienskin.com.

Fireworks ships with a preview, or "LE" (limited edition) version of Eye Candy 4000. It allows you to sample three of the many effects the full version offers. If you like the sample filters, you can purchase the full version for a reasonable price.

Let's explore the effects included in Eye Candy 4000 LE:

- **Bevel Boss**. This effect works similar to the Fireworks Inner and Outer Bevel filters, except you have many more styles and varieties from which to choose. Bevels are particularly useful for creating buttons for a Web site interface.

Example of the Bevel Boss effect.

- **Marble**. This filter creates the appearance of marble in a bitmap image. It is mainly used to create pure marble patterns. It is not generally used to retouch an image. Its many parameters allow you to create a faux-marble appearance of virtually any variety.

Example of the Marble effect.

- **Motion Trail**. Motion Trail is an unusual filter. It produces a blur that extends past the edge of the image, suggesting a blur caused by rapid movement. You can set the Motion Trail parameters in so many ways that you will almost always be able to produce a convincing blur for your image.

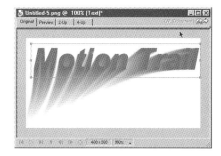

Example of the Motion Trail effect.

Alien Skin Splat LE

Alien Skin Splat LE is the sample version of a new set of filters from Alien Skin. You only receive one effect in this LE version, called the Edges filter.

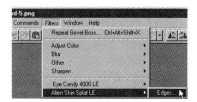

This filter is quite versatile, and can be regarded as many filters in one. With it, you can alter the appearance of the outside edges of an image. You can choose from many edge effects, including Pixelated and Small Tear. Small Tear simulates the appearance of worn parchment.

Example of an Alien Skin Splat LE Edges "Pixelated" effect.

If you want to use the other filters in Splat, you must purchase the full-featured version from Alien Skin.

Applying Touch-Ups

Fireworks ships with an impressive assortment of tools that can be used to retouch an image. Unlike using a filter as a Live Effect, these tools permanently change the pixels of the image; because of this, it is recommended that you always save a backup copy of the original image.

You can maintain precise control over the size, edge feathering, and intensity of these tools from the Properties panel.

Touch-Up Tools

Unlike the filters, you access these tools from the Tools panel. You can selectively apply them to parts of an image as small details, or apply them to large areas. They can all be accessed from the Bitmap section of the Tools panel under the Pencil tool. You can click and hold on the tool that is currently visible to gain access to the other tools.

The touch-up tools in the Tools panel.

These tools are different from filters because you "draw" the effect with your mouse or graphics tablet pen. This allows for a high degree of control. Let's examine each of the touch-up tools:

- **Blur Tool**. The Blur tool is used to soften the focus of selected areas of an image. The more you draw over a selected area, the more it is blurred.

- **Sharpen Tool**. The Sharpen tool is used to sharpen the focus of selected areas of your image. The more you draw over a selected area, the more it is sharpened. Use this tool when you need a bit of sharpening applied to selected areas.

- **Dodge Tool**. The Dodge tool lightens parts of an image while it decreases the saturation of colors. You can draw over the area you want lightened. More passes with the mouse produce more lightening. There are many ways to lighten part of an image, but this tool does the most convincing job. Use restraint, and your viewers won't know that the Dodge tool was applied.

- **Burn Tool**. The Burn tool darkens parts of an image while it increases the saturation of colors. You draw over the area you want darkened. More passes with the mouse produce more darkening. It is best to use restraint with this tool — a little burning goes a long way.

- **Smudge Tool**. The Smudge tool actually pushes pixels in the direction you drag, slightly blurring them in the process. It's the digital equivalent of a traditional artist's smudge stick. If you use it to retouch photographs, restraint is recommended.

"Dodge" and "Burn" are terms taken from the photographer's darkroom, to lighten and darken images.

The Rubber Stamp tool is a good choice for removing wrinkles and tears from scanned versions of old photographs.

- **Rubber Stamp Tool**. The Rubber Stamp tool allows you to copy an area of pixels from one area of an image and paste them in another. This is perhaps the favorite tool of the photo retoucher. With it, you can add selected portions to an image, or remove sections from an image. The Rubber Stamp tool is in a class by itself. It can be used in a subtle way, such as to remove dust and imperfections from a scanned image. It can also be used to make radical photo alterations, creating images that could never be produced by photography alone.

Exercise Set-Up

In the next exercise, we will practice using the Fireworks color-adjustment filters. In subsequent exercises, we will practice using the other filters we discussed in this chapter, including the sample plug-ins from Alien Skin.

If you are familiar with adjustment layers in Photoshop, then you will feel right at home with Live Effects in Fireworks.

Adjust the Color of an Image

1. Open **white_vanda.tif** from the **RF_Fireworks** folder. This orchid image is rich in color and high in contrast, making it a good candidate for the Fireworks color-adjustment filters.

2. With the Pointer tool (black arrow), select the image so you see a blue border around it.

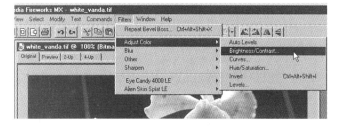

3. Click on the Effects plus (+) sign and choose Adjust Color>Brightness/Contrast.

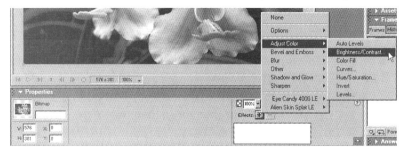

Although it is possible to apply the filters from the Main menu, (Filters>Adjust Color> Brightness/Contrast), that would permanently alter the pixels of the image, creating a problem if you change your mind later on. You have more flexibility if you apply the filters as Live Effects from the Properties panel.

4. The Brightness/Contrast dialog box appears. Move the Brightness slider to 50, or enter a value of 50 into the Brightness field. Notice the change. Change the value to -50 and note the effect. Do the same with the Contrast slider, noting the changes. Enter a value of 20 into both the Brightness and Contrast fields. Click OK. You now see the effect as listed in the Properties panel. You can toggle the effect on or off by clicking the small checkmark in this field. It turns to a red "X" when not in use.

5. Click the blue circle with the "i" in the middle. This brings up the Brightness/Contrast dialog box, allowing you to change the settings as you prefer.

6. Click the actual words in the Brightness/Contrast field. The field is highlighted. Once selected, click the minus (-) sign (Delete Current Selected Effect) to delete the effect. Now we are back to where we began.

7. Next, let's explore the Curves filter. From the Properties panel, click the plus (+) sign (Add Effects or Choose a Preset) and choose Adjust Color>Curves. The diagonal line is straight, telling you that no changes have been made. Make sure the RGB channel is selected in the Channel field. The Input and Output fields have values of 0 (zero). Click once on the diagonal in the middle of the curve. A point is created. You can drag this point toward the upper left to lighten the image, and toward the lower right to darken it. Move the point toward the lower right, or enter a value of 100 in the Input field and 150 in the Output field. Click OK.

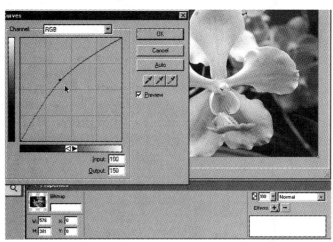

8. Notice the effect this has on the image. Remember that the horizontal axis depicts the original brightness of the pixels and the vertical axis shows the new edited values. This is indicated by the concavity or convexity of the curve.

In this example, we only edited the RGB channel. You can have more control by editing the individual R (red), G (green), and B (blue) channels. You can also add more than one point to your curve (usually, one is enough). The best way to get comfortable with the Curves filter is to experiment with it.

While you experiment with the Curves filter, don't worry about harming your image. These are Live Effects and can easily be edited, hidden, or discarded.

For nature photography, try increasing the Saturation a little bit for more vibrant colors.

9. You can hide the effect by clicking the checkmark, or edit it further by clicking the blue and white "i" (Info) icon. Try clicking the eyedropper icons to set the shadow, midtone, and highlight points for the image. (Click the eyedropper icons and then the corresponding point of your image to set the tonal range.) Select the Auto button to see how Fireworks would handle the adjustment on its own. After you have tried some of these suggestions, click on the effect, and then click the minus (-) sign (Delete Current Selected Effect) to remove it from the Properties panel. The image returns to its original state.

10. Now let's use the Hue/Saturation filter. From the Properties panel, click the plus (+) sign (Add Effects or Choose a Preset) and choose Adjust Color>Hue/Saturation. Move the Saturation slider to the right, or enter a value of 50 in the Saturation field. The colors become very vivid. Now drag the Hue slider back and forth and notice the changes. For a realistic effect, you would normally stay close to a value of 0. For now, set it to a value of -10. Notice how the overall color becomes warmer. Drag the Lightness slider to the right and left and notice the effect this has on the image. When you are done experimenting, leave the slider at its default setting of 0.

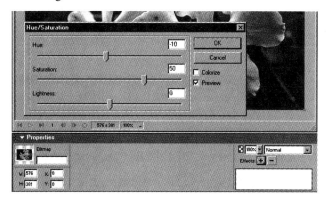

11. Select the Colorize check box from the Hue/Saturation dialog box. Drag the Hue and Saturation sliders in both directions. As you may have guessed, these settings are useful for colorizing black-and-white photographs. To manually do so would require isolating individual areas and colorizing each one separately. When finished, click Cancel, or delete any Hue/Saturation effects you saved. We want to keep the image in its original state for the next step of the exercise.

12. From the Properties panel, choose Adjust Color>Invert. Notice the dramatic change in the image. This is an all-or-none filter — it's either on or off. You can click the checkmark in the Effects field to hide the Invert effect, or eliminate it entirely by clicking the minus (-) sign in the Properties panel.

13. Select the Invert effect from the Effects field. Click the minus (-) sign in the Properties panel to delete it.

14. Now let's experiment with the Levels filter. This filter is similar to the Curves filter, but it is more intuitive. From the Properties panel, click the plus (+) sign, select Adjust Color>Levels, and note the Levels dialog box that contains the histogram for the image.

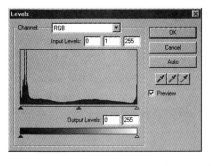

Levels adjustments should not be considered substitutes for a good scan. Always try to produce the best possible scan.

Levels provides more control than Brightness/Contrast.

15. Move the left (black) and right (white) sliders below the histogram. Any values outside of these two margins are discarded. In this example, nothing is discarded. Try moving the center (gamma) slider to the left a little bit. This sets the midtones. By moving the slider to the left, you include more values between this slider and the white (right) slider. Notice how the image brightens.

16. Now experiment with the Output Levels sliders at the bottom of the dialog box. By default, they are at the extreme ends of the grayscale. Moving these effectively lowers the contrast.

17. With the Levels dialog box still open, click the Auto button. This allows Fireworks to automatically correct the image. Notice that not much happens. This means the image had a good histogram, and did not need much correction. When you are finished experimenting, remove the Levels effect from the Properties panel, and return the image to its original state. Keep the file open for the next exercise.

Blur an Image

1. Continue working in the open document, or open **white_vanda.tif** from the **RF_Fireworks** folder. Let's run the blur filters on the image.

2. From the Properties panel, click the plus (+) sign icon and select Blur>Blur. Notice how the image blurs slightly. You can see the effect is now listed in the Properties panel. Click the minus (-) sign to delete the effect. Now select Blur> Blur More. The same effect, but more intense. Click the minus (-) sign to delete the effect.

3. Now select Blur>Gaussian Blur. The Gaussian Blur dialog box appears. You can move the Blur Radius slider, or enter the amount of blur you want to apply. Click the blue and white "i" on the Properties panel to try a few different values. For a strong blur, enter a value of 10. Click the check box in the Properties panel next to the "i" icon to hide the blur. When you use Live Effects, you can change your mind at any time, and return to the original image to continue your work.

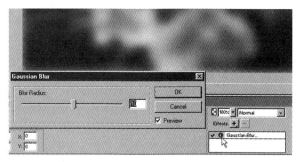

4. When you are finished, delete the effect and leave the file open for the next exercise.

Use the Convert to Alpha Effect

1. Open **white_vanda.tif** from the **RF_Fireworks** folder if it is not already open.

2. In the Properties panel, click the Effects plus (+) sign, and select Other>Convert to Alpha. You can see how the image was converted to grayscale, with black showing as opaque, white as transparent, and everything in between as proportionately transparent.

3. Delete the effect and leave the file open for the next exercise.

Find Edges

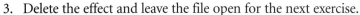

1. Continue working in **white_vanda.tif.** From the Properties panel, click the plus (+) sign and select Other>Find Edges.

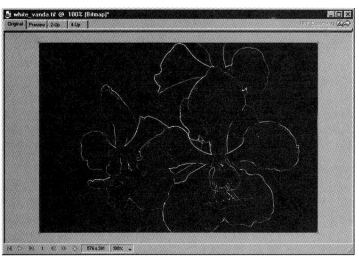

2. You probably won't use this effect very often, but it is there for the rare occasions when you need it.

3. When finished, delete the effect, and leave the file open for the next exercise.

Try using the Unsharp Mask filter for intentional distortion effects.

As a guideline, remember that the Pixel Radius value determines the width of the sharpened "halo" that surrounds edges, and the Threshold value determines what is considered an edge. Threshold also determines where the first two settings (Amount and Pixel Radius) are applied.

Using Numeric Transform is an excellent way to scale down an image to make a thumbnail. This way, all of your thumbnails can be of consistent height and/or width.

When you scale down an image to a very small size, only a fraction of the pixels remain. Thus, only a fraction of the "information" remains. By giving an image a strong dose of sharpening, you can give the illusion of greater detail.

Sharpen an Image

1. Continue working in the open **white_vanda.tif.** From the Filters menu, select Sharpen>Sharpen. Notice how the flower seems to display more detail. Look at the blurred background. It appears grainy.

2. Delete this effect from the Properties panel by clicking the minus (-) sign. From the Filters menu, select Sharpen>Sharpen More. You see the same effect as with the Sharpen filter, but it's about three times more intense. The Sharpen More filter probably applies more sharpening than you would need under normal circumstances.

3. Delete the Sharpen More effect. From the Filters menu, select Sharpen>Unsharp Mask. The dialog box that appears offers more control of the effect than you have with either Sharpen or Sharpen More.

4. In the Unsharp Mask dialog box, set the Sharpen Amount to 100, Pixel Radius to 2, and Threshold to 25. Notice that with these settings, the edges of the flower are sharpened more than the rest of the image. You could not achieve this effect with the regular Sharpen filter.

5. Try some different settings on your own and notice the effects.

6. Move the Threshold slider to 0. With this setting, everything gets sharpened. Move the Threshold slider back to 25. When satisfied with the result of the sliders working together, delete the Unsharp Mask.

7. Select the image. From the Main menu, select Modify>Transform>Numeric Transform. From the pop-up menu, select Scale, and enter 20% for the vertical and horizontal values. Click the Scale Attributes and Constrain Proportions check boxes to ensure the image scales correctly. Click OK.

8. You are left with a thumbnail, the sort of image that would be useful in an on-line photo gallery menu. (Each thumbnail would link to the full-sized image.)

9. From the Main menu, select Modify>Canvas>Trim Canvas. This command trims away the excess canvas to prepare the image for export.

10. Select the image, and from the Properties panel, select Sharpen>Sharpen More. Examine the result.

11. When finished, close the file without saving.

Use Eye Candy 4000 LE

1. Open **gull.tif** from the **RF_Fireworks** folder.

2. From the Properties panel Live Effects, select Eye Candy 4000 LE>Bevel Boss. A pop-up window appears, allowing you to set the Eye Candy parameters. On the Basic tab, set the Bevel Width (pixels) to 12, Bevel Height to 50, Smoothness to 75, Bevel Placement to Inside Marquee, Darken Deep Areas to 0, and Shade Interior should be unchecked. (These values should be the defaults.) You see a basic bevel, similar to what Fireworks can create on its own.

3. Keep the file open for the next exercise.

Eye Candy 4000 LE's Bevel Boss works similar to Fireworks Bevel effects, but you get more options with Eye Candy, chief among them the ability to custom- make a bevel of your own design.

There are numerous settings in Eye Candy 4000; exploring them all is beyond the scope of this book. For all but the occasional "gimmicky" Bevel effect, the regular Fireworks Live Effects are sufficient.

Use Alien Skin Splat LE

1. In the open **gull.tif** file, select Alien Skin Splat LE>Edges from the Properties panel as a Live Effect. This effect alters the edges of your image. Choose Settings>Dot Edge. As you can see, it would be difficult to manually produce an effect such as this.

Alien Skin Splat LE is a good tool for creating interesting borders around images.

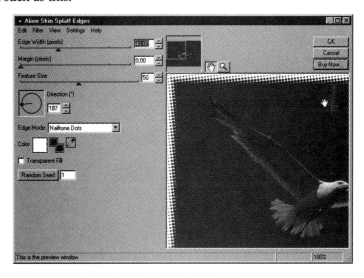

When designing a Web page, remember that this third-party plug-in is included with Fireworks. Many more effects are included in the full version of the product, available directly from Alien Skin.

2. Now try increasing the values of the Edge Width, Margin, and Feature Size using the appropriate sliders.

3. Change the Edge Mode to Torn Paper. Notice what happens. As you can see, this filter offers plenty of control.

4. Select Settings>Ink Spill, and note the effect.

5. Click OK or Cancel.

6. Close the file without saving.

With the exception of the Rubber Stamp tool, all of the bitmap retouching tools are grouped under the Pencil tool. You can also access these tools by pressing the "R" key ("R" for "Retouch") on your keyboard. Then press the "R" key to toggle through the tools until you find the one you need.

Apply Touch-Ups to an Image

1. Open **sailboat_beach.tif** from the **RF_Fireworks** folder. One by one, let's use the bitmap retouching tools, located on the Tools panel.

2. Select the Blur tool from the Tools panel. If you don't see it, click and hold on the tool below the Pencil tool.

3. In the Properties panel, set the Size to 40, Edge to 50, Shape to Round Brush Tip, and Intensity to 80. Drag the tool over the white clouds and notice how they soften. If you prefer to work slower, choose a lower Intensity. More passes with the tool are required at a lower Intensity level, allowing for more control.

4. Select the Sharpen tool from the Tools panel. From the Properties panel, set the Size to 20, Edge to 50, Shape to Circle, and Intensity to 20. We are using a lower Intensity because the Sharpen tool quickly produces unwanted artifacts when overused. Run the Sharpen tool around the edges of the sails. This will draw greater attention to the sails, and create a better "snap." Drag the Sharpen tool over the boats out toward the horizon. They appear to brighten as their pixels increase in contrast to the surrounding blue water. Next, touch-up the hulls of the boats on the beach, and finally the horizon itself. This causes it to appear crisper.

Dodge and Burn are good tools for making small contrast adjustments in tight areas.

A general rule-of-thumb is that when retouching, you don't want viewers to notice your efforts. The idea is to make viewers think the photo is in its original state.

5. Select the Dodge tool from the Tools panel. Set the Size to 40, Edge to 100, Shape to Round Brush Tip, Range to Midtones, and Exposure to 10 (this low Exposure allows you to work slowly). Let's bring out the light areas of the clouds by "painting" these areas brighter with the Dodge tool. To make the effect more realistic, lower the Size setting as you bring out the brightest areas. This produces a more natural look.

6. Select the Burn tool from the Tools panel. This tool has the opposite effect of the Dodge tool. It's used to reinforce the shadow areas. Set the Size to 60, Edge to 100, Shape to Round Brush Tip, Range to Shadows, and Exposure to 30. By choosing Shadows for the Range, we can darken the shadows without adversely affecting the highlights.

7. Let's increase the footprint shadows on the sand. Drag the Dodge tool over the sand. More passes with the tool produce a more pronounced effect. If you apply too much of this effect, it won't look realistic.

8. Select the Smudge tool from the Tools panel. Set the Size to 40, Edge to 10, **Shape** to Round Brush Tip, and Pressure to 50. Do not click the Use Entire Document or Smudge Color check boxes. Place the tool over the main powerboat at sea, then click and drag slightly to the left. This simulates a motion blur, making it appear that the boat was moving when the photo was taken.

9. Finally, select the Rubber Stamp tool, located in the Bitmap section of the Tools panel. This is the tool you would use to clone one area of an image and use it on another part of the image. Let's clone the boat we just smudged. Set the Size to 40, Edge to 50, Opacity to 100%, Blend Mode to Normal. Do not click the Source Aligned or Use Entire Document check boxes.

The Rubber Stamp tool is probably the best tool for fixing problem areas in an image. It's the perfect tool for retouching an area of a scanned photo that has dust or other blemishes. It's just a simple matter of finding a "good" area, cloning it, and applying the good pixels to the blemished area.

When using the Dodge tool, selecting Highlights from the Range field allows you to adjust the highlights without adversely affecting the shadows.

10. Select the area to be cloned by holding down the Option/Alt key and clicking right in the middle of the boat. Paste the cloned area by releasing the Option/Alt key and clicking in the area where you want to paste the pixels. Put the boat copy to the left of the original boat by moving the cursor to the left of the boat and clicking.

11. Take care to preserve the horizon line. If you clicked too high or too low, undo the step (press Command/Control-Z) and try again. See if you can make yours match the image below.

12. Let's clone a cloud. To do this, you need a Size setting of 80 for the medium-sized clouds. Hold down the Option/Alt key, select the area to be cloned, then release the Option/Alt key and paste the pixels elsewhere in the sky.

13. When you are satisfied that you understand how the Rubber Stamp tool works, close the file without saving.

Creating a Vignette

A *vignette* is a cropped selection of an image with a feathered edge. The most common vignettes are oval in shape, but you can use any of the bitmap selection tools to define the area you want to include in your vignette. Once the vignette selection has been made, virtually anything can be done with it. It can become part of a montage or placed over a background of any color and/or texture.

To create a vignette, you can use the bitmap selection tools, such as the Lasso, Marquee, and Magic Wand tools. The selection is then masked from its surroundings. The best way to ensure a successful vignette is to start with a quality selection.

Create a Vignette

1. Open **mountain_child.tif** from the **RF_Fireworks** folder.

2. Select the Oval Marquee tool from the Tools panel, or press the "M" key on your keyboard. If the Oval Marquee tool is not selected, continue to press the "M" key until you toggle to the Marquee tool. In the Properties panel, set the Style to Normal, and the Edge to Feather with a value of 25. Make a circular selection by dragging your marquee directly from the middle of the boy's nose. Press the Shift-Option/Alt keys as you drag so your selection starts from the center and is constrained to a perfect circle. Drag out enough of a marquee to encompass most of the boy.

The next chapter of the book focuses on the concept of layers, a core part of the Fireworks workflow. You will soon see how easy it is to take a selection such as this vignette and modify it in many ways using layers.

3. From the Main menu, choose Modify>Mask>Reveal Selection. This masks your marquee without discarding the surrounding pixels. This is the preferred way to make a vignette because the mask itself can be edited. You can enlarge or reduce your selection at any time. Surrounding the vignette, notice the gray-and-white checkerboard pattern. This means you are looking right through the image to a transparent background.

Vignettes offer an excellent method of creating montages with many component images.

4. Close the file without saving your changes.

Chapter Summary

In this chapter, you learned that Fireworks provides an extensive collection of image-retouching tools. You found you can adjust the brightness and contrast of an image, and the hue and saturation, using convenient slider controls. You also learned how to perform sophisticated adjustments using the Levels filter. For even more sophistication, you found that Fireworks offers a Curves filter that provides the highest level of control over the colors in your images.

Due to the special requirements for Web graphics, you learned that the Fireworks filters are indispensable. You learned that the Unsharp Mask filter can effectively produce the illusion of higher resolution in your Web graphics.

You worked with the comprehensive set of touch-up tools. Previously available only in Photoshop, Fireworks now allows you to Blur, Sharpen, Dodge, Burn, and Smudge images — all with pixel-perfect precision.

You learned that the Rubber Stamp tool allows you to quickly remove problem areas in your images, and add missing elements.

Finally, you learned how to create a vignette. This technique is especially useful when creating montages — collections of images you want to appear together as part of a composition.

Complete Project B: Image Retouching Advertisement

8 Layers

Chapter Objectives:

Fireworks allows you to create a full range of documents — from very simple to very complex. As the complexity of a document increases, the need for layers becomes apparent. Layers allow the designer to organize files, and quickly locate a file when it is needed. The Fireworks Layers panel allows you to effectively manage the layers in your documents, which enhances your overall workflow. In this chapter, you will:

- Review the Layers panel, and find out how to use its features and functions.

- Find out how to create and modify layers.

- Discover the benefits of locking layers.

- Learn the differences between Single-Layer and Multi-Layer Editing modes.

- Find out how to apply blending modes and opacity to layers, and what effects these properties produce.

- Learn about the Web Layer, and why it is needed in every Fireworks document.

Projects to be Completed:

- Globe Illustration (A)

- Image Retouching Advertisement (B)

- Animated Banner (C)

- The Cable Store Web Site (D)

Layers

At the heart of Fireworks is the concept of *layers*. Layers divide Fireworks documents into separate planes, similar to individual sheets of acetate that are stacked one on top of the other.

Most graphics applications — such as Photoshop — rely heavily on layers. Fireworks is no different in this regard. You can use layers to organize a document into separate editable areas that can be hidden and/or locked as needed. Layers also make it easy to change the stacking order of the images and objects in a document. In short, layers allow you to organize Fireworks documents and make it possible to effectively manage even the most complex files.

Layers Panel Overview

The Layers panel has a logical set up, designed to allow you to manage your documents with ease. If it is not visible, you can view the Layers panel by choosing View>Layers or pressing the F2 key on your keyboard. Using Layers is essential when working on Fireworks documents of any appreciable complexity. You will appreciate the new-and-improved Fireworks MX interface that allows you to easily locate this important panel.

Creating Layers

To create a layer, you would select Edit>Insert>Layer, or click the New/Duplicate Layer button located at the bottom of the Layers panel. By default, Fireworks automatically creates Layer 1 for all new documents. If you were to add another layer, it would be named Layer 2, then Layer 3, and so forth.

Duplicating Layers

It is very common practice to duplicate a layer. Let's say you have worked very hard on a bitmap image or object that resides on a particular layer. Before attempting any further work, you can duplicate the layer for back-up purposes, ensuring your work is not lost due to any unforeseen problems. Duplicating layers adds to the file size of your document, but with the large amount of RAM in most of today's computers, this is usually not a problem.

To duplicate a layer, you would select the layer and drag it to the New/Duplicate Layer button located at the bottom of the Layers panel. As an alternative, you can select Duplicate Layer from the Layers panel Options menu. This would display the Duplicate Layer dialog box.

Use Layers to better organize your documents.

From this dialog box, you can choose the number of duplicate layers you need, and you can specify where you want the layers to reside in the stacking order. You can drag a layer into a different position in the stacking order at any time (this will be covered in more detail later in this chapter).

Naming a Layer

It's a good idea to assign unique and descriptive names to your layers. This helps with document organization. Even though each layer is automatically assigned a generic name of Layer 2 or Layer 3, these names don't tell you very much about the content of the layer. A layer name such as "Product Logo" tells you exactly what is on the layer, and saves a lot of time searching for the specific layer you need.

To name a layer, you would double-click a layer in the Layers panel, and then enter a new descriptive name. If you decide to rename the layer again, double-click the layer in the Layers panel, enter a new name, and press the Return/Enter key to change the layer name.

Selecting a Layer

Before you can do anything to a layer, you must first select it. To do this, you would simply click the layer you want to modify. In the Layers panel, a pencil icon appears to the left of any layer that is selected. The pencil icon signifies that the layer can be edited. When the layer is not selected, the pencil icon is not visible, and the layer cannot be edited.

Organizing Layers

You can alter the stacking order of your layers for better organization. Layers are stacked from the top-down. A layer that is positioned above another layer in the stacking order overlaps the layer that lies below it, as viewed on the canvas. If one object overlaps another on the canvas, and you want to remove the overlap, you can drag the overlapping layer to a lower position in the stacking order in the Layers panel.

The Footer Bar layer is being placed lower in the stacking order, between the Navigation Menu layer and the Product Logo layer. Navigation menu will be at the top of the stacking order after this change.

To move a layer to a different position in the stacking order, simply drag it to the new location in between two other layers. When you see a bold line appear in the *target area* (new location), you can release the mouse button and the layer is dropped into its new position.

Viewing/Hiding Layers

During development of complex documents, it can be helpful to hide some of the layers in the document. You might find it easier to work on a particular layer with nothing else visible on the canvas. When you hide a layer, all of the objects that are on the layer become invisible.

When you export a document, only the visible layers are exported. You can have alternate versions of a document, each with various visible layers. If you later decide to export a different version of the document, it's as easy as making other layers visible, and exporting that version of the document.

Hiding the footer bar layer.

To hide a layer, click the eye icon in the Layers panel. To view the layer, toggle the eye icon on again. You can show/hide all of the layers at once by clicking the Layers panel Options menu (top-right corner of Layers panel) and choosing Show All/Hide All.

Collapse/Expand a Layer

More than one object can exist on a layer. You can expand any layer to view each individual object it contains. To save space on your monitor, you can collapse the layer.

The expanded Navigation Menu layer.

To expand a layer, you can click the plus (+) sign on the left side of the layer. Once the layer is expanded, it displays a minus (-) sign where the plus sign used to be. You can also select the size of the thumbnails by clicking the Layers panel Options menu and selecting Thumbnail Options. From there, you can choose not only their size, but whether you want to view them at all.

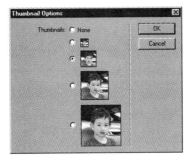

The Thumnail Options dialog box.

As you can see, Fireworks offers a significant amount of flexibility when organizing layers. This helps to increase your efficiency and boost productivity.

Locking a Layer

It's a good idea to lock a layer when you are satisfied with it and you want to make sure you don't mistakenly change it in any way. You might need an object to be in an exact location; if the layer is not locked, you could accidentally move the object without knowing it. Locking the layer prevents errors such as this from occurring.

When a layer is selected, a pencil icon appears to the left of the layer on the Layers panel. When you click the pencil icon, it turns into a padlock icon, signifying the layer is locked. You can lock any layer, even if it is not selected. To do this, click in the column where you find the pencil icon, and the padlock icon appears to tell you the layer is locked. To unlock a layer, click the padlock icon, and the layer can be modified.

Single-Layer Editing

Single-Layer Editing is a feature you may or may not choose to activate. It is one of those features that designers either like to use, or refuse to use. Normally, when you select an object or bitmap image on the canvas, the layer on which it resides is activated and you can edit or move the object. When you are in Single-Layer Editing mode, in order to select an object on the canvas, you must first select the layer on which it resides.

For example, if Layer 2 is selected, and you go to the canvas and try to select an object on Layer 3, you won't have success. You must first return to the Layers panel and select Layer 3 (Layer 2 is automatically deselected). The objects on Layer 3 then become editable.

To activate Single-Layer Editing, go to the Layers panel Options menu and choose Single-Layer Editing. You will see a checkmark next to this option. You can click the checkmark again to turn off Single-Layer Editing.

It's worth taking a moment to discover which option (Single-Layer Editing vs. Multi-Layer Editing) you are most comfortable using. Our experience has shown that it's better to select one option and stay with it; it can get confusing if you switch back and forth between editing modes.

Deleting a Layer

You can delete any layer in a Fireworks document except the Web Layer (used to store image hotspots and slices). As we discussed earlier, Fireworks forces you to keep at least one other layer in every document. If you need to delete any other layer, you would select it, and then click the Delete Selection (trash can) icon at the bottom of the Layers panel, or drag the layer directly to the Delete Selection icon. As an alternative, you can choose Delete Layer from the Options menu. It is immediately removed from the Layers panel.

Layer Properties

Fireworks supports full or partial transparency for any bitmap image or vector object. What's more, in addition to controlling the amount of transparency, you can also control the way the transparency behaves. This is accomplished by applying two layer properties — blending modes and opacity.

Blending Modes

You can choose a blending mode when you have at least two layers (not including the Web Layer, which will be explained shortly) in your document. When you change the blending mode in the top layer, it determines how the layer interacts (blends) with the layer beneath it. The result color for each pixel in the blend is based on the color of that pixel and the blending mode you select.

If you're having trouble selecting objects, check to see if you accidentally left the Single-Layer Editing feature activated, or if the layer is locked.

As you examine the many blending modes, try not to be overwhelmed — you don't have to memorize them. The best way to learn about the blending modes is to use them in different situations. To find the mode that produces the effect you are seeking, apply one to your document, and if it is not the correct effect, try another.

The blending modes are discussed below. For clarity, we refer to the top layer as the *blend color*, and the layer underneath it as the *base color*. The combination of the blend and base colors is the *result color*:

- **Normal**. Normal applies no blending mode. This setting is suitable for many purposes.
- **Multiply**. This mode multiplies the base color by the blend color. This generates a darker result color. This mode is often used for shadow effects. Using Multiply, black will remain black, and white will become completely transparent.
- **Screen.** The Screen blending mode multiplies the inverse of the blend color by the base color. This produces a lighter color than either the blend or the base color. Using Screen, white will remain white, and black will become completely transparent.
- **Darken.** This mode selects the darkest of either the blend or base color, pixel by pixel, to arrive at the result color. Only pixels that are lighter than the blend color are replaced.
- **Lighten.** The Lighten blending mode selects the lighter of either the blend or base color, pixel by pixel, to arrive at the result color. Only pixels that are darker than the blend color are replaced.
- **Difference.** This mode subtracts the blend color from the base color, or vice-versa.
- **Hue.** The Hue blending mode combines the hue of the blend color with the luminance and saturation of the base color.
- **Saturation.** Use this mode to combine the saturation of the blend color with the luminance and hue of the base color.
- **Color.** The Color blending mode combines the hue and saturation of the blend color with the luminance of the base color.
- **Luminosity.** This mode combines the luminance of the blend color with the hue and saturation of the base color.
- **Invert.** Use this blending mode to invert the base color. This would only be used in circumstances where you need the inverse color.
- **Tint.** This mode adds gray to the base color.
- **Erase.** You can use this blending mode to remove all base color pixels.

The Multiply blending mode is an excellent method for creating cast shadows.

Opacity

Once you have chosen a blending mode, the next step is to select how much of it you wish to apply. This is done with the opacity slider on the blend (upper) layer. By default, an object or bitmap image is set to 100% opacity, which can also be thought of as 0% transparency (you can't see through it). To lower the opacity (increase the transparency), you would lower the value with the slider, or manually enter a number into the value field.

Web Layer

The Web Layer cannot be deleted from a Fireworks document.

When you start a new Fireworks document, by default there are two layers. One of them, Layer 1, is the layer you can use to add objects and/or bitmap images to the new document. The other layer is different. It's called the *Web Layer*, and is used to store image hotspots and slices. (These two concepts will be addressed in more depth in Chapter 10.)

You can't delete the Web Layer, nor can you rename it. The purpose of this layer will become clearer in Chapter 10. For now, you don't need to do anything with this layer, simply understand that it needs to be included in every Fireworks document.

Exercise Setup

Understanding how layers work is critical to mastering Fireworks MX. In the next exercise, you will import a vector file and a bitmap file, each on its own layer. You will then add some text on another layer, and review ways you can work with multi-layered documents.

Work with Layers

1. Open a new document with a Size of 500 × 500 pixels and a White Canvas Color. If the Layers panel is not visible, choose Window>Layers from the Main menu or press the "F2" key. By default, you see two layers — the Web Layer and Layer 1. Leave the Web Layer alone. Fireworks stores information for slicing and hotspots in this layer.

Fireworks can import Illustrator files up to version 8 and still maintain the vectors.

2. Let's import an Illustrator 8 document into this Fireworks document. From the Main menu, select File>Import, and then navigate to the **RF_Fireworks** folder. Select **salad_special.ai.** The Vector File Options dialog box appears, allowing you to edit the file before it is actually placed on the canvas. Leave the default settings as shown below. Click OK.

3. Your cursor changes to an inverted "L," as seen below.

Where you click on the canvas with this cursor determines the placement of the upper-left corner of the imported file. Click toward the upper-left corner of the canvas to place the file. The canvas should now resemble the illustration below. Note the Layers panel. Even though the file is on Layer 1, each individual object in the file resides on its own sub-layer. This allows you to click the eye icons to selectively hide the objects on the layer. Click one of the eye icons associated with a sub-layer and notice how that object is hidden from view. Click the same eye icon to return the sub-layer to view.

It is recommended that you name your layers. A file with many layers can get confusing if you do not assign unique names to the layers.

You can collapse the entire layer to save space on your monitor by clicking the minus (-) sign to the left of the layer name.

4. Click the minus (-) sign for Layer 1 and leave the layer collapsed. Double-click the words "Layer 1" in the Layer Name field. A dialog box appears. In the Layer Name field, enter "vector" as the new name for Layer 1. Click away from the Layers panel or press the Return/Enter key to apply the name.

5. There is another layer called Layer 2 in the Layers panel. Fireworks created this layer when you imported the Illustrator file. Select Layer 2. Let's import a bitmap image onto this layer. Select File>Import and navigate to the **RF_Fireworks** folder. Select **salad_plate.tif.** You again see the inverted "L" cursor. Click on the canvas between the "L" and "A" in the word SALAD to place the upper-left corner of the image in the middle of the text as shown below.

6. As you see, the edge of the bitmap file overlaps the text. To fix this problem, we must drag the new layer below the vector layer on the Layers panel. To do this, select Layer 2 and drag it under the vector layer. Do not release the mouse button until you see a black line and an icon as shown below. The black line tells you where the layer will be placed when you release the mouse button. Release the button and you see the text is now correctly covering the edges of the bitmap image.

Think of layers as pieces of see-through acetate that contain the various objects in your file. The file appears as if you were looking down from the top layer to the other layers below.

Another advantage of using layers is that you can lock a layer to keep its content secure.

7. Collapse Layer 2 by clicking the minus (-) sign to the left of the layer name. Rename Layer 2 "bitmap" (as described in Step 4). Drag the bitmap image so it is positioned in the middle of the text. You can use the Arrow keys to move the image one pixel at a time to fine-tune its position. Position everything as shown so there is room for some text at the bottom of the canvas. Click to the right of the eye icons on the Layers panel to lock the layers.

8. Add a new layer by clicking the New/Duplicate Layer icon at the bottom of the Layers panel. It resembles a manila file folder. Name this new layer "footer text".

9. With the footer text layer selected, choose the Text tool from the Tools panel. In the Properties panel, choose a 70-pt. Arial Font, set the Color to Black, Bold, Smooth Anti-Alias, and other settings as shown below in the Properties panel. Type the words "TODAY ONLY" all in capital letters so the text appears similar to the illustration below. When you are satisfied with the placement of the text, lock the layer as described in Step 7.

It is helpful to occasionally hide a layer while you are designing. An example of this would be when the objects on that layer are partially overlapping other objects that require attention.

10. Add another new layer and rename it "test". Drag it to the top of the layer stack in the Layers panel. Notice that the Web Layer always remains at the very top of the stack. Drag the test layer directly below the Web Layer. With the test layer selected, choose the Rectangle tool from the Tools panel. Set the Fill to Red #FF0000 and the Stroke to None. Draw a rectangle that covers the right side of the canvas as shown below. Since the layer is placed at the top of the layer stack, the red rectangle hides the content of the layers below it in the layer stack.

11. With this layer still selected, look at the Layers panel and notice the top-left Opacity field. To the right of it is a slider. Move the slider to 50, or manually enter a value of 50 in the field. This causes the rectangle to be half transparent and half opaque.

Access the blending modes from the Layers panel.

12. Notice the field to the right of the Opacity field. It is set to Normal. This is the default blending mode. Change the blending mode setting to Screen. Notice how only the non-white areas are affected, while the white areas remain white. Experiment with the various blending modes to become familiar with their affects on an image.

13. When you are finished experimenting, close the file without saving.

Chapter Summary

In this chapter, you learned how to use layers, and learned the benefits of using layers as part of your Fireworks workflow. Layers allow you to keep your work well organized, which helps increase your efficiency.

You also learned about the Fireworks blending modes and how transparency effects can be achieved by choosing the right blending mode for the task at hand.

It takes extra effort to create separate layers for the vector objects and bitmaps in a Fireworks document. You realize the payoff for the additional work when your design becomes very intricate and you need to make extensive edits. At times such as these, you will be glad you took the time to stay organized, and included individual layers for the elements of your design.

9 Animated GIFs

Chapter Objectives:

Fireworks is perhaps the best available tool for creating animated GIFs. While other image editors (such as ImageReady) allow you to create animated GIFs, Fireworks was designed from the ground up as a Web graphics tool. This is not the case with other image-editing tools. Once you've created an animation with Fireworks, you may find it's the only tool you need (or want) to use.

It's easy to create animated GIFs with Fireworks. As you will discover, Macromedia included many excellent features into this application that allow you to design professional-looking animations quickly and easily. In this chapter, you will:

- Learn about the Fireworks Library panel.

- Discover how to create frame-by-frame animations.

- Find out how to use the Frames panel.

- Learn what it means to "tween" animations, and how Fireworks automates this process.

- Find out how to create symbols and why they are so useful when developing animations.

- Discover how to export your animations for use on the Web.

Projects to be Completed:

- Globe Illustration (A)

- Image Retouching Advertisement (B)

- Animated Banner (C)

- The Cable Store Web Site (D)

Animated GIFs

The animated GIF is perhaps the most common form of animation on the Internet today. While there are plenty of sophisticated new tools for creating animation — including Macromedia Flash — the animated GIF is still the format of choice in many instances. It offers many advantages over alternative methods: no browser plug-ins are required, and no special code is needed to embed animated GIFs in your Web pages. Everything you need for the animation is self-contained in the file.

The GIF and animated GIF formats are both 8-bit (maximum of 256 colors). Each pixel is a discrete unit. In an animated GIF, if a color of a particular pixel stays the same throughout the animation, there is no increase in file size. It is recommended that you create animated GIFs with this idea in mind. You will most likely identify additional ways to minimize the final file size of your documents. Every Web designer is acutely aware of the importance of keeping file size to a minimum.

Libraries

Graphic symbols simplify the creation of animated GIFs. They are reusable elements that are stored in the Library panel. After you place a symbol in the library, it can be reused any number of times, simplifying animated GIF development. Fireworks can also animate objects — moving, rotating, and otherwise changing them over time. To accomplish this, the object is first converted to a symbol. This process is called "tweening" and will be covered later in this chapter.

You can drag instances of graphic symbols onto the canvas for animation. You can also make global changes to any of your graphic symbol instances by editing the graphic symbol itself. Once the symbol is modified, you can apply the changes to the instances on the canvas. Graphic symbols will be covered in-depth later in the chapter.

Frame-by-Frame Animation

A major distinction can be made between frame-by-frame animation and animation using tweening (more on this in a moment). In *frame-by-frame animation*, each frame is drawn separately, and is slightly different from the frame before it. When viewed at sufficient frame rate (speed), the illusion of motion is created. Without motion, there would be no animation; you would simply have a series of still images.

Before we actually create a frame-by-frame animation, it is necessary to become familiar with the Frames panel. From here, you organize animations.

In an animated GIF, if a color of a particular pixel stays the same throughout the animation, there is no increase in file size. It is recommended that you create animated GIFs with this idea in mind.

Understanding how to work with frames is essential to creating animated GIFs.

Frames Panel

By default, every Fireworks document has one frame. You can look at the Frames panel to see the default frame, named Frame 1.

Up until now, all of the examples in this book have been static (still) imagery with one frame. We can move beyond still images and create documents that contain more than one frame. The Frames panel can be accessed from the Main menu by selecting Window>Frames.

As you build an animation, it's helpful to name the frames. You can do that by double-clicking the default name (Frame 1) and entering a new descriptive name for the frame. As we found when working with layers, descriptive names help you quickly find the correct frame when you need to work with it.

To add a frame, you can click the New/Duplicate Frame icon found at the bottom right of the Frames panel, next to the Delete Frame (trash can) icon.

Alternatively, you can choose Add Frames from the Frames panel Options menu, and then click OK in the dialog box that appears.

The Frames panel Options menu allows you to duplicate an existing frame as well as add a new frame. This feature can be useful when you want to modify the artwork on an existing frame rather than start a new frame from scratch. The other Frames panel options will be discussed later in the chapter.

You can add more than one frame by entering the required number of frames in the Number value field. The radio buttons in the Add Frames dialog box allow you to insert the frame(s) in a variety of locations within the animation.

You can specify how many times an animation will loop by clicking the GIF Animation Looping icon at the lower left of the Frames panel.

The menu that appears allows you to choose how many times you want the animation to loop.

Before exporting the file, you can preview the animation from the canvas. In the Document window, you can see the playback controls, which resemble those on a VCR. You can view individual frames, rewind, fast-forward, play, and stop the animation. Click the white Play/Stop icon to make the animation play. As it plays, each frame in the Frames panel highlights accordingly. While playing, the white Play button turns to a black Stop button. Clicking the Play/Stop icon again stops the animation preview.

You can tell Fireworks how long to play each frame. The default time setting is 7/100 of a second. The value is entered in hundredths of a second; a value of 50, for example, would be a half second; a value of 100 would be one second.

The Include When Exporting check box allows you to decide whether or not the frame should be included in the exported GIF. This feature is useful when you don't want the frame to be exported, but you still want to keep the frame as part of the Fireworks document.

Onion Skinning

The term *onion skinning* is derived from traditional cel animation. Each frame was drawn on thin tracing paper, making it possible to see several frames of the animation at one time. This technique provided an excellent way to ensure proper timing of the movement in the animation.

In Fireworks, onion skinning is a powerful tool that enables you to simultaneously view objects across multiple frames. This feature allows you to see the movement of an entire animation, all in one frame, making it a very useful aid in animated GIF development.

To view onion skinning in Fireworks, you can click the Onion Skinning icon, located in the bottom-left corner of the Frames panel.

The menu that appears allows you to select from different onion skinning options:

- **No Onion Skinning.** No onion skinning is visible.
- **Show Next Frame.** This option shows only the current and the next frames.
- **Before and After.** This selection shows one frame, the frame before it, and the frame after it.
- **Show All Frames.** This option shows every frame in the animation.
- **Custom.** Use this option when the other options do not meet your needs. Selecting this option causes a dialog to appear, allowing you to choose the number of frames before the current frame and the number of frames after the current frame. It also allows you to choose the opacity of these onion-skinned frames, providing greater control. The Multi-Frame Editing check box allows you to select and edit any of the onion-skinned frames without leaving the current frame.

Construct a Frame-by-Frame Animation

1. Open a new document with a Size of 200 × 200 pixels and a White Canvas Color.

2. Select the Brush tool from the Tools panel. Set the Tip Size to a 10-pixel Width. Choose a dark color to create good contrast on the white canvas. Use the Brush tool to draw a circle. Use most of space on the canvas. Don't worry if it's not perfect; it's the concept that is important in this exercise.

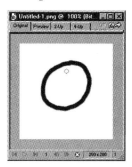

3. On the Frames panel, double-click Frame 1 and rename it "circle". Then press Return/Enter, or click away from the field to enter the new name. Click the New/Duplicate Frame icon at the bottom of the Frames panel, and name the new frame "triangle". Add a third frame and name it "square".

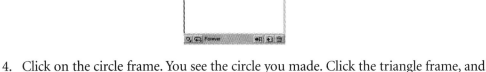

4. Click on the circle frame. You see the circle you made. Click the triangle frame, and with the same Brush tool settings, draw a triangle on the canvas. Click the square frame, and draw a square with the same Brush tool settings.

5. Click the Onion Skinning icon found in the bottom-left corner of the Frames panel. The Onion Skinning dialog box appears. Choose Show All Frames, which allows you to see all three frames of the animation at once.

6. Look at your canvas. The selected frame is visible, but the other frames are also visible. Notice that the unselected frames are lighter than the selected frame so you can distinguish one from the other. Select the different frames and notice how the canvas changes. Here, we selected the circle frame.

7. Now set the animation to Loop, and choose Forever from the GIF Animation Looping pop-up menu.

8. When finished, close the file without saving your changes.

To keep file size low, keep bitmaps in one position throughout the animation, and animate smaller elements, such as text.

Onion skinning is a good method for creating cartoon-style animations. You can base each new frame on the one before it.

This was a simple example, but the process is the same regardless of the length of the animation, or the sophistication of the artwork. You might prefer to duplicate a frame rather than draw each one from scratch as we did here. Remember that you can just as easily use vector tools, text tools, and imported bitmap images to create an animation. In short, if an object can be placed on the canvas, it can be used in an animation.

Animation Using Tweening

Tweening is an old term derived from traditional cel-based animation. Animators found that it was very time-consuming to draw each and every frame in an animation. In an effort to save time, the master animator would draw the *keyframes* (the most important frames) where major changes take place in the animation. "Tweeners," usually apprentices, would then draw the frames in between the keyframes. Tweening eased the traditional animation process, but it was still very difficult and required significant amounts of time.

Fireworks removes the difficulty from the tweening process. The digital artist creates the keyframes, and Fireworks automatically completes the tweening. In other words, you create the beginning and the end of a sequence, and Fireworks takes care of everything in between. This allows you to be more efficient and more productive.

In Fireworks, you don't create keyframes in the traditional sense of the word. Instead, you create graphic symbols, which, as we learned earlier, are stored in the Library panel.

Creating Graphic Symbols

In order for Fireworks to tween elements in your animation, they must first be converted into graphic symbols. You can start with anything — bitmaps, blocks of text, vector objects, or a combination of any of these — as the initial elements in the animation. Then you would designate those elements as graphic symbols.

To create a graphic symbol, you can choose any object on the canvas, and then press the "F8" key on your keyboard, or choose Modify>Symbol>Convert to Symbol from the Main menu. The Symbol Properties dialog box appears.

To create a graphic symbol, choose that option from the Symbol Properties dialog box and click OK. The object becomes a symbol, and appears in the Library panel.

After you create a graphic symbol and store it in the Library panel, you can drag instances (copies) of the symbol onto the canvas, delete instances, or add more instances to the animation. It's this kind of flexibility that makes Fireworks such a useful tool for creating animations.

Animating Symbols

After an object has been converted to a graphic symbol, it can be animated. An example would be to place a symbol on the canvas, and then create a second frame with the symbol placed in a different location. The animation would take place when Fireworks tweens the symbol over a specified number of frames.

When you tween a graphic symbol, it can move — scale or rotate as it moves, fade the color or change the color as it moves, or a combination of any of the above.

Create an Animation Using Tweening

1. Open a new document, with a Size of 468 × 60 pixels, the standard size for a Web banner ad. Choose White for the Canvas Color.

2. Select the Text tool from the Tools panel. Choose a large font (we chose 25-pt. Arial Black, Black color), and type in a short phrase, such as "Tweening is cool!" Place it on the left side of the canvas. We will animate the phrase, moving it across the canvas.

3. Let's convert the text to a graphic symbol so Fireworks can tween it. Select the object, and from the Main menu, choose Modify>Symbol>Convert to Symbol. You can also do this by pressing the "F8" function key.

When tweening bitmap images, file size can get very large if you are not careful.

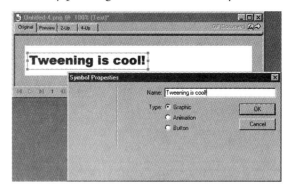

4. In the dialog box that appears, enter a unique name for your symbol, and choose the Graphic radio button for the Type of symbol. Click OK.

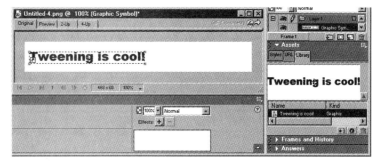

You can view the Library panel by opening the Assets panel and clicking the Library tab.

5. Note what happens on the canvas. The object now has a different border. The little arrow in the bottom-left corner tells you that this is an instance of a symbol. The symbol is now visible in the Library panel, as well as its name and description. Here it's a graphic symbol, but it could also be an animation symbol or button symbol.

6. With this graphic symbol instance selected, hold down the Option/Alt key and use the Pointer tool to drag the instance toward the right of the canvas. This makes a copy. Or you can copy the symbol (press Command/Control-C) and paste it (press Command/Control-V), or select Edit>Copy and then Edit>Paste from the Main menu. Press the Right Arrow key to move the copy to the right.

7. To make the tween, we must ensure both objects are selected. Shift-select the first instance so both instances are selected. Then select Modify>Symbol>Tween Instances from the Main menu.

8. In the Tween Instances dialog box that appears, enter 10 for the number of Steps. Click the Distribute to Frames check box. If you don't click this check box, the tweened instances will all be placed on one frame. It is possible to choose Distribute to Frames from the Frames panel Options menu, but it's easier to let Fireworks do it now.

9. Look at the Frames panel. There are a total of 12 frames, which include the first two instances you made, and the 10 steps of tweening you specified.

Shift-click frames to change the timing of all the frames at one time.

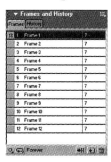

10. You can play your animation by pressing the white Play button at the bottom of the canvas.

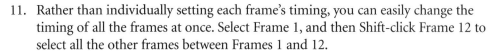

Once clicked, the Play button turns into a black Stop button, which you can click to stop the animation.

11. Rather than individually setting each frame's timing, you can easily change the timing of all the frames at once. Select Frame 1, and then Shift-click Frame 12 to select all the other frames between Frames 1 and 12.

12. Now double-click the right column for Frame 1 (where the 7 is displayed). In the dialog box, change the number to 10 (10/100), so the animation plays a little bit slower. Play the animation again (click the Play button), and notice the slower pace. Close the file without saving.

Making an Object Fade In or Fade Out

In the previous exercise, you learned how easy it is to tween an object across the canvas. Easy, that is, once you converted your object into a symbol. Causing an object to fade in or fade out is based upon the same principle. Instead of moving the object, however, it remains in the same place; the opacity of the object changes over time.

You do not have to decide on moving versus fading — it's just as easy to do both at the same time. You can tween a symbol's location, size, color, rotation, opacity, or any combination of these attributes. If you can imagine it, you can tween it.

Fade an Object Using Tweening

1. Open a new Fireworks document with a Size of 200 × 200 pixels, and a White Canvas Color.

2. Choose the Brush tool from the Tools panel and draw the word "fade" on the canvas.

3. Select the object, and choose Symbol>Convert to Symbol from the Modify menu or press the "F8" function key. In the dialog box that appears, name your symbol "fade", and click the Graphic radio button for the Type of symbol. Click OK.

Tweening is used to fade an object even if it does not move as it fades.

4. Copy the instance of the symbol to the clipboard by choosing Copy from the Edit menu, or by pressing Command/Control-C. Make a duplicate by choosing Paste from the Edit menu, or by pressing Command/Control-V. With the copy selected, move it down the canvas with the Down Arrow key, or drag it with the mouse.

5. In the Properties panel, set the object you just moved to an Opacity of 0 (zero). The object disappears. It's still there, of course, but it is now transparent.

6. Select both objects by pressing Command/Control-A. Once both objects are selected, you can tween them.

7. Select Symbol>Tween Instances from the Modify menu. Enter 5 as the number of Steps, and click the Distribute to Frames check box. Click OK.

8. Press the white Play button at the bottom of the canvas to view your animation. If you want to change the timing, review how this was done in the previous exercise.

9. Leave the file open for the next exercise.

In this example, you tweened the symbol instances with a fade and movement. As you gain proficiency in tweening, you can experiment with scaling, rotating, or whatever you prefer. Breathe new life into the animated GIFs you create for the Web — due to its many advantages, this technology will be in use for a long time.

Exporting Animated GIFs

The process of exporting an animated GIF is practically the same as for its non-animated counterpart. The file format is still GIF and 8-bit (256 colors). We are working with animation, however, so you must specify the timing. This is the only difference between the two, but it is an important one.

As you have seen, the Frames panel is important when creating animated GIFs because this is where you control the order of the frames while they play. You can also specify the timing of each frame in the Frames panel, as we learned in the first exercise of this chapter. By default, the exported animated GIF plays each frame at the speed you initially set, and loops the specified number of times. You can change the timing information upon export, allowing for more flexibility.

Export Options

Selecting File>Export Preview from the Main menu brings up the Export Preview dialog box. Let's take a look at the three tabs in this dialog box: Options, File, and Animation.

Options Tab

The Options tab is found on the upper-right side of the canvas. In the Options Format field, you must select Animated GIF. The other fields — Palette, Loss, and Dither — are the same as for the non-animated GIF format. A good choice for the Palette setting is WebSnap Adaptive. It chooses Web-safe colors whenever possible, but keeps the appearance of the animation as close to the original as possible.

Upon export, choose fewer colors (if possible) to keep the file size low.

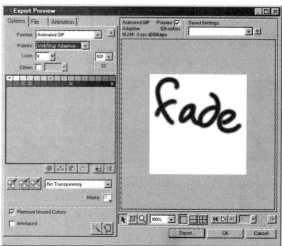

You can lower the file size of a GIF by lowering the total number of colors. This is even more pronounced with an animated GIF, especially one with many frames. If, for example, you were creating an animated GIF banner ad for a client and you were over the file-size limit by a small amount. You could work with the number of colors to reduce the file size.

It's highly recommended that you don't select any Dither with an animated GIF, as this considerably increases the file size, and can negatively impact the quality of the file.

You can set Transparency for an animated GIF the same way you would for a regular GIF. It is recommended to choose No Transparency whenever the canvas color of your document will match the background color of your Web page.

File Tab

The File tab for an animated GIF is the same as a regular GIF. You can change (scale) the size of your animation from this dialog box. If you design the file for the proper export size, scaling is not an issue; but if you need a smaller animation, you can resize the file from the File tab without difficulty.

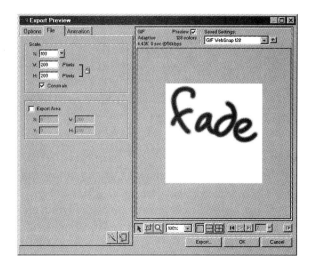

If you have to scale up the animation, keep in mind that the image quality will degrade as Fireworks tries to interpolate the pixels. Again, create your design in the intended export size whenever possible to avoid image quality degradation.

Animation Tab

The Animation tab is specific to the animated GIF format. As you can see, most of the information is similar to what you entered in the Frames panel when you originally created the animation.

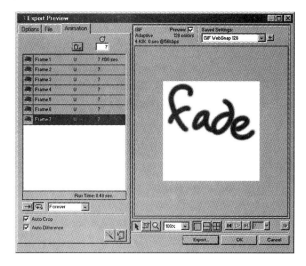

This dialog box allows you to override the frame timing. Here, all frames are set to the default 7/100 second. To change any frame, you would simply choose the frame and enter a new value in the Frame Delay field.

At the bottom of the dialog box are the Looping fields. We set it to Loop Forever, but you can change that setting when necessary.

The Auto Crop field trims away any of the canvas that does not contain pixel information for any of the frames. This would be very labor intensive to perform manually. If your animation needs to remain at the original size (such as a banner ad), you should uncheck this box.

The Auto Difference option tells Fireworks to export only the pixels that change between frames. Keep this option selected, as it lowers the file size of your animated GIF.

The Export Wizard icon is not applicable in this situation, as you already know what you want — an animated GIF. If you were not familiar with the export process, or weren't sure of what export format to choose for the situation at hand, clicking the Export Wizard icon would walk you through it, step by step.

The Optimize to Size Wizard allows you to lower the file size by entering a new value in the Target Size field. When you use the Wizard, however, you don't have control over how this is accomplished. Instead, it is recommended that you selectively lower the number of colors in the animation from the Options tab as we discussed earlier.

Export the Animated GIF

1. With the file from the previous exercise still open, select File>Export Preview from the Main menu. The Export Preview dialog box appears.

2. In the Options tab, make sure the Format field is set to Animated GIF.

3. Click the Export button at the bottom of the dialog box. Navigate to your **Work_In_Progress** folder and click Save.

4. Close the Fireworks file without saving.

Chapter Summary

In this chapter, you learned all about the animated GIF file format. With it, you can add visual interest to a Web site. No browser plug-ins are required to play an animated GIF, which makes it an attractive format for many designers.

You learned how to create frame-by-frame animations where you individually create each frame. You also found that when you create what Fireworks calls "symbols," you can tween objects for smooth effects such as motion, fade-ins, and fade-outs.

Finally, you learned how easy it is to export an animated GIF.

Complete Project C: Animated Banner

10 Image Maps and Slices

Chapter Objectives:

When you develop content for the Web, you must consider the best way to present the information to viewers, while you provide the quickest possible download times. An excellent way to present compelling graphics that also contain necessary links to other Web pages is to utilize image maps — graphics that contain multiple links to multiple Web pages. Each linked area contains a hotspot that when clicked, takes the viewer to a new Web page. Image slices are used to optimize files that are placed on the Web, allowing each slice (piece) of an image to be saved at an optimized setting that allows for much quicker download than when the whole image is saved at one setting. In this chapter, you will:

- Find out about image maps and how they are used.

- Discover more about hotspots.

- Learn how to create static navigation bars.

- Find out how to export HTML.

- Discover how to export Fireworks files to other compatible applications.

- Learn about image slices and why they are so useful for Web-based content.

- Increase your knowledge of rollovers.

Projects to be Completed:

- Globe Illustration (A)

- Image Retouching Advertisement (B)

- Animated Banner (C)

- The Cable Store Web Site (D)

Image Maps and Slices

Up until this chapter of the book, we have focused on the various vector and bitmap tools we can use to create Web graphics in Fireworks. In this chapter, we shift our focus and create actual Web content that consists of image maps, image slices, and Web pages that contain these components.

The first Fireworks Web tool we are going to explore can be used to create image maps. An *image map* is an image on a Web page that contains multiple links. The linked areas on the image are called *hotspots*. Image maps are different than simply placing an image onto a Web page and linking it to a page; that makes the entire image link to one Web page.

There are many situations when image maps are useful, including linking areas of an actual map to related Web pages. For example, if you had a Web page that contained an image of the United States that needed to be linked to fifty other Web pages — one page for each of the states — you could draw a hotspot on each of the states on your image map that linked to its respective Web page. You can also use image maps to create static navigation bars. A *static navigation bar* is a group of buttons that do not have any special effects, such as rollovers. You can use Fireworks MX to define hotspots on an image, and the program then generates the requisite HTML code when you export the image to the Web.

The other Web tool we are going to examine in this chapter is called the Slice tool. It allows us to use a Web design technique called *image slicing*. Image slicing allows us to cut an image into pieces (slices). Each slice can be saved with its own unique settings to allow for quicker download time, to add text to a portion of an image, or to include rollover effects. The HTML file that is created during the export process reassembles the image slices using HTML tables.

Creating Hotspots

The hotspot tools allow you to create multiple links on a single image. These tools work similar to the vector shape tools. There are three different hotspot shapes you can create using these tools. The Rectangle Hotspot tool allows you to draw rectangular-shaped hotspots, and the Circle Hotspot tool allows you to draw perfect circles for your hotspots (it cannot draw ellipses). The Square and Circle Hotspot tools work in a very similar fashion to the shape tools — you simply click and drag.

The final hotspot tool, the Polygon Hotspot tool, allows you to draw a hotspot of any shape you prefer. The Polygon Hotspot tool is a little more complicated, though. When you draw a shape with the Polygon Hotspot tool, you would click a single point on the object and then follow its outline, clicking to add another point whenever the direction changes. As you go around curves, you must be certain to leave a small amount of space between the points. This ensures a smooth curve is created.

When you draw a hotspot, you see a semi-transparent blue object with a small target symbol on it. The blue overlay helps you identify the shape as a hotspot; the target symbol is called the *behavior handle*. We explore how to use the behavior handle later in the chapter. These visual cues are visible only when viewing the image in Fireworks; they do not display in your final image.

Add Hotspots to a Map

You may encounter a dialog box that requests you to replace fonts or maintain appearance. This occurs if the fonts used in the file are not active on the system.

1. Open **zoo_map.png** from the **RF_Fireworks** folder. As you can see, this is a mock-up map for a zoo. Let's link the different areas of the zoo to their associated Web pages.

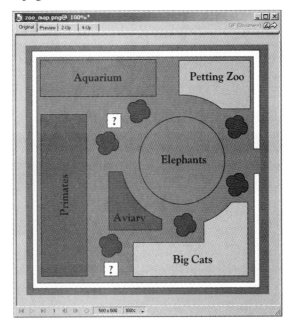

2. Start with the circular area that is labeled Elephants. Select the Hotspot tool from the Web section of the Tools panel. Click and hold on the Hotspot tool until you see the pop-up list of optional tools. Select the Circle Hotspot tool from the list.

3. Use the Circle Hotspot tool to draw a circle over the existing circle on the map. Press the Option/Alt key while you draw with the Circle Hotspot tool to draw from the center outward. This is similar to the work we did with the vector tools.

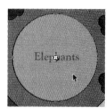

4. Select the Rectangle Hotspot tool from the Hotspot tool pop-up menu. Use the Rectangle Hotspot tool to draw a hotspot over the Primates section of the map.

5. Select the Polygon Hotspot tool from the Hotspot tool pop-up menu. Use the Polygon Hotspot tool to draw a hotspot over the Aviary section of the map.

6. Use the Pointer tool to select the Big Cats area of the map. Control/right-click on the shape and select the option to Insert Hotspot from the pop-up menu. (This shortcut for creating hotspots on a selectable vector object is not available on a bitmap.)

7. Use the shortcut method in Step 6 to insert hotspots over the two remaining areas of the map — Petting Zoo and Aquarium.

You can also insert a hotspot over a selected object with the keyboard shortcut Shift-Command/Control-U.

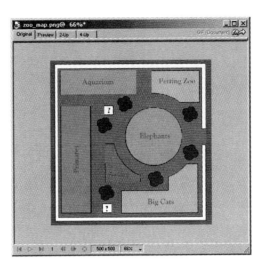

8. After you insert hotspots over the Aquarium and the Petting Zoo areas of the map, choose File>Save As from the Main menu. Save the file as "zoo_imagemap.png" to your **Work_In_Progress** folder. Leave the file open for the next exercise.

Setting Hotspot Properties

A screen reader is software that "reads" information on the screen in a computer-generated voice. Screen readers allow those who are visually impaired to successfully access and use the Internet.

After a hotspot has been created, some information must be provided before it can work properly:

- The most important piece of information is where users will go (the new Web address) when they click the hotspot.

- It is also very important to identify the alternate text for every hotspot. For most users, *alternate text* (also called "alt text") is a small pop-up box that contains additional information about an image or a hotspot. For a visually disabled user, however, alternate text provides the information that a screen reader "reads" aloud to the user. Without alternate text, visually impaired users could not successfully use an image map.

- The Target option allows you to specify where the new page opens. You can use the Target option with frames (more on frames later in the chapter).

Add Hotspots to an Image Map

1. Continue working in the open **zoo_imagemap.png** from the previous exercise.

2. Use the Pointer tool to select the hotspot over the Elephants section of the map.

3. We do not have other Web pages to link to; instead, let's link to other Web sites. In the Properties panel, set the Link to http://www.save-the-elephants.org/.

4. The Alt text should provide a very descriptive phrase or sentence that describes the hotspot. It may be tempting to simply enter the word "Elephants" as the Alt text, but that would force the user to rely on the visual clues on the map to explain the rest. A person using a screen reader cannot see those visual clues. Enter the following for the Alt text: "This link will take you to Save the Elephants dot Org."

5. Add the following link to the Primates hotspot: http://www.primarilyprimates.org/.

6. Enter the following as the Alt text for the Primates hotspot: "This link will take you to Primarily Primates dot Org."

7. Save the file in your **Work_In_Progress** folder. Keep the file open for the next exercise.

Exporting HTML

In previous chapters of this book, you learned how to optimize and export images in the various Web formats. Now that you want the final output in the form of Web content, you must export it to HTML. You can optimize graphics using the Optimize panel, since the Web content includes images. When you export the initial image maps, you will have an HTML file and a single image. When you create image slices later in this chapter, the process will become a bit more complicated because you will work with multiple images.

When you perform an export with Web objects defined in your image, the Save As dialog box automatically saves the file as HTML. The result of the export is a Web page you can open in any browser with fully functional links. There are many options you can set for the HTML file and the image. These include:

- Save the image in a subfolder.
- Copy the HTML onto the clipboard instead of copying it to a file.
- Image-naming conventions for slices.
- Alternate text for the entire image.

To view the HTML Setup dialog box, you can select File>HTML Setup from the Main menu. The various options are divided into three categories that can be accessed from the tabs found at the top of the dialog box.

The HTML Options dialog box is also available when you are going through the export process. Access HTML Options by clicking the Options button in the Save As dialog box.

General Tab
The General tab allows you to:

- Change the style of HTML. We will explore the HTML style in depth when we export to other applications.
- Choose the file extension. An extension consists of three characters that follow the dot in a file name. For HTML files, the extension is most commonly .htm or .html, but you may need another extension in more advanced situations.
- Include HTML Comments. The HTML Comments are instructions in the code that tell you what to copy in case you want to paste the code into another document.
- Force an all-lowercase file name (no uppercase characters).

Table Tab

The Table tab allows you to apply specific settings to a table on a Web page:

- The Space With option allows you to choose how Fireworks will force certain cells to maintain their proper size and shape. Data tables were not originally intended for the complex layout schemes that are used on the Web, so it is often best to use a Spacer image. This setting creates a 1 × 1-pixel image that is saved with all the other images and is used to hold the table together. If you have a simple table, you may try to set this value to either Nested Tables-No Spacers or Single Table – No Spacers. The Nested Tables option creates multiple tables nested inside one another.

- The Cell Color option allows you specify a particular color for the cells in the table.

- The Use Canvas Color option applies the background color you chose when you created the document to the background color of the table.

- The Contents pop-up menu allows you to designate what is placed in empty cells. Empty table cells are closed by the Web browser; this can result in the table appearing a little strange. To avoid this situation, you would place content into the empty cells. The two options are a 1-pixel transparent GIF or a non-breaking space. The default of using the GIF spacer image works well in most situations.

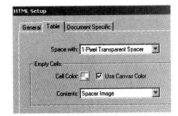

Document Specific Tab

The Document Specific tab allows you to select some advanced document settings:

- The first option allows you to define a naming convention for image slices (we explore slices in depth later in the chapter). This naming convention defines how the names are assigned to the multiple files. This option is necessary only when you are using a Web server that is limited to eight-dot-three naming conventions (eight-character file name with a three-character file extension). There is also the option to change the naming convention for situations where you want to export a separate image for each of the frames in an animation.

- The other option is the Alternative Image Description or Alt text. This option defines the default alternative text for the whole image when there are no hotspots in an image map.

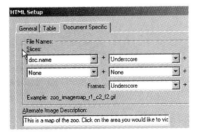

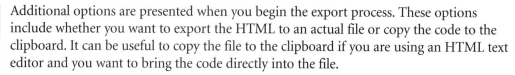

If you navigate to a folder for image placement, make sure the images directory and the HTML file are under the same directory; otherwise, an absolute path to your hard drive will be placed in the code. If this happens, the images will not show up when viewers look at the page.

Additional options are presented when you begin the export process. These options include whether you want to export the HTML to an actual file or copy the code to the clipboard. It can be useful to copy the file to the clipboard if you are using an HTML text editor and you want to bring the code directly into the file.

You also have the option to export slices as they are drawn or use guides. (We will discuss these slice options more thoroughly later in the chapter.) Finally, you can choose a subfolder for your images, which is especially useful when you are working with slices — the slicing process can result in quite a few images. If you do not have a folder for the images, the default option creates the folder for you. Otherwise, you can simply navigate to the proper folder and place the images.

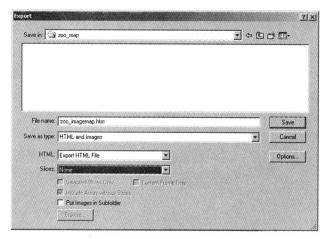

Exercise Set-Up

Using the information we learned on HTML, let's turn our map of the zoo into a working HTML image map.

Export the Zoo Map to HTML

1. Continue working in the open **zoo_imagemap.png**, or re-open the file from your **Work_In_Progress** folder.

2. Select Export from the File menu to access the Export dialog box.

3. Navigate to your **Work_In_Progress** folder and create a new folder named "zoo_map".

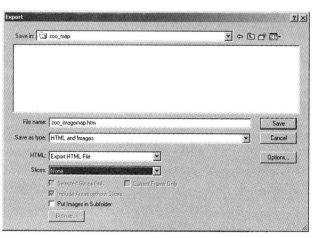

4. Make sure the File Name is **zoo_imagemap.htm** and the Save as Type value is set to HTML and Images.

5. Click the Put Images in Subfolder check box.

6. At the bottom of the dialog box, do not change the default images/ directory name. It creates an **images** directory inside the current directory.

7. Click the Options button on the right side of the dialog box under the Cancel button.

8. Make sure the Include HTML Comments check box is selected.

9. Click the Document Specific tab at the top of the dialog box.

10. Set the value of the Alt text to: "This is a map of the zoo. Click on the area you would like to visit."

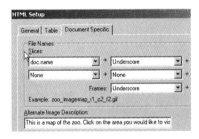

11. Click OK to accept the options and close the Options dialog box.

12. Click Save to save the HTML file and the image. Close the file.

Viewing the Web Page

Now that you have exported your content as a Web page that includes an image map, you can view it in a browser. At this point, you can't view it from the Internet, but you can view it locally from your Work_In_Progress folder.

If you want viewers to have access to your Web page from any computer, you must secure space on a Web server and upload the HTML file and the image file (or files) to that Web space. You must also be very sure to maintain the directory structure — if you place your images in the Images subfolder on your system, you must place the images into a subfolder of the exact same name (Images) when you upload to the Web server. There are many free Web space agencies available on the Web and most Internet Service Providers (ISPs) also provide free Web space to their customers. Once you secure Web space, ISPs usually offer a tutorial on how to post your files on the server using the File Transfer Protocol (FTP).

For the remainder of the book, we will view all of our pages from the Work_In_Progress folder, since individual Web-server access may vary.

View Your Web Page from the Work_In_Progress Folder

1. Open your preferred Web browser. Our screen shots show Microsoft Internet Explorer, but any browser is suitable for this exercise.

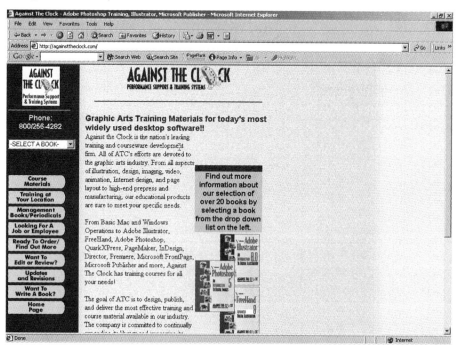

2. From the File menu, select Open.

3. In the Open dialog box, navigate to the **zoo_map** folder located inside the **Work_In_Progress** folder and select **zoo_imagemap.htm**.

4. Click OK and the image map opens in your browser.

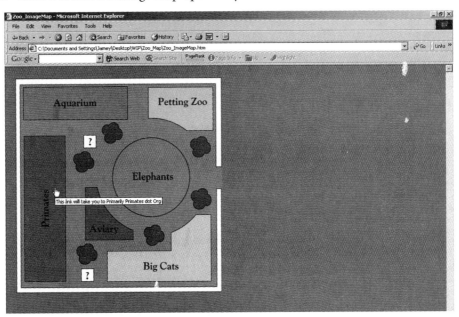

5. Click the Elephants hotspot to test your link. This link sends you to a page that is on the Internet, so you must be connected to the Internet for the link to work. If you are not connected to the Internet, connect and retest your link.

6. Click the Back button on your browser and test the Primates hotspot.

7. Close you browser when you are done testing your links.

Exporting to Other Applications

You may have noticed that there are limitations to how much you can modify Web content using Fireworks. In fact, Fireworks was designed more for creating Web objects (image maps and buttons) then for creating and managing full-blown Web sites. There are many Web-development products on the market today, but three of them are considered the industry standards: Macromedia Dreamweaver, Adobe GoLive, and Microsoft FrontPage.

In Fireworks MX, many options are available for exporting HTML code. Since HTML is a standard maintained by the World Wide Web Consortium, the differences in the code that is generated for each of the export options are primarily stylistic when it comes to basic HTML. When you use Firework's more advanced Web features, such as rollover effects, the output file can be very different for each of the various Web editors. Luckily, Macromedia made the wise decision to allow Fireworks to generate HTML code in styles that are compatible with all three industry-standard editors. If you use Fireworks to create Web images and objects, but prefer to use Adobe GoLive as your Web-development tool, your Fireworks code can be seamlessly imported into GoLive.

To see the various HTML output options, you can open any Fireworks .png file or create a new file. Once a file is open, you can select File>HTML Setup. The HTML Setup dialog box should look familiar to you — it is the same dialog box you see when you click the Options button in the Export dialog box.

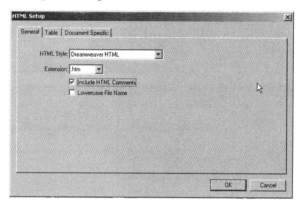

If you click on the pop-up menu labeled HTML Style, you see various available options. There is an HTML version for each of the three standard editors, as well as a generic HTML option. The generic HTML does not insert any of the stylistic differences found in the three editors; it is a good choice when you intend to manually edit the code.

You will also notice that there is a dotted line followed by three XHTML options. XHTML (eXtensible HTML) is the newest version of HTML. Including XHTML is Macromedia's way of helping you remain current with the latest technology. As of the release of Fireworks MX and the writing of this book, Microsoft has not yet developed a version of FrontPage that supports XHTML.

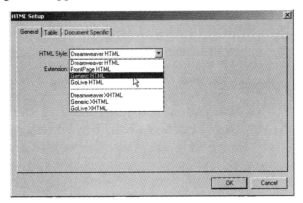

Exporting Dreamweaver Library Items

As mentioned above, the basic differences between the three applications' code is primarily stylistic; however, Fireworks allows you to export your code as a Dreamweaver Library item.

When you use Dreamweaver to develop a Web site, you set up a local folder to act as a mock-up of the completed site. This mock-up area, called the "local root", can contain bits of HTML code that can be repeatedly used throughout the Web site. If a library item is updated, every instance of that item on the site is automatically updated. If you want to use this functionality, you must use Macromedia Dreamweaver and follow these steps:

- In Dreamweaver, set up your Web site using the site management tools.

- Create a folder named Library inside the local root directory.

- Export your Web content, such as the image map you created earlier, and change the Save as Type setting from HTML and Images to Dreamweaver Library, which includes the .lbi file extension.

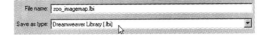

- Once you select the Dreamweaver Library type, you are asked for a valid Library directory located inside the local root of the site where you want to use this object. Navigate to your Library directory.

- After you save the Library item into the appropriate directory, open Dreamweaver and you should have the Web object available to you in the Library panel. Simply drag and drop this object onto any page where you want to use it.

- If you make any changes to the Library item, Dreamweaver automatically asks if you want to update all instances of the object.

Understanding Slices

As mentioned earlier, image slicing is a technique used to slice (cut) a single image into many smaller images. After you slice the image, it is then reassembled in an HTML table — a grid-like structure that holds the image slices in place. One of the fundamental reasons for using slices instead of an image map is that it allows you to turn pieces of the sliced image into rollovers. If you are familiar with the Internet, you have probably used rollovers many times. *Rollover images* change their appearance when the user places the mouse over the image. This functionality is especially useful for buttons because it signals the user that an image (or part of an image) is clickable.

Many Web interfaces are built using image slicing techniques. One might think it would be easier to simply place text on an image rather than creating slices that may be replaced by HTML text. but keep in mind that image data is always larger in file size than HTML textual data. Another reason for using image slicing rather than creating image maps is that slicing allows you to include textual content in an image. Slices ensure that text is visible to screen readers and search engines; they cannot "read" the pixels of an image to determine what letters you used.

An additional benefit is that slices can decrease the amount of time a Web page takes to download, since most modern browsers and Web servers are capable of transmitting and receiving multiple files simultaneously. This means that many small files (slices) should download faster than one large file. When a Web server is busy and overloaded, some of the smaller image slices will not be transmitted right away; this can cause only parts of the interface to download. Most viewers know about this problem and it is unlikely they will leave your Web page when they experience it.

A good example of this type of slicing is a tabbed interface such as those on amazon.com or apple.com. One way to minimize the amount of redundant image loading on each page is to make sure the images that remain the same in appearance on each page are assigned the same file name from one page to the next. This technique stores the image in the browser's cache so it won't download again as the user visits a new page. This saves considerable download time for the user.

Using Guides to Create Slices

There are two methods you can use to create image slices. One way is to use guides to define your slices. This method is only effective if you are slicing a simple image. If you have a complex image with areas that overlap, you cannot use guides to define your slices.

As you can see in the screen shot below, the guides were drawn to slice both the Cats tab and the Furniture sub-element. Since these slices overlap, the left guide correctly slices the Furniture tab, but it also incorrectly slices the Cats tab.

This is not an acceptable way to slice this image. The Cats tab would be broken into two images, each requiring a link. This method does not allow you to add behaviors such as rollovers and pop-up menus (we explore these functions in the next chapter).

Image slicing is when you cut a single image into parts and reassemble the parts inside an HTML table.

Using the Slice Tool

The other method of creating slices is to use the Slice tool. The Slice tool offers complete control over the slices you create.

As you add slices, you will see they resemble the hotspots on images maps — but slices are identified by their green color rather than the blue color that signifies a hotspot. An image slice has a behavior handle, which you can use to add interactive behaviors to slices. As you draw slices, you will see that red lines are added to the image. These red lines provide a preview of the table cell border locations.

There are two variations of the Slice tool:

- The standard Slice tool can be used to draw rectangular slices.
- The Polygon Slice tool works similar to the Polygon Hotspot tool, but the end result is not a polygon. It is a rectangular-sliced image that outlines the shape you draw. Tables and bitmaps are essentially grids, so they can only be made of rectangles.

While you are working on a sliced image, you may find that you need to modify the image. It is much easier to edit an image with slices turned off. You can turn off the slices in one of two ways. You can make the Web Layer invisible in the Layers panel (click the eye icon) or you can hide the slices using the Hide Slices and Hotspots option found under the Slice tool.

Slice an Image

1. Open **tabs_cats.png** from the **RF_Fireworks** folder.

2. This is a tabbed interface similar to the interface we discussed earlier. Let's begin by placing guides where we want our slices to be positioned. Make sure the Rulers are visible. Use the Pointer tool to drag a horizontal guide across the top and bottom of the interface.

3. Draw five vertical guides on the ends of the tabs and where one tab meets the next tab in line. Don't worry if the guides are not exact. We will fine-tune them later.

4. Draw a vertical guide in between each of the links in the second row, and draw a vertical guide at the beginning and end of the second row.

5. While this may look chaotic, it will ensure our slices are precisely aligned and do not overlap. If the slices are not exactly aligned, you will create unnecessary slices; if they overlap, you will get very unexpected results in the final table. Select the Zoom tool from the Tools panel. Zoom in to ensure the guides are aligned correctly. In the screen shot below, notice that the horizontal line is cutting off part of the beige tabs. This is clearly an error. Attention to the smallest detail is crucial when adding rollovers.

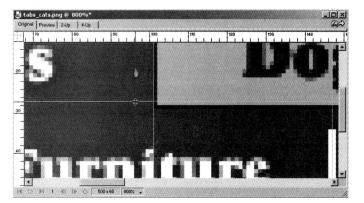

Press the "K" key to switch to the Slice tool.

6. Once your guides are in place, create a folder in your **Work_In_Progress** folder named "Tabs". Save this file into the **tabs** folder.

7. Select the Slice tool from the Tools panel.

8. Use the Slice tool to draw a slice over the Cats tab. Use the guides to make precise slices that do not overlap.

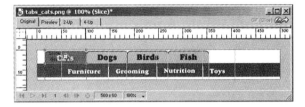

9. Use the Slice tool to draw slices over the three remaining tabs (Dogs, Birds, and Fish).

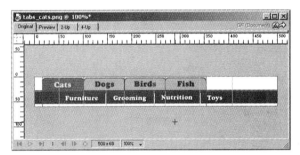

10. Draw a slice for each of the sub-elements in the second row (Furniture, Grooming, Nutrition, and Toys).

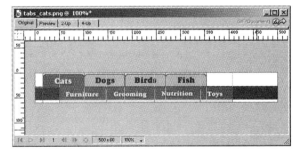

11. Select Save from the File menu to save the file into your **tabs** directory. In the next exercise, we will set options for the slices and export this file to HTML. Leave the file open for the next exercise.

Setting Slice Options

When you select a slice and look at the Properties panel, you see the various slice options. You can set any of the preset Optimize options for a selected slice. By default, a slice has the same Optimize options as the entire document, but you can modify the settings for each slice if necessary. This can be especially useful when you have a photograph or a gradient as part of an interface. You can set those particular slices to JPEG, and all of the other slices can be set to GIF. If one of the presets does not provide what you need, a slice can be optimized from the Optimize panel instead.

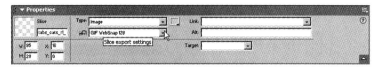

Another slice setting is for the Type of data for that particular slice. The two options are Image and HTML with Image, the latter being the default setting. The Image setting creates an image when you export the slice. The HTML with Image setting allows you to place HTML code into your slice.

If you know HTML, you can add the page content in the Fireworks editor. If you don't know HTML, you can still set the slice to HTML with Image, but it will not create an image from that slice. Instead, you can place text into that cell of the table using your favorite WYSIWYG Web-page editor. The Link, Alt, and Target options work the same as they did for hotspots, but these settings would be applied to the sliced image, not a hotspot.

WYSIWYG is short for "What You See Is What You Get." WYSIWYG editors are Web-page editors that work similar to word processors.

Set Slice Options

1. If you closed **tabs_cats.png** after the previous exercise, open the file from the **tabs** folder, which you created in your **Work_In_Progress** folder.

2. Use the Pointer tool to select the slice that is over the Dogs tab.

3. Since we do not have any of our own content Web pages, set the Link for this slice to "http://www.akc.org/".

4. Set the Alt text for the tab to, "This tab is for the dog section of our site."

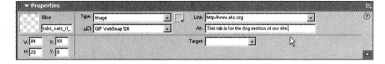

5. Select Export from the File menu.

6. In your **tabs** folder, create a new folder named "cats" and make it the current directory.

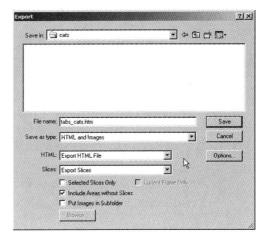

7. Set the Save as Type to HTML and Images, and set Slices to Export Slices.

8. Click the Put Images in Subfolder check box.

9. Leave the default path as images/. We do not have an **images** folder in the current **cats** folder, so Fireworks will create one for us.

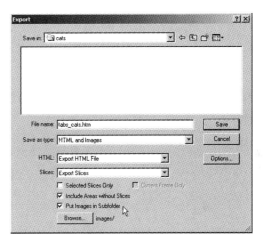

10. Click Save.

11. Open **tabs_cats.htm** in your browser. Ensure you are connected to the Internet, and then check the link to make sure it is working properly.

12. Leave the file open for the next exercise.

Rollovers in Slices

As mentioned earlier, one reason for using slices rather than image maps is so you can add rollover effects to parts of an image. The tabs in the interface we worked on in the previous exercise would be much more interesting if they changed color when you placed your mouse on them.

To create this effect, you must use an animation tool. You will create a duplicate of the current frame and apply your rollover effect to the duplicate. Then you will add a behavior to cause the image to change when the user places their mouse pointer over it. This will be accomplished using the behavior handle.

Add Rollover Behaviors to Slices

1. Continue working in the open **tabs_cats.png**.

2. In the Frames panel, choose the Duplicate Frame option from the pop-up menu.

3. In the Duplicate Frame dialog box, set the Number of frames to 1, and click the After current frame radio button. Click OK.

4. In the Tools panel, click the Hide Slices and Hotspots button.

5. Make sure you are on Frame 2 in the Frames panel. Select the rounded rectangle used to define the Dogs tab and select a new fill color.

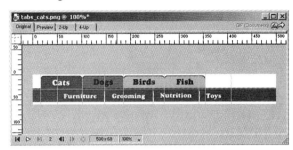

6. Change the colors for the Birds and Fish tabs, applying any colors you prefer.

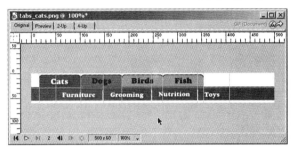

7. Click on Frame 1 in the Frames panel. Notice that the three tabs you changed returned to their original color.

8. Return the slices to their visible state (click the Hide Slices and Hotspots button) and select the slice over the Dogs tab.

9. Drag the behavior handle to the Dogs slice, and drop it. This should open the Swap Image dialog box.

If you simply click the behavior handle, a pop-up menu appears. Make sure you drag the behavior handle away from its origin and release it while it is over the Dogs tab.

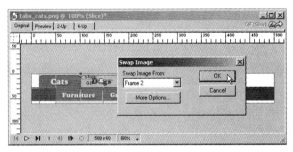

10. Make sure the Swap Image From option is set to Frame 2, and then click OK.

11. Repeat Steps 9 and 10 for the Birds and Fish tabs.

12. Save the file, and leave it open for the next exercise.

Previewing a Web Page and Updating HTML

There are times when you might want to view a Web page before exporting it. You can preview Web pages with the Preview in Browser option located in the File menu. After you export a file, you will most likely need to update the HTML (content) from time to time. Rather that create an all-new file, you can update the existing HTML file and its associated images.

Press the "F12" key to preview a document in your primary Web browser.

You can set the primary and secondary browsers by using these options on the Preview in Browser menu.

Preview Web Pages in a Browser

1. Continue working in the open **tabs_cats.png** file.

2. Choose Preview in Browser from the File menu. This opens a submenu. You should have at least one browser listed in this submenu. Click a browser from the list.

3. Test to make sure your rollovers are working correctly, and then close the browser window.

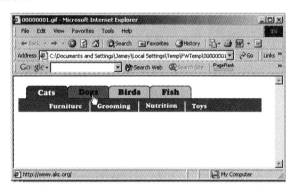

4. Leave the file open for the next exercise.

Update an HTML File

1. Continue working in **tabs_cats.png**. From the File menu, choose Update HTML.

2. This first dialog box asks you to locate the HTML file you want to update. Navigate to the **tabs_cats.htm** file located in the **Work_In_Progress/cats** folder.

3. Click Open.

4. Click the Replace Images and their HTML radio button. Click OK.

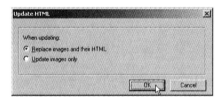

5. The next dialog box prompts you to identify the location of your images. Navigate to the **images** directory so it becomes the current directory. Click the Select "images" button located at the bottom of the Select Images Folder dialog box.

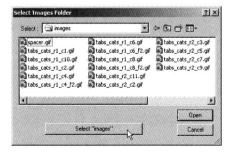

6. Your HTML file is now updated. Save your .png file and check your HTML file in your browser. If you want a refresher on how to open a file in a browser, refer the section of this chapter where we discussed opening a file from the **Work_In_Progress** folder.

Chapter Summary

In this chapter, you learned how to build Web page content. You explored image maps, which allow you to create a single image that has multiple hypertext links to various locations. An image map is an excellent choice for static navigation that does not need to include actual text. If you need to include text elements in an image, or you want to add rollover effects, image slicing is a better choice than image maps. Slices cut images into many smaller images; when exported to HTML, they are reassembled using HTML tables.

Navigation Bars and Pop-Up Menus

Chapter Objectives:

Web pages are not considered complete without navigation bars and pop-up menus. These Web page elements are standard fare for virtually every site on the Internet. You will find it easy to develop complex navigation bars and pop-up menus using Fireworks advanced features — specifically designed for these purposes. With them, you can create rollovers effects, apply up to four different states to buttons, and create both HTML- and image-based pop-up menus. In this chapter, you will:

- Find out how to create a button symbol.

- Discover how to apply four states to your buttons.

- Learn how to set a disjointed button rollover, where you click on one button, and another button changes its appearance.

- Explore the different types of pop-up menus you can create using Fireworks.

- Find out how to apply advanced attributes to your pop-up menus.

Projects to be Completed:

- Globe Illustration (A)

- Image Retouching Advertisement (B)

- Animated Banner (C)

- The Cable Store Web Site (D)

Navigation Bars and Pop-Up Menus

Now that you know how to use Fireworks to create Web content, let's explore some advanced options including the Button Editor, navigation bars, disjointed mouse-overs, and pop-up menus. These advanced options allow you to create complex Web content, even if you have very little knowledge of the underlying technology. Fireworks can actually generate complex HTML, JavaScript, and DHTML that, up until very recently, was impossible to accomplish unless you completed the programming yourself. Using one or many of these options can save significant development time.

Button Editor

The *Button Editor* is a very powerful tool that allows you to generate complex buttons in a short period of time. To make use of these objects on a Web page, you need to export the images and their appropriate HTML. You can use a Web page editor to incorporate these objects.

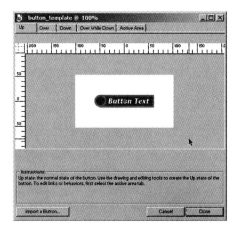

Keep in mind that a button on a Web page is essentially a graphic with a link applied to it. Using the Button Editor, you can make your buttons dynamic and interactive.

Creating dynamic buttons is a fairly straightforward process. You can start by drawing a button, which would then be converted into a symbol. When you used symbols for animation, you used graphic symbols. When you create buttons, however, you use interactive button symbols. After you create the button symbol, you can use it as many times as necessary by creating multiple instances of the button.

These symbols allow you to set the different states of the button. *States* are essentially event-driven appearances of the button. For instance, you can set one appearance for the button when a user places the cursor over the button (the Over state), and another appearance when the user clicks the mouse on the button (the Down state).

Creating a Button Symbol

The first step in developing a button is to create a symbol. The symbol type is, of course, the button symbol. This symbol type allows you to set various interactive options for the button.

If you do not set a specific link for a button, it will use the default link of #, which in HTML means "self." This means when the user clicks the link, the browser loads the current page.

Before you can create a button symbol, you must first design your template button. The template button can be converted into a button symbol, which can then be edited to represent the various button states. Once you have a button symbol, you can use it many times in a document by creating multiple instances of the symbol. To convert a graphic into a symbol, you can select the entire image that you want to use for the button. If the shapes and text are not grouped, make sure you select each part of the shape; otherwise, your button will be incomplete. Once all the elements are selected, you can click Modify>Symbol>Convert to Symbol, or you can Control/right-click on the object and choose the Convert to Symbol option from the pop-up menu.

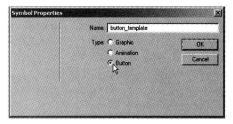

The keyboard shortcut to convert the current selection to a symbol is pressing the "F8" key.

This command opens the Symbol Properties dialog box. From there, you can choose button options to select a name for the symbol. Once you click OK, you will see that the object you turned into a symbol is now a slice, with one minor difference from other image slices.

If you were to look closely in the lower-left corner, you would notice a new icon on this slice. This icon tells you that the slice is actually a button symbol.

Create a Button Symbol

1. Open **button.png** from the **RF_Fireworks** folder.

2. Use the Pointer tool to select all of the elements of the button.

You may encounter a dialog box requesting you to replace fonts or maintain appearance. This occurs if the fonts used in the file are not active on the system.

3. From the Main menu, select Modify>Symbol>Convert to Symbol.

4. In the Symbol Properties dialog box, name the symbol "Button_Template".

5. Click the Button radio button to select the symbol Type.

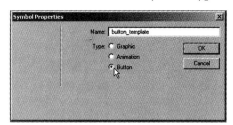

6. Click OK.

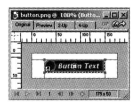

7. Save **button.png** in your **Work_In_Progress** folder. Leave the file open for the next exercise.

Your button symbol is complete. Next, let's examine how to make buttons more interactive and dynamic.

Understanding Button States

In the previous chapter, you created a simple rollover in an image slice. When you looked at the content in a browser, the image with the rollover property changed to another state when you hovered your cursor over the image. This type of rollover is also called a *mouse-over event*.

When you create buttons using the Button Editor, you can add a total of four states to the buttons — the Up, Over, Down, and Over While Down states. Even though all of these states are available, you should weigh the option of using all of them against the additional download time they would add to your pages.

When a user loads a page, an image is downloaded for each state of the button. All the states have to be downloaded at the very beginning of the process. When a user places his mouse over a button, the change in state occurs immediately. If the states were not downloaded at the beginning of the process, a user would hover the mouse over the image and it would request the image from the Web server. The rollover effect would probably be lost since the user would most likely click on the image before the browser was able to download the image from the server.

Let's explore each of the button states:

- **Up State**. The Up state is how the button appears when the user is not interacting with the image. You could say a button that is in no other state is, by default, in the Up state. This state is required in every button.

- **Over State**. The Over state is how the button looks when you hover your cursor over it. Of the three interactive states, this is the most useful state. It signals the user that this button is a clickable object. If you are not going to add an Over state to a button, there is little reason to use the Button Editor — but it is likely you will always add an Over state on a button.

- **Down State**. The Down state is how the button looks when the user clicks the button. In most cases, this state automatically reverts to the Over state after the user removes the mouse from the button. The only time a clicked button remains in its down position is when you are using frames, and the frame where the button resides does not change. It is recommended that this option only be applied in a multi-button navigation bar that is used in conjunction with frames. If the Down state is not applied to a button, the button remains in the Over state when the user clicks the button.

- **Over While Down**. The Over While Down state is how the button looks when the button is in the down position and a user hovers the mouse over it. This is a very rare situation, since the only time that the button stays in the down position is when it is used in frames and the button's frame does not change. It is recommended that this option only be applied in a multi-button navigation bar that is being used in conjunction with frames. If the Over While Down state is not applied to a button, the button remains in the Over state when the user clicks the button.

Setting Button States and Properties

Now that you know how to convert an image into a symbol, you can set up the various button states. Let's examine how to add each of the states to a button. As mentioned earlier, it is not practical to use all states for all buttons. In many situations, using all of the states may cause viewers to download images they will never see.

To begin, you must first open a button symbol. This can be accomplished in many ways. All of the options listed below open the Button Editor:

- Select the button and choose Modify>Symbol>Edit Symbol.
- Control/right-click the button and choose Symbol>Edit Symbol.
- Double-click the button to select it.
- Edit a button symbol from the Library. You will explore this option later in the chapter.

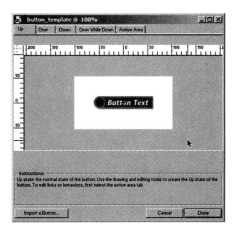

The Button Editor includes tabs that allow you to edit each of the button states. You can also copy the state of the button to the other states of the button. This feature is very useful because it allows you to keep your buttons consistent through all of the states. Copying the previous state to another state also helps you avoid jumping, which can occur if the graphics in the various states are not all aligned. Once you copy the previous state to the current state, you can make the changes you want in that particular button state.

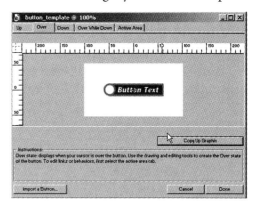

An additional tab, called the Active Area tab, allows you to change the size of the active area on the button (by default, the entire button is the active area). When the user clicks in the active area, the mouse turns into a hand symbol, and the user is taken to a new Web page. When you click the Active Area tab and select the slice object, you can set the link properties for the button in the Properties panel. These properties are the same as for hotspots. You can set links for each button instance as it is added to the document.

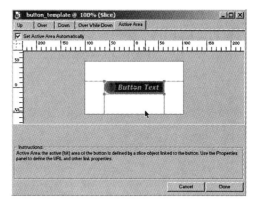

Fireworks includes a feature that allows you to import complete, pre-made buttons that come in two-, three-, and four-state variants. There is a small number of these pre-made buttons, but they are completely editable; you can start with one of the pre-mades and modify it to precisely suit your needs. If you do not want to use pre-made buttons, you can easily create a new button symbol from the Symbol menu instead of converting image elements into a symbol.

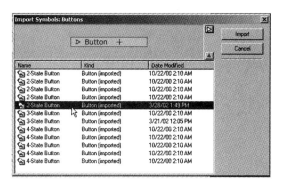

Add the Over State to a Button

1. Continue working in **button.png** from the previous exercise.

2. Double-click the slice object to open the Button_Template symbol in the Button Editor.

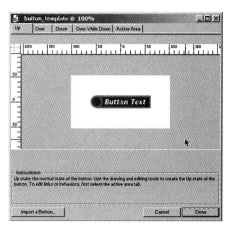

Double-clicking the behavior handle does not open the Button Editor. Make sure you double-click the slice itself and not the behavior handle.

3. Click the Over tab.

4. Click the Copy Up Graphic button below the work area of the Button Editor.

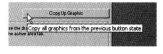

5. You should now have a copy of the Up state in your Over state. In the Over state, use the Pointer tool to click the small black circle on the button.

You do not need the other states for this exercise, so you are not going to create them at this time. To create them, you would follow the same steps you used for the Over state.

6. Use the Properties panel to change the Fill color to White #FFFFFF.

7. Click Done.

8. Click File>Preview in Browser, and choose one of the available browsers. This opens the button in the browser and shows you how the file would look if you exported it at this point in development.

9. Close your browser and save **button.png**. Leave the file open for the next exercise.

Making Use of Button Symbols

Once you have created a button symbol, you can use it in a document as many times as you prefer. This feature allows you to create navigation systems for Web pages that have a consistent appearance throughout the site.

A navigation system can be included as a library item in Dreamweaver; when edited, every instance of the library item on every Web page of the site is automatically updated. If you use Dreamweaver as your Web-page editor, consult Dreamweaver's documentation or the Against The Clock book, *Creating Web Pages Using Dreamweaver MX*, to learn how to use Dreamweaver libraries. It is important to note that exporting HTML to a Dreamweaver library object and using the Fireworks library are different operations. Each product in the Macromedia MX suite has its own library.

To add an instance of a button to a Web page, you can open the Assets panel, click the Library tab, locate the button in the Library, and then drag an instance of the button to the canvas.

Once the button is on the canvas, you can use the Properties panel to set the properties for the button. After the properties are set, any new buttons you copy to the canvas would have identical settings, including the text on the button. Those settings are not permanent, however; you can change the normal slice properties — Alt text, Link, Export options, and Target for frames — and you can change the text that appears on the button. If you prefer, you can set a button to the Down state when the page loads. This can be useful if you want to let users know where they are in the navigation scheme.

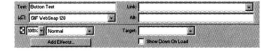

When you change the text in this way, you are only changing it for that particular instance of the button, and it automatically updates all the states that are in use.

Create and Edit Button Instances

1. Continue working in the open **button.png** from the previous exercise.

2. Select Modify>Canvas>Canvas Size. Change the canvas Height to 250 pixels. Set the Anchor point to the top center so the new canvas space is added below the button.

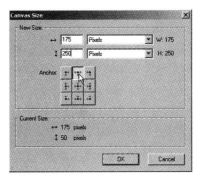

3. Click OK.

4. In the Assets panel, click the Library tab.

5. Drag a copy of the button from the Preview pane in the Library panel to the canvas.

6. After you drop the object on the canvas, you see that it did not drop where you expected. Use the Pointer tool to move it until it snaps into place under the first button.

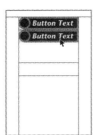

7. Repeat Steps 5 and 6 until you have a total of 5 buttons on your canvas.

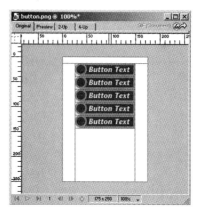

8. Select the first button. From the Properties panel, set the Link to "http://www.againsttheclock.com", and Button Text to "ATC". Add appropriate Alt text, such as, "This link takes you to the Against The Clock Web site at A T C dot com."

9. Pick four more sites to use as links, and set the Link, Alt text, and Button text for each. We chose four popular search engines for our links.

10. Select File>Preview in Browser and choose one of the available browsers. Yours should resemble ours, but your links are probably different than ours.

11. Save the file and keep it open for the next exercise.

Editing and Updating Buttons

If you were using a set of buttons that were manually created, and then you decided to change the color scheme of the site and the buttons, you would be forced to edit each of the buttons, one at a time, in order to update them. This could be a very time-consuming effort. When you use the Button Editor to create buttons, however, you can simply edit the button symbol and all the instances of that symbol are automatically updated. This is an excellent timesaving benefit for Web designers.

Modify Buttons

1. Continue working in the open **button.png** from the previous exercise.

2. Double-click any of the button objects to open the Button Editor.

If you want to change only one instance of a button, turn off the slices and make your changes directly to that button instance.

3. Change all the green on the Up state to any color you prefer.

4. Click the Over tab and then click the Copy Up State button. This copies the new color from the Up state.

5. Change the color of the fill of the circle in the Up state.

6. Click Done. The color should be changed on all your button instances. Notice that the color you chose may be obscured by the green overlay that the slice places on the button. Remember that you can hide the slices if you want to look at the page without the green overlay. To hide the slices, click on the Hide Slices and Hotspots button located in the Web section of the Tools panel.

7. Save your file and preview it in your browser.

8. After you have seen the changes, close your browser and **button.png**.

Creating a Disjointed Rollover

In Chapter 10, you added a simple rollover effect to an image slice. You did this by using the Pointer tool to grab and slightly drag the behavior handle so it was released on top of the original slice. This opened the Swap Image dialog box, allowing you to identify which images to swap.

As an alternative, you can click the behavior handle. This opens the Behavior menu, which allows you to apply behaviors to the selected slice.

Selecting the Add Swap Image Behavior option opens a different Swap Image dialog box. As you can see, you still have the option to set a frame as the swapped image, but you also have a number of other options.

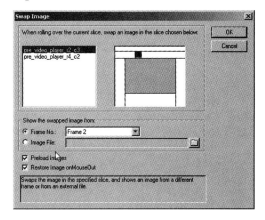

The top of the dialog box has two windows that allow you to identify which image is swapped when the mouse is placed over the selected slice. You can choose to have another image act as the rollover, rather than the image you mouse-over. In a case such as this, the image is called a *disjointed rollover*.

The two windows allow you to choose the swapping image either by name or location. You can click on the outline of the slice to choose it by location, or click the name of the slice that should change when the mouse-over event occurs. If you use a rollover image that is not in the same file as the slice, be certain the image is the same size as the slice. Otherwise, your browser will force it to fit in the allocated space, which can cause unexpected and poor results.

Preload and Restore

The last two options in the Swap Image dialog box are for preloading the images and restoring the images on *mouse-out* (the mouse is moved away from the button).

If the Preload Images option is unchecked, the browser will not download the swap image until the user places the mouse over the slice. In this case, the user will most likely not see the image change to the new state. The user will either click on the link or move the mouse elsewhere before the browser retrieves the image from the server.

Checking the Restore option returns the image to its normal state when the user moves the mouse off of the slice. Uncheck this option if you do not want the image restored on the mouse-out event.

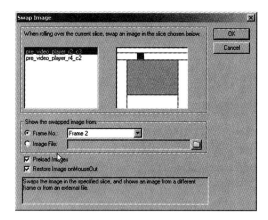

When you dragged the behavior handle to the current slice, the simpler Image Swap dialog box was displayed because you had already chosen which slice would be swapped on the mouse-over event. By dragging the behavior handle to the current slice, you selected that slice. If you want to quickly create a disjointed rollover, drag the behavior handle to the other slice. This opens the simpler Swap Image dialog box that has a More Options button.

Clicking the More Options button opens the dialog box that you used with the Behavior menu. From the More Options dialog box, you can choose to add multiple rollover behaviors — a regular rollover and a disjointed rollover —to a single slice.

Add Disjointed Rollovers

1. Open **video_player.png** from the **RF_Fireworks** folder. This is mock-up of a video player. Let's add a preview to each of the channels in the Channel Picker.

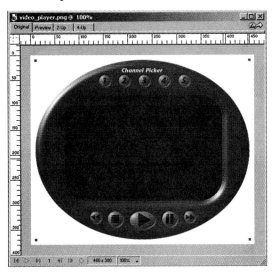

2. Use the Slice tool to slice a square around the screen and around each of the numbered buttons (1-5).

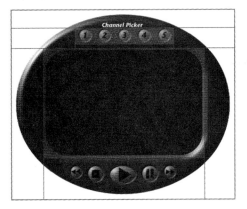

3. Click the Hide slices and hotspots button to hide the slices so you can modify the interface. We will modify each button in a different frame, each of which will serve as a rollover state.

4. Use the Frames panel to create 5 duplicate frames that are inserted after the current frame.

5. Click OK.

6. In Frame 2, set the Fill for Button 1 to Black and the Text Color for Button 1 to White.

7. Perform Step 6 for Frames 3 through 6, where the frame number is 1 more than the button number. This would make Frame 6 the frame for Button 5.

8. When all the buttons are set to the correct color in the appropriate frames, save the file, and then return to Frame 2.

9. In Frame 2, delete the black square that is acting as the screen.

10. From the File menu, select Import, and import **lions.jpg** from the **RF_Fireworks** folder. Once the cursor changes into two lines joined in a 90-degree angle, click on the canvas and use the Pointer tool to move the image so it is centered over the screen area.

11. With the bitmap image still selected, select Send to Back from the Modify menu.

12. Repeat Steps 9 through 11 for Frames 3 through 6. Place **fball.jpg** in Frame 3, **bike.jpg** in Frame 4, **fishing.jpg** in Frame 5, and **balloons.jpg** in Frame 6. All of these images are located in the **RF_Fireworks** folder.

13. Save the file.

14. Return to Frame 1 and click the Show Slices and Hotspots button.

15. Click the slice that is positioned over Button 1 and drag the behavior handle to the slice that is positioned over the screen. You should see a blue line indicating the screen slice will be the rollover image.

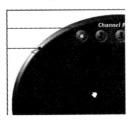

16. Chose Frame 2 from the Swap Image dialog box and then click OK.

17. Drag the behavior handle from the slice that is positioned over Button 1 and release it over the slice that is positioned over the screen. You should now see two blue lines: one line should go from the behavior handle to the slice positioned over the screen, and the second line should point to the current slice. These lines indicate that both of these images will rollover when the mouse-over event occurs.

18. Repeat Steps 14 through 17 for the remaining four buttons. Remember that the frame number is one more than the button number.

19. Preview the file in a browser and test your buttons.

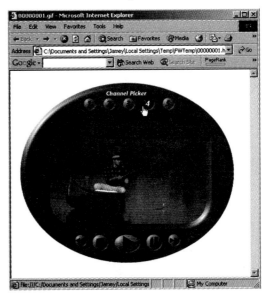

20. Save and close the file.

Pop-Up Menus

Pop-up menus have become a very popular method for organizing large amounts of content on the Web. Due to this popularity, they are quickly becoming a convention that most users recognize and know how to use. You can use Fireworks to quickly and easily build very complex DHTML pop-up menus. These pop-up menus work in any of the 4.0 or later browsers. You have the option of making pop-up menus from images or from plain text.

To create a pop-up menu, you can click the behavior handle for either a slice or a hotspot, and choose the Add Pop-up Menu option. This opens the Pop-up Menu Editor. This editor has four tabs that allow you to choose from many options for the pop-up menu. The four tabs include Content, Appearance, Advanced, and Position. Let's take a closer look at each of these tabs.

Content Tab

The first of the pop-up menu tabs allows you to add content to the menu. There are three columns that allow you to:

- Insert the text that will be visible to the user.
- Insert the link to the Web page where the user will be sent.
- Identify the target that the link will open.

To add content to any of these value areas, simply double-click in the blank space and add the desired information. If you want to edit an existing value, double-click that value and change it to a new value. If you want to add another menu element, click the plus (+) sign; if you want to remove a menu element, select it and click the minus (-) sign.

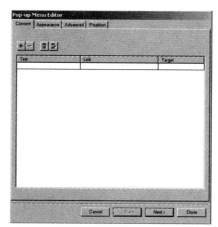

If you want to include nested menus and submenus in your pop-up menu, select the menu item you want to place under another and click the Indent Menu button (shown below). If you want to return it to its original position, select the item and click the Outdent Menu button (shown below). Finally, if you want to change the order of an item in the list, click the item and drag it to the new position. When you move an item, its indentation level may change; you can select the item and set it to the correct level of indentation.

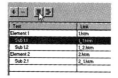

It is possible to include more than one level of submenus in a pop-up menu. Users will most likely find such a complicated menu difficult to navigate and will be unable to find what they are looking for.

Appearance Tab

The next tab on the Pop-up Menu Editor is the Appearance tab. When you get to this point in development, you need to make a decision: Do you want the menu to include images or HTML?

The Image option allows you to add styles, such as bevels and textures, to each of the menu items. Styles do not add much to the overall file size because the text is still dynamically created on a separate layer. This means that there are only two extra images (the buttons) created for the image-based menus; it also means that you must use the basic cross-platform Web fonts to ensure your text is displayed correctly on every machine.

When a Web page loads, the browser requires that every font you used in your design must be present on the user's system. The only way you can ensure this is to limit your design to the standard cross-platform fonts. This may seem to be a major limitation of image-based menus, but it actually helps to save file size and download time. It would be extremely inefficient to have two images (one each for the Up and Over states) for each of the menu items.

If you want plainer-looking pop-up menus, the HTML option offers all of the same options except the beveling and texture styles. HTML menus have an added benefit of downloading slightly faster than image-based menus.

Let's focus on the image-based pop-up menu options, since the HTML options are only slightly different. Below the choice for Cell type on the Pop-up-Menu Editor, you can see a number of options for setting the appearance of the menus. Below that is a Preview window that updates as you make changes to the Appearance settings.

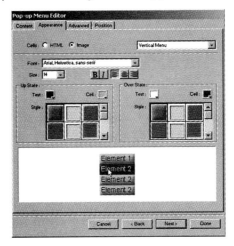

- The first option allows you to choose whether the menus pop up vertically or horizontally. In most cases, you are likely to use the default vertical menu.

- Below that, you can set text options such as Font, Size, Bold, Italic, and Alignment.

- Two boxes are located under the Font section. The one on the left is used to set the attributes for the Up state; the one on the right is used to set the attributes for the Over state. Here you can set the colors for the Text and the Cell. The *cell* is the square that contains the text.

- Finally, you have the option to set a Style that can apply a beveled or textured appearance to the buttons.

When you look at the HTML menu options, you see the same options are available for text-based menus, except there are no styles. Text-based menus can look just as professional as image-based menus, as far as the text is concerned. If you don't require beveling or textures on your buttons, HTML-based menus are a good choice.

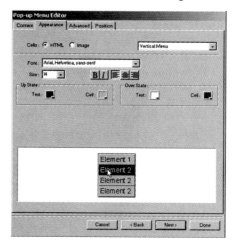

Advanced Tab

The next tab in the Pop-up Menu Editor is the Advanced tab. This tab allows for greater control over the appearance of the cells.

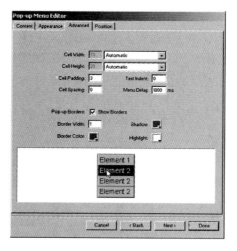

Here is a list of all the Advanced options:

- **Cell Width**. Cell width can be used to create a static width for a menu. This is set to Automatic by default, which uses the longest string of text in the given menu for the width of the cells. One problem with Automatic width is that each menu could be a different width.

- **Cell Height**. Similar to Cell Width, this option is set to Automatic by default. It uses the font size to determine the height of the cell.

- **Cell Padding**. This option sets the amount of space between the cell content and the cell border. This options uses pixels as the units of measurement, with 3 pixels being the default.

If you include submenus, you must set the Cell Padding to a value larger than 3 pixels, or the submenu arrow may overlap your text.

- **Cell Spacing**. As the name implies, this option is used to set the amount of space between cells. This is typically best left at the default value of 0, since it would break apart the menus if it were set higher. The value is presented in pixels as the units of measurement.

- **Text Indent**. This option allows you to insert a space on the left side of the menu item. It is presented in pixels and has a default value of 0.

- **Menu Delay**. This option allows you to set the number of milliseconds the menu will wait before appearing. This is done so the menus do not pop up when users touch one menu item on their way to another item. The user must place the mouse on the menu item for a specified period of time before the item pops up. This is set to 1000 by default (1/10th of a second).

- **Pop-Up Borders**. This check box allows you to turn the borders off and on.

- **Border Width**. This value is presented in pixels and is only available in HTML-based menus. It has a default value of 1 pixel.

- **Border Color**. You can use this option to set the color of the border on HTML-based menus. This option is not available for image-based menus.

- **Shadow**. This option is available in both image- and HTML-based menus. It can be seen on the bottom and right edges directly inside the border. It creates the appearance of a drop shadow.

- **Highlight**. This option is only available for HTML-based menus. It can be seen on the top and left sides of the cell directly inside the border. When used with a drop shadow, this option can create a three-dimensional appearance.

Position Tab

The final tab in the Pop-up Menu Editor allows you to choose where the menu items appear. It is important to carefully place the menu items so they do not obscure other elements on your Web page.

There are two options for setting the locations of menus and submenus. The first option is to set the position graphically by choosing one of the preset options. The blue rectangle shows where the menu will be placed.

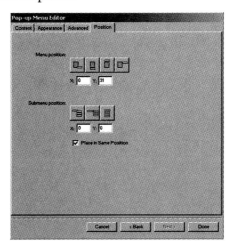

The second option is to set the X and Y coordinates for the menu. You can make your best guess on the correct location of the menu, and then test it for accuracy. If you need to fine-tune the location, you can do so by changing the numbers in the value fields for the X and Y coordinates. The units of measurement are the number of pixels from the left- and top-most points of the image.

If you want to set the position relative to the pop-up menu that triggers it, you can click the Place in Same Position check box; otherwise, it is set relative to the entire pop-up menu.

Add Pop-Up Menus

Notice that you are leaving the Link value fields empty in this exercise. You would normally enter a path in each of these fields. Fireworks will enter the default link, which is a pound sign (#). You will not see this in the interface, but when you turn it into HTML, the link will be set to the default link, and will not change the current document.

1. Open **menu_bar.png** from the **RF_Fireworks** folder. Notice that this menu was already sliced into sections. Let's add a pop-up menu to the Mammals slice.

2. Click the behavior handle on the Mammals slice.

3. Choose Add Pop-up Menu from the Behavior menu.

4. Add the following Text elements on the Content tab:

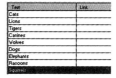

5. Click the Lions text item and click the Indent Menu button in the Add Pop-up Menu dialog box.

6. Repeat Step 5 so Tigers, Wolves, and Dogs are all indented under their main menus.

7. Click the Appearance tab in the Add Pop-up Menu dialog box.

8. Choose Image as the Cell type.

9. Choose 12-pt. Verdana, Bold, and Italic for the Text options. While this is not the exact font found in the menu, it is a close approximation.

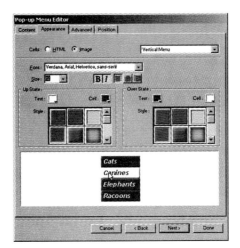

*You may have noticed
that a list is displayed
whenever you choose a
font. If a user does not
have the first font in the
list, their computer will
search the list until it finds
a font that it has, and use
that font instead.*

10. For the Up state, select the Text Color of #FFFFCC. For the Cell Color, choose #663366. These are the same purple and cream colors used in the actual menu.

11. For the Over state, swap the colors used in Step 10. Your Cell Color should be #FFFFCC and your Text Color should be #663366.

12. Choose Styles for the Up and Over states. We used the first style in the example. This option creates a clean, squared-off bevel.

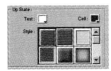

13. On the Advanced tab, set Cell Padding to 5 pixels.

14. On the Position tab, choose Bottom of Slice for the Menu position. This should set the X position to 0 and the Y position to 31.

15. Set the Submenu position to the top right of the menu. This sets its X and Y location coordinates to 0.

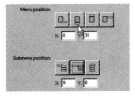

16. Click Done.

17. Preview the file in a browser to test your pop-up menu.

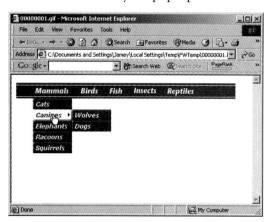

18. Save the file in you **Work_In_Progress** folder and close it.

Chapter Summary

In this chapter, you learned how to add more advanced behaviors to images and HTML pages. First, you explored the Button Editor, which is a very powerful tool for creating stand-alone buttons and complex navigation systems. Then you learned how to create more complex rollovers where you could make one slice change its appearance when the mouse rolled over a totally different image. Finally, you learned how to make complex HTML pop-up menus using the Pop-up Menu Editor.

Complete Project D:The Cable Store Web Site

Free-Form Project #2

Assignment

You work for a Web-design firm that specializes in creating banner advertisements. Against The Clock hired your firm to design a creative banner for the redesign of their Web site. They asked you to use an animated GIF in the banner advertisement that continually changes while the user views the site. Against The Clock did not provide any files or graphics for this project, knowing that your company worked best when given free rein to design innovative ideas. Against The Clock suggested you review their current Web site for ideas about their company and their products.

Applying Your Skills

To complete this project, use the following functions, methods, and features:

- The size of your banner ad should be 468 pixels wide by 60 pixels high.
- Begin with a simple bitmap image and enhance it until you have designed a complex animated GIF.
- Use descriptive names for each frame using the Frames panel.
- Use tweening in your animated GIF.
- Include at least 12 frames.
- Add appropriate text to your banner ad.
- Include a fade-in at the beginning of the animation, and a fade-out the end to allow for a smooth transition at the beginning/end of each loop.

Specifications

- The final size of this animated GIF should be no more than 300K.
- Use the vector drawing tools and the Text tool to create portions of the animated GIF.
- Utilize tweening, fade-in, and fade-out techniques to stimulate viewer interest.
- The animated GIF should loop continually while the user is viewing the site.
- Set the viewing speed relatively slow, at about 12/100 of a second per frame.
- Visit www.againsttheclock.com for information on the company so you can apply appropriate images and text to the GIF file.

Included Files

No files are included for this project. You should create the design from scratch. You can gather ideas from the exercises and projects in this book and from the Web, but be sure the design you create for this free-form project is original.

Publisher's Comments

If you begin to pay attention to the various Web sites you visit, you may notice that embedded motion is found quite commonly. Many Web users have to come equate motion on a page with the quality of the Web site. One of the ways to provide this movement is through the use of animated GIFs. As a Web designer, you must be able to apply your skills and use your business sense to develop animated GIFs that are appropriate for your client's business, while they stimulate interest in the company's products. You must be mindful of the file size, knowing that big files will extend download times, use bandwidth, and frustrate viewers — all of which your client wants to avoid.

Review #2

Chapters 6 through 11

In the second half of the book, you learned how to manipulate bitmap images —
with no image degradation — using Fireworks bitmap tools. You found you
can remove flaws from images using the new image-retouching filters and tools,
and create the perfect image for the job at hand. You discovered that layers allow
the designer to organize files, quickly locate a file, and effectively manage
documents — all of which enhance the overall workflow. You found out why
Fireworks is considered the best tool for creating animated GIFs — it was
designed from the ground up as a Web graphics tool. You learned that using
image maps is an effective method of presenting compelling graphics and links to
other Web pages. You also learned that image slices can be used to optimize files
that are placed on the Web, allowing for much quicker download times. And
finally, you explored the development of navigation bars, rollovers, disjointed
rollovers, and pop-up menus, all of which are Web components you can create
with Fireworks advanced features and functions. Through this series of discussions, exercises, and projects you should:

- Be familiar with selecting, creating, and modifying bitmap images using
  the bitmap tools.

- Be able to edit your images using the adjustment filters and re-touch tools.

- Know how to create, copy, delete, lock, unlock, and rename layers using
  the Layers panel.

- Understand how to use the Frames panel to create frame-by-frame
  animation, and to develop "tweened" animation.

- Be capable of creating hotspots, image maps, rollover effects, pop-up
  menus, and navigation bars.

- Be comfortable developing, copying, and editing Web buttons, applying the
  Up and Over states to buttons, and placing buttons in navigation bars.

Project A: Globe Illustration

One of your friend's parents owns a travel service and is in desperate need of a new globe illustration to act as a simple logo for letterhead, advertisements, and the Web. As a favor for your friend, you've offered to take on the task. The job is all yours, with no team members to assist in completing the project.

In order to make your job a bit easier, you were given a piece of clip art that illustrates the shape of the continents. You know the logo will be used to target a variety of people — children, teens, adults, and senior citizens — of all socioeconomic levels.

Get Started

1. From the File menu, select Open and navigate to the **RF_Fireworks** folder. Select **globe.png**. From the File menu, choose Save As, and save the document to your **Work_In_Progress** folder using the same file name of "globe.png".

2. This document contains a template of the globe. You will work on top of this template, using it as a guide for the creation of the globe portion of the logo.

Remember to frequently save your changes.

Create the Globe

1. Select the Ellipse tool from the Vector Tools section of the Tools panel. In the Properties panel, set the Stroke to 2 pixels and the Stroke Color to Red. First, let's create the outline of the globe and the outline of the continents. Set the Fill to None so it does not obscure the template.

2. From the View menu, select Guides>Show Guides if it is not already checked, and ensure the Rulers are checked and showing. Position a vertical guide at the vertical center of the globe template, and a horizontal guide at the horizontal center of the globe template. We will use these "crosshairs" to approximate the globe template's center point.

To position guides, "pull" them from the rulers surrounding the canvas after having selected View>Rulers. See Chapter 2 for further instruction on how to view and position guides.

If you want to reposition your ellipse while still drawing it, simply hold down the Spacebar in addition to the Shift and Option/Alt keys. With the Spacebar depressed, use your mouse to reposition the circle. When you release the Spacebar, you can continue drawing the ellipse.

We will eventually change the stroke color and width and add a fill color to the continents and the circle of the globe. These aspects of the logo will change, so you can initially work with any stroke color and width you prefer.

You may find it easier to work with individual points and reshape the line segments when viewing the document at a magnification greater than 100%. Throughout this project — and all other projects and exercises in this book — feel free to view your document at any zoom level.

3. Position your cursor where the two guides meet. Hold down the Shift-Option/Alt keys to draw an ellipse from the center of the globe template with a 1:1 aspect ratio (a circle). It should be the size of the black-and-white background image. If your circle is slightly off center, use the Pointer tool and/or the Arrow keys to reposition it. Hide the guides if you do not want them visible on the screen.

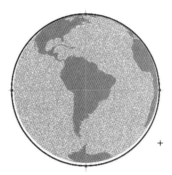

Drawing the circle from the center.

4. If your new ellipse is noticeably larger than the globe template's circumference, use the Scale tool to resize it so it is exactly the same size or just slightly larger than the outside stroke of the globe template.

5. Let's draw South America. Select the Pen tool from the Tools panel. In the Properties panel, set the Stroke to 2 pixels and choose Red as the Stroke Color.

6. Use the Pen tool to mark the key points of what will be your continent. Insert a point at every place along the perimeter of the continent where a relatively significant curve – either concave or convex — straightens or changes direction. There are at least eight of these points along the perimeter. Close the continent's border by ending your path at the point where you began.

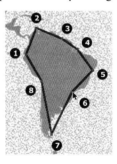

Eight key points around the perimeter of South America.

7. Use the Pen tool to pull out the point handles and use them to curve the line segment between Points 5 and 6 along the perimeter of the continent as shown on the globe template.

8. Use the point handles associated with Point 4 to curve the line segment between Points 3 and 4. Then use the point handles associated with Point 2 to curve the line segments between Points 1 and 2, and Points 2 and 3.

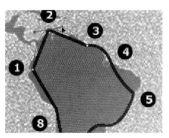

9. With the Pen Tool still selected, add an additional point to the path between Points 6 and 7. Let's call this Point 6.5. Drag the point handles from Point 6.5 to create appropriate curves between Points 6.5 and 7, as well as between Points 6.5 and 6.

Adding Point 6.5.

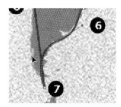

Creating curves between Points 6.5 and 7, and Points 6 and 6.5.

10. Use the point handles at Point 5 to curve the line segments between Points 4 and 5, and Points 5 and 6.

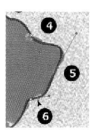

11. Edit the point handles at Point 8 to affect the final straight-line segment. Shorten the handle pointing to the right in order to decrease the curve jutting into the continent. When this step is done, the abstract outline for South America is almost complete. If necessary, use the Pen and Subselection tools to make final adjustments to the shape.

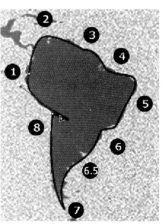

12. Create the outlines for the visible portions of the other continents, applying the same methods we used to create the South America perimeter. Use the Pen tool to place points along the coastlines of the globe template wherever a curve or straight line takes a different direction. Then, use the Pen tool to adjust various point handles and add or remove points along the path as necessary. Use the Subselection tool to reposition any points along the line.

13. After you have successfully created outlines for each remaining continent, select the Pointer tool from the Tools panel. Select the red elliptical vector shape, and then choose Edit>Copy followed by Edit>Paste to duplicate the ellipse. Deselect the new circle. Hold down the Shift key and click on each of the continent shapes you created. From the Modify menu, select Combine Paths>Join. After ensuring the newly joined path is still selected, hold down the Shift key and use the Pointer tool to select the duplicate red ellipse. Finally, select Combine Paths>Crop from the Modify menu to crop the portions of the North America, Europe, Africa, and Antarctica continents that lie outside the red ellipse.

14. Use the Pointer tool to select the red circle that marks the outside of the globe-in-progress. In the Properties panel, set the Fill to a bright blue (#0000FF). Use the Pointer tool to select the joined continent shapes before setting their Fill to a bright green (#009900). Finally, use the Pointer tool to draw a bounding box around all of the items on your canvas to select them all. Set the Stroke to Black, and change the Tip Size to 1, with a Stroke Category of 1-Pixel Soft.

Setting the Stroke attributes.

15. Use the Pointer tool to select the blue globe background. In the Properties panel, set the Fill Texture to Swish with a 21% Texture Amount. Set the Fill Category to Radial. Select the Fill Color swatch so you can edit the radial gradient. Set the right color tip below the sliding scale to Blue #0000FF. Set the left color tip to White. Click outside the dialog box to apply the radial gradient changes. With the blue circle still selected, the gradient handles should now be visible. Place the circular end of the handle on the black circle outline at a South East (-45 degree) position. Place the square end of the handle straight across the globe at the edge of the canvas.

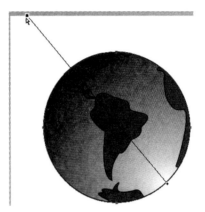

16. Use the Pointer Tool to select the joined continents, then choose Modify>Combine Paths>Split. Next, use the Pointer tool to select the South America shape as well as all portions of the North America shape. From the Modify menu, choose Combine Paths>Join. With the resulting shape still selected, set the Fill to Radial, and select the Fill Color swatch so you can edit the radial fill. As we did with the blue globe radial fill background, pull the initial shape color (Green #009900) to the right of the slide, and set the left color to White. Position the radial fill handles as shown in the illustration below.

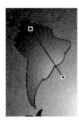

17. Select the Europe/Africa shape, and set the Fill to the same radial gradient as the joined America shape. Position the handles in approximately the same position as shown.

18. Click on Antarctica. Apply the same radial gradient we used previously, and then set up the gradient handles as shown.

19. Finally, hold down the Shift key and then select all of the shapes using the Pointer tool. In the Properties panel, set the Texture to 33% Plaster.

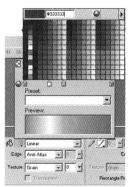

Globe Stand

1. As you watch the width and height specifications listed in the left corner of the Properties panel, use the Rounded Rectangle tool to draw a rectangle approximately 475-pixels high and 35-pixels wide, with a roundness setting of 100. This will act as the axis of the globe. In the Properties panel, set the Fill to Linear, and apply the Silver preset gradient from the Edit Linear Gradient dialog box. When the Silver preset gradient slide is displayed, set the second color tip box from the left to White, and remove the fourth and fifth boxes from the left by dragging them down from the underside of the slide. Finally, set the left-most color swatch to gray #333333.

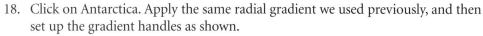

Unless otherwise specified, any shape with a fill other than None should have a texture attribute of 0 — no texture.

Make sure you draw the rounded rectangle at an initial size of approximately 35 pixels in width by 475 pixels in height, watching the dimensions in the Properties panel as you draw. If you manually edit the dimensions of the rectangle after creating it with very different dimensions, the roundness of your rectangle may be quite different from those illustrated.

2. With the rounded rectangle still selected, click the Scale tool in the Tools panel. Hover near the bottom-right corner of the rectangle until the cursor changes to indicate the Rotate function. Rotate the rounded rectangle so it angles from North West to South East at an approximately –45-degree angle. Double-click or press Return/Enter to apply the rotation.

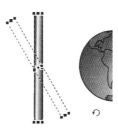

Rotating the rounded rectangle.

3. Use the Pointer tool to position the rounded rectangle over the globe as shown.

4. Next, let's create the semi-circular portion of the globe stand. If your guides are hidden, select View>Guides>Show Guides to display the "crosshairs" we set up at the beginning of the project. In the Properties panel, set the Fill to None, and the Stroke to 1-Pixel Soft Black. Use the Ellipse tool and the Shift key in conjunction with Option/Alt key to draw an ellipse with a 1:1 aspect ratio from the center of the guide crosshairs. End the ellipse just short of the left canvas edge. Draw another circle with a 1:1 aspect ratio from the center of the crosshairs. Use your artist's eye to make this ellipse bigger than the globe by approximately the same distance that separates the left edge of the canvas from the closest point of the outer circle.

5. If your rulers are not visible, select View>Rulers. Move the vertical guide so it is positioned at 180 pixels, and shift the horizontal guide to 370 pixels. Add an extra vertical guide at 370 pixels, and a second horizontal guide at 20 pixels. With only the outer circle selected, use the Knife tool to draw a line from the top-left intersection point to the bottom-right intersection point of the guides. Next, use the Pointer tool to select and delete the top-right sliced portion of the circle. Finally, Shift-select the two circles, then choose Combine Paths>Punch from the Modify menu to create a C-shaped vector.

Selecting Modify>Combine Paths>Punch removes the center circle portion from the outer region. It also defines the edges of the form.

6. Deselect the new form. Click on the globe's axis (the rounded rectangle). Choose the Scale tool from the Tools panel, and hover the cursor over the lower-right corner of the axis until the cursor changes to signify the Rotate function. Freely rotate the rectangle until it is parallel with the imaginary line running through the two tips of the new C-shaped object.

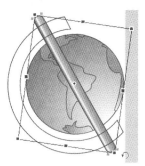

7. Set the Fill of the new semi-circular shape to Linear, and then select the Silver preset from the dialog box that is displayed after clicking the gradient color swatch. Position the gradient handles with the circular end at the center of the outer edge of the form, and the square end in line with the tips of the semi-circular shape. The gradient handle line should be positioned perpendicular to the globe's axis.

8. Select the Rectangle tool from the Tools panel and draw a vector shape that is approximately 40-pixels Wide by 80-pixels High. Set the Fill to Silver Linear and the Stroke to 1-Pixel Soft Black with Tip Size of 1. Edit the Silver Linear preset gradient by removing the left-most color tip on the gradient slide. Move what is now the left-most color swatch all the way to the left of the slide, and remove the middle color swatch. Position the rectangle so it is touching the bottom-center of the C-shaped globe holder.

9. Select both the new rectangle and the axis of the globe. From the Modify menu, choose Arrange>Send to Back to place those elements in the lowest position in the document's stacking order.

To complete Step 10, it can be helpful to place a horizontal guide running through the left and right blue points that are used to describe the circle while it is selected. This tells you where to begin your slice when the selection outline is hidden. You may also find it convenient to hold down the Shift key while using the Knife tool to simplify the task of slicing in a straight horizontal line.

10. Use the Ellipse tool to draw an oval that has a 225-pixel Width and 150-pixel Height. With the ellipse still selected, use the Knife tool to horizontally slice the ellipse in half. Delete the bottom portion of the sliced oval. Horizontally center this semi-circle above the bottom portion of the rectangle created in Step 8; this acts as the base of the globe stand.

In the Ripples Properties dialog box, you may find there are more or less color chips along the gradient slide than we want. If there are only two color chips, follow Step 12 as written. If you find more than three color chips, remove the extra chips so only three remain. If there are precisely three chips, you do not need to add a gray #666666 point; simply set the middle chip to gray #666666 and position it as instructed in Step 12.

11. Ignore the inappropriate fill on the globe stand base. Select the Rounded Rectangle tool from the Tools panel and set the Fill to Linear with the Silver preset. Set the Stroke to 1-Pixel Soft Black with Tip Size of 1. Set the Roundness of the rectangle to 100. Draw a thin horizontal rounded rectangle along the bottom of the globe stand base that extends slightly beyond the edges of the semi-circle. We recommend a Height of 8-10 pixels.

12. Select the semi-circle globe stand base. In the Properties panel, set the Fill Category to Ripples and click the associated color swatch to access the Ripple Properties dialog box. Set the left color swatch to dark gray #454545. Select White as the color of the right color swatch. Add another point on the color slide by clicking just beneath it. Set the new color point to medium gray #666666. Move this middle point until it is positioned about a quarter of the way from the left-most point toward the right-most point.

13. With the base semi-circle still selected, reposition the Ripples handles as shown.

Finishing Touches

1. Use the Ellipse tool to draw a small circle with a diameter that is approximately equal to that of the globe's axis. This circle will act as a decorative sphere on the tips of the globe stand's axis. Set the Stroke color to Black and Stroke Category to 1-Pixel Soft with a Tip Size of 1. Set the Fill Category to Radial, and select the Silver preset. Use your knowledge of radial fills to position the gradient handles so the circle appears spherical with light shining from a South East direction. Edit the gradient slide if necessary. After you have perfected the sphere, select Edit>Copy and Edit>Paste to create a duplicate sphere. Position one sphere at the bottom tip of the globe axis and the other at the top tip.

2. Let's add a bit of texture to a few of the globe stand elements to give the impression of brushed steel. Select the globe axis and the short vertical shaft of the stand. Set the Texture to Grid 3 with a Weight of 50%. Select the semi-circular base of the globe stand and apply the same Texture, with a Weight of 71%.

3. The artwork is now complete. Save your changes, and close the document.

You successfully completed a logo using a variety of tools. You should now have a complete understanding of fills, strokes, textures, the Knife tool, and all of the vector tools. Additionally, you now have a good grasp of the way items can be stacked on top of one another within a Fireworks document, know the different methods of combining paths, and have a thorough understanding of the Pen tool. All of these abilities — in addition to other skills required to complete this project — provide a firm foundation so you can tackle the more complicated features of this program.

Project B: Image Retouching Advertisement

The Ladies Spa of East Boston hired you to create an advertisement that will be used to spread the word about their limited-time discount for mothers of all ages. The company provided a photograph and logo for the project, and told you they want relaxation and rejuvenation to be the themes of the ad.

Unfortunately, the photograph needs quite a bit of enhancement before it is ready to be used; in its current state, it does not set the proper mood for relaxation or rejuvenation. In addition to creating the advertisement, you decided to retouch the photograph so the woman in the image appears younger and more energetic.

Getting Started

1. From the File menu, select Open and navigate to the **RF_Fireworks** folder. Choose **photo_retouch.png**. From the File menu, choose Save As, and save the document in your **Work_In_Progress** folder using the same file name.

2. When the document is first opened, the bitmap image is automatically selected. Choose Deselect from the Select menu, and then click the Image Size button in the Properties panel. Set the image Width to 750 pixels, and the image Height to 500 pixels. Click OK to apply the changes. Save your document.

Retouch the Photo

1. Use the Zoom tool to zoom in on the eyes, nose, and eyebrows of the woman, whom we'll call Maggie. Select the Rubber Stamp tool from the Tools panel. In the Properties panel, set the Size to 16, Edge to 100, and Transparency to 33%. Ensure the Source Aligned check box is selected, and the Use Entire Document check box is not selected.

The Rubber Stamp tool properties.

In the Retouch the Photo exercise, we provide instruction for those users with no photo-retouching experience. If you already have experience with photo retouching, you may simply read through Steps 1-5 to discover the portion of the image that should be retouched, and then perform the tasks on your own. Begin again at Step 6. If you do not have any experience with photo retouching, Steps 1-5 offer very detailed instruction on how to retouch a portion of this image. Beginning at Step 6, use the techniques described to continue editing the image with only minimal instruction.

Retouching Maggie's image is a crucial part of creating the Ladies Spa of East Boston advertisement. Eliminating the wrinkles at the corners of her eyes and lightening the dark circles below her lower lashes creates an inviting picture of a woman who is relaxed, refreshed, calm, and friendly — exactly the image that a spa advertisement should project.

Image retouching is a very subjective art. Use your artist's eye while applying the tools to produce a realistic-looking image. While this project offers good suggestions on how to edit Maggie's image, feel free to deviate from the instructions if you want to apply your own artistic view to the image.

You can always select a new focal point for the Rubber Stamp tool by holding down the Option/Alt key and clicking in a new beginning spot.

2. Single-click directly inside the upper-left curve of the apple of Maggie's cheek to set the Rubber Stamp tool's initial point (see the image below for a rough placement suggestion). A circle and small crosshairs appear where you click; the crosshairs indicate the region to be cloned by the Rubber Stamp tool, and the circle indicates your brush tip.

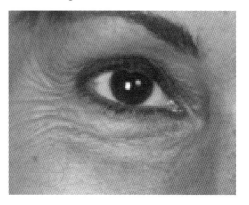

Circular cursor and crosshair-point indicator immediately after placing the initial click of the Rubber Stamp tool.

3. Click your cursor at the left corner of the circle beneath Maggie's eye. Apply the Rubber Stamp tool throughout the area beneath Maggie's eye from left corner to right. Notice how the crosshairs move to show you what is being cloned. We set the Rubber Stamp tool intensity to a relatively low opacity to ensure the tones applied by the tool blend well. If you find the opacity is less than what you want to correct the area below Maggie's eye, feel free to increase the intensity of the tool or apply the tool more than once on a specific area.

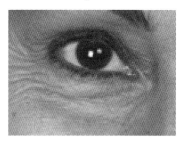

Area where you begin to apply the Rubber Stamp tool.

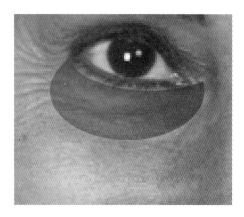

Shading shows the area where you should apply the Rubber Stamp tool.

Completely removing all of Maggie's wrinkles and darker shadows would make her look unnatural — not to mention that the retouching efforts would be obvious. Don't worry about removing every line and shadow on her face; instead, concentrate on giving her skin a "toned" look that is even in color while still displaying some variation to show contour. You may want to frequently toggle between a magnified view and one that shows the image at 100% to ensure your retouching efforts look realistic.

If necessary, reapply the Rubber Stamp tool to camouflage any of the shadows or wrinkles that are too dark to mask with the Blur tool. You can use the Dodge tool with a low Intensity – we recommend a setting of between 5 and 10 – to bring out the highlights on these areas and lighten the shadows.

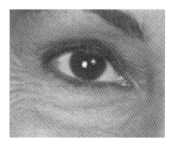

The under-eye area after applying the Rubber Stamp tool.

4. Select the Blur tool from the Tools panel. Set the Size to 18, Edge to 100, and Intensity to 34. With this tool selected, run your cursor over any wrinkles or dark marks that still stand out beneath Maggie's eye after applying the Rubber Stamp tool.

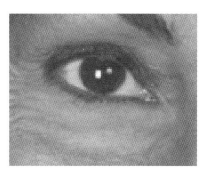

Applying the Blur tool to the region below Maggie's eye blends the shadows into the rest of her skin.

5. Press Command/Control-1 to view your document at 100% magnification. Notice how retouching one small portion of Maggie's image made a significant improvement in her overall appearance.

6. As image retouching is such a subjective task, it is not in your best interest to follow a step-by-step guide for working with the rest of Maggie's image. Use the skills you acquired using the Rubber Stamp and Blur tools to retouch the areas of Maggie's face that are shaded in the image below. You can enhance any other areas you think need attention. The Burn, Dodge, and Smudge tools can be helpful; experiment with the retouching tools to find which ones are most useful for your individual retouching technique.

Remaining areas of Maggie's portrait that require retouching to give her a younger, more relaxed appearance.

As with all other aspects of Maggie's retouching, the appropriate level of darkening for her lips is quite subjective. If you feel an Exposure level of 50 creates a color that is too dark or otherwise inappropriate for Maggie's image, simply select Edit>Undo or use the keyboard command Command/Control-Z, lower the Exposure level, and reapply the Burn tool on that portion of her image.

7. Select the Burn tool. In the Properties panel, set its Exposure to 50. The Edge should be set to 100, and though we recommend an initial Size of 13, you may find another setting more convenient. With these settings in place, run your cursor over the pink of Maggie's lips to darken the hue of her lipstick while keeping the tones similar to those already found in the image.

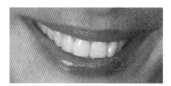

8. Select the Rubber Stamp tool from the Tools panel. In the Properties panel, set the Size to 9, Edge to 100, and Opacity to 33%. Single-click the dark grey area of Maggie's lower eyeliner on the left eye to set that area as the initial point. Use the Rubber Stamp tool on this area to extend the outer corner of Maggie's eye, adding a soft corner to the edge of her eye that lifts slightly upward. This addition emphasizes Maggie's smile by making her eye seem more friendly and distinct. Repeat this process on the outer corner of Maggie's right eye.

Extending the outer corner of Maggie's left eye.

9. This is how the image should look at this point.

The retouched image.

Create the Advertisement

1. Use the Pointer tool to click and drag Maggie's bitmap image. Drag it to the left of the canvas, ensuring the top and bottom of the bitmap are still aligned with the top and bottom edges of the canvas. Select View>Rulers (if the rulers are not already in place) to display the document's measurements. Move the image so the right edge lies at approximately 720 pixels; this placement provides a tighter margin between Maggie's left ear and the edge of the ad.

2. Select the Marquee tool from the Tools panel and use it to select a vertical slice of the bitmap that is at least as tall as the height of the image itself, and is wider than the width of white canvas showing beside Maggie's picture. Select Edit>Copy and then Edit>Paste to duplicate the portion of the background you selected. Reposition the new portion of background on the canvas so it covers the white canvas showing at the right side of the document.

3. Use the Rectangle tool to draw a rectangle that spans the entire width of the canvas and is 45-pixels high. Position this rectangle so it is flush with the bottom of the canvas. In the Properties panel, set the Fill to Linear. Click the Linear Color swatch to set the gradient attributes. Set the left-most color tab to #FFFFCC. Click to create a tab that is midway between the right and left ends of the gradient slide, and set its color attribute to #FFFFCC as well. Drag the right-most color point so it is approximately an eighth of the way in from the right end of the color slide. Set this swatch to #FF6666, a color that is similar to the shade of Maggie's lipstick.

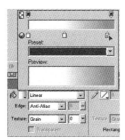 

4. Use the Text tool to create a text block that contains the word "you" in all lower-case letters. Next, create three more text blocks that contain the words "deserve", "to", and "relax", respectively. Create these in all lowercase characters as well. Apply the following text attributes to each of the words:

- you: Size 20; Color #FFFFCC; ATC Font Pine Normal.
- deserve: Size 41; Color #FBE2D0; ATC Font Elm Italic, Bold.
- to: Size 20; Color #FFFFCC; ATC Font Pine Normal.
- relax: Size 66; Color #FF6666; ATC Font Pine Heavy Italic.

Use the Pointer tool to select the words "deserve" and "relax." Use the Effects portion of the Properties panel to apply a Drop Shadow with a Distance of 5, Opacity of 65%, Softness of 4, and Angle of 315 to these text blocks.

If you do not have the Against The Clock (ATC) fonts installed on your system, you can use standard Windows/Macintosh fonts instead. You can use Times or Times New Roman in place of the ATC Pine family, and Verdana instead of the ATC Elm family.

Use the Pointer Tool to position the words as shown in the figure below.

Positioning the words in the image.

5. After positioning the headline correctly, create a new text block using a Font of Bold Elm Normal, Size of 17, and Color of White. In the text block, insert the following sub-heading for the advertisement: "You're a homework tutor and a doctor, and a friend. You're a chef and an entertainment director, a chauffeur and a maid. You're all this and more… but to your children, you're simply". (Note that there is no punctuation at the end of the word "simply".) Position this text so it lies in the top-right corner of the advertisement. If necessary, use the Pointer tool to adjust the dimensions of the text block so it fits in a more aesthetically pleasing manner.

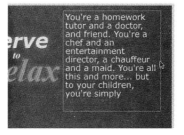

6. Create another text block containing the word "MOM." Set the Size to 27, Font to Bold Elm Normal, and Color to #FCFCCA. Use the Pointer tool to position this text just below the last line of the text block created in Step 5. Align the text so "MOM." sits a little beyond the right-most edge of the text block above it.

7. Next, make another text block with Size of 12, Color of White, and Font of Elm Normal. Additionally, click the Right Alignment button in the Properties panel so the text inserted in this field is flush right. In the text block, enter "And the Ladies Spa of East Boston knows that Moms deserve to be pampered too. That's why, from". Use the Pointer tool to position the text block so the right edge of the text aligns with the right edge of the "MOM." text above it. Use the Pointer tool to resize the text block if necessary, and ensure the left edge of the new text block does not extend significantly farther than the left edge of "MOM."

8. Select the Line tool from the Tools panel and set the attributes of Tip Size 1, Color of #FF6666, and Stroke Category of Hard Line. Hold down the Shift key to draw straight horizontal paths that run beneath "MOM.", down the right side of the text block created in Step 7, horizontally beneath that text block to a point just below Maggie's earring, vertically down to just barely touch Maggie's shoulder, and then horizontally to end just below the beginning of the "MOM." field. See below for an illustration of these paths.

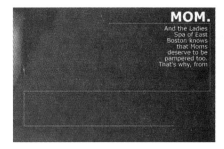

Paths drawn with the Line tool.

9. Create four single-line text blocks for the rest of the main advertisement text as follows:

   - "October 27 – November 4": Size of 21; Color of #EDDED1; Font of Pine Bold Italic.
   - "we're offering special rates on": set all text to Size of 12; Color of White; Font of Elm Normal.
   - Then select "special rates" and set the Size to 17; Color to #FFE7B3; Font to Bold Elm Normal.
   - "Full and Half-day spa packages": Size of 21; Color of White; Font of Pine Bold Italic.
   - "for all Moms who need a break": Size of 12; Color of White; Font of Elm Normal.

You can also create the lines on the canvas using the Pen tool while pressing the Shift key to draw straight lines. This would create one continual path rather than several segments. The choice should be based on your personal preferences.

Position these vertically in the order listed above so the first line lies just above the second horizontal section of the pink path, and the last line of text lies just above the bottom horizontal section of the pink path. Space the middle two lines of text evenly between the first and fourth lines. Use the Pointer tool to center the "for all Moms who need a break" line in relation to the bottom horizontal section of the pink path. Center the top three lines of text in relation to the newly centered bottom line. See below for an illustration of these changes.

All main text included on the advertisement.

Logo, Final Text, and Finishing Touches

1. Open **spa_logo.png** from your **RF_Fireworks** folder. Use the Pointer tool to select the group of items in the document. Select Edit>Copy from the Main menu. Select Window>**photo_retouch.png** to return to your advertisement document. Select Edit>Paste to paste a copy of the logo onto your canvas. Use the Pointer tool to position the logo in the bottom-left corner of your document so the black rectangle of the logo has the same margin of off-white on the top, left, and bottom sides.

2. Use the Subselect tool and the Shift key to select the "S", "P", and "A" vector shapes in the logo. In the Properties panel, add an Inner Shadow with a Distance of 6, Opacity of 65%, Softness of 4, and Angle of 315.

If you have ever looked at professional portrait photography, you may have noticed that some photographers shoot with a slightly soft focus. This can add a certain amount of warmth or friendliness to the expression on the subject's face. Our final step is to borrow that concept to visually soften the advertisement to better imply the feelings of happiness and restfulness for our spa advertisement.

3. Create a text block and enter "Check out our Web site at www.ladiesspaofeast-boston.com, or call 555-1212 to find out about all the special services we have in store for you, Mom!" Set the Size of this text to 12, Color to #474055, and Font to Elm Normal. Use the Pointer tool to adjust the text block so the text falls into two relatively even lines, and vertically center the height of the words in relation to the black box of the spa logo. The left edge of the text should lie next to the black box in the logo, leaving approximately the same margin between the two items that is between the black box and the top, left, and bottom edges of the horizontal rectangle it lies upon.

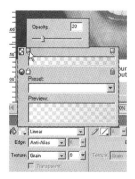

4. Select the Rectangle tool from the Tools panel. Choose a Linear Fill in the Properties panel, and set its attributes so the left end-point shows 20% Opacity and Color of #FFFFCC, and the right end-point displays 20% Opacity and Color of #FE6565. Use these settings to create a rectangle that covers the entire upper portion of the advertisement, ending vertically where the completely opaque footer rectangle begins.

You finished a very detail-oriented photo-retouching project that allowed you to gain experience using the photo-manipulation tools, inserting text, and customizing an image. These skills are very useful and you will probably rely on them quite frequently.

Project C: Animated Banner

You can't surf the Web for long without encountering an animated GIF. This common file format has been around for a long time, and shows no signs of disappearing any time soon. It does not require a browser plug-in, so the widest possible audience can view and enjoy the files.

Perhaps the most popular use of the animated GIF is in the typical Web banner ad. This project provides an opportunity to experience a typical workflow for creating a standard-sized (468 × 60 pixels) animated GIF banner ad. The subject of the advertisement is a sale offered by a framing gallery.

First, we will build the animated GIF with the goal of keeping the file size under 20K, knowing that there are file-size restrictions on banner ads. No company wants to include a 200K "masterpiece," no matter how beautiful it is, because it would cause a very negative impact on download speed. We will aim for economy of size.

After we complete the animated GIF, we will have a little fun with some tweening effects. The file size of this effort will be about 50K.

As a banner ad designer, you will often be placed under a file-size restriction. If your completed banner were under the size limit, you would have the luxury of embellishing it, and pushing the boundaries of the size limit. When you complete this project, you will have an idea of what this might entail.

Getting Started

Using the same border on every page saves file size because any pixels that repeat throughout the frames of an animated GIF do not add extra file size. In other words, this border will be "paid for" in Frame 1, but comes "free-of-charge" in Frames 2 through 4.

1. Open a new Fireworks document. Set the Size to 468 × 60 pixels, Resolution of 72 Pixels/Inch, and a Canvas Color of White. Click OK.

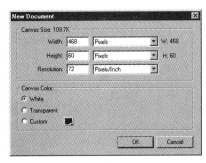

2. Save the file as "banner_ad.png" in your **Work_In_Progress** folder. Even though we have not started to build the file, it's a good idea to get into the habit of saving your file from the outset. Since this banner is being developed for a framing gallery, let's "frame" the animation with a beveled border so it resembles a picture frame. The border will be included in every frame of the animation.

Save time when creating GIF animations by mapping out everything ahead of time on scratch paper.

3. Begin the border by selecting the Rectangle tool from the Tools panel. Choose a Stroke of None and a Red (#FF0000) Fill. On the canvas, draw a small rectangle. Make it any size you prefer. In the Properties panel, reset the rectangle with the following attributes: W of 468, H of 60, X of 0, Y of 0, and the other settings shown below. This rectangle will define the outer edge of the beveled border.

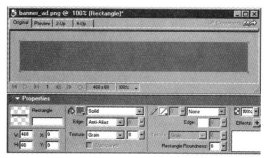

4. To achieve a border of 5 pixels, it's a simple matter of making another rectangle 10 pixels smaller in width and height, and then moving the new rectangle down and to the right by 5 pixels. To do this, draw another rectangle and set its properties to W of 458, H of 50, X of 5, Y of 5.

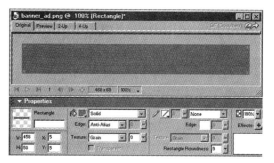

5. Press Command/Control-A to select both rectangles, or choose Select>Select All from the Main menu. With both objects selected, choose Modify>Combine Paths>Punch from the Main menu. This leaves only the intersection of the two objects as the selection.

To achieve a desired effect, it's often faster to modify simple shapes rather then draw complicated shapes from scratch. The Combine Paths options (including Punch) are good choices for this.

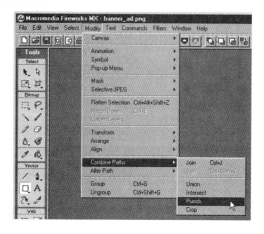

6. From the Properties panel, select Effects>Bevel and Emboss>Inner Bevel. Set the Bevel Edge Shape to Flat, Width to 1, Contrast to 100, Softness to 0, Angle to 135, Button preset to Raised. Since the border is only 5 pixels wide, these settings provide a thin, crisp bevel that is perfect for our needs.

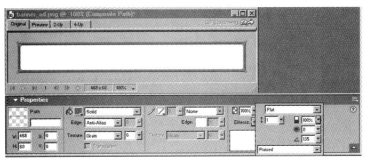

Lock layers you are not currently editing. This prevents you from accidentally moving or deleting objects on those layers.

7. Since this border will appear in every frame of the animation, we need to name it and lock it. On the Layers panel, rename Layer 1 "Border", and click the pencil icon to lock it. Since this border will frame all of the content to follow, subsequent layers will be added under this layer (placed lower in the stacking order).

8. Save the file to the **Work_In_Progress** folder. We are now ready to create the main content for each of the four frames of the animated GIF.

Create the First Frame of the Animation

1. Our banner will feature a Labor Day sale, so we will use a stars-and-stripes motif. First, let's divide the content area into red, white, and blue sections. Begin by adding a new layer. Click the New/Duplicate Layer icon at the bottom of the Layers panel. Name the new layer "Content Area". Drag it to the bottom of the layer stack. Fireworks is a vector-based program, so it's not necessary to make a separate layer for every object. This allows you to keep the number of layers in the document to a minimum.

2. We already have a red border and a white canvas, so all we have left to do is make a blue area. Select the Rectangle tool from the Tools panel. In the Properties panel, select a Blue Fill of hexadecimal code #0000CC and a Stroke of None. Draw a small rectangle in the middle of the canvas. It should cover the left half of the canvas. This is easily accomplished by going to the Properties panel and setting the W to 234, H to 60, X to 0, and Y to 0. The width is set to 234 pixels because that is half the total width of the banner (468 pixels). Since this layer falls under the Border layer, the border is still visible above the blue rectangle.

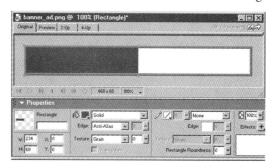

3. Select the Text tool from the Tools panel. Choose Arial or any other sans-serif Font you prefer, with a Size of 45 pt. and a White Fill. Choose Bold and Italic Styles. Over the blue area, enter the word "LABOR". Over the white area, use the same font, but apply a #FF0000 Red Fill. Enter the word "DAY", and position the words to look similar to what is shown below. Depending upon the actual font you use, you may need to choose a different font size.

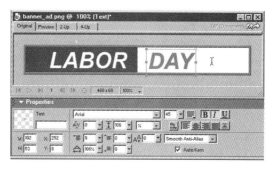

4. Add a subtle drop shadow to the text. Start by selecting the Pointer tool from the Tools panel. Select the LABOR text, hold down the Shift key, and then select the DAY text. From the Properties panel, choose Effects>Shadow and Glow>Drop Shadow. Set the Distance to 2, Color to Black (#000000), Opacity to 65%, Softness to 2, and Angle to 315.

It's easy to get carried away with drop shadows; used with restraint, they can enhance a design.

This subtle effect adds the benefit of a drop shadow without being too obvious. As with many design issues, less is often more.

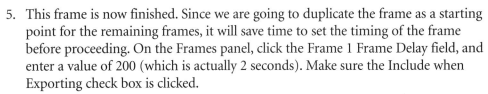

5. This frame is now finished. Since we are going to duplicate the frame as a starting point for the remaining frames, it will save time to set the timing of the frame before proceeding. On the Frames panel, click the Frame 1 Frame Delay field, and enter a value of 200 (which is actually 2 seconds). Make sure the Include when Exporting check box is clicked.

Duplicate frames when-ever possible to save time and effort. It's easier to edit an existing frame than to start from scratch.

6. In the Frames panel Options menu, choose Duplicate Frame to access the Duplicate Frame dialog box. Set the Number to 1, and click the After current frame radio button. Click OK. Save the file in your **Work_In_Progress** folder. You're ready to create content for the other frames.

Create Content for the Remaining Frames

1. Select Frame 2 from the Frames panel. You can now easily edit this frame and keep the same drop shadow settings used in the text. With the Text tool, select the word LABOR, and replace it with the word "FRAME". From the Properties panel, change the text Fill color to #FF0000 Red. You may need to switch to the Pointer tool to select the new color.

Notice that the drop shadow remains, since we only edited the text, not the Live Effect.

2. Use the Pointer tool to select the blue rectangle, making sure it is the only object selected. In the Properties panel, enter a new X value of 234. This moves the blue rectangle to the right side of the canvas.

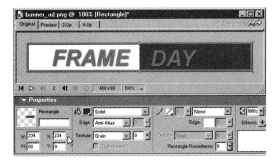

3. Use the Text tool to select the word DAY, and replace it with the word "SALE". From the Properties panel, change the Fill color to White #FFFFFF. You may need to switch to the Pointer tool to select the new color. As before, the drop shadow remains.

4. In Frame 2, you reversed the color scheme from Frame 1. You can easily reverse the colors again for the next frame by duplicating the original Frame 1. On the Frames panel, select Frame 1. From the Frames panel Options menu, select Duplicate Frame. Set the Number to 1 and click the At the end radio button. The duplicate frame is named Frame 3.

5. Select Frame 3. Use the Text tool to select the word LABOR, and replace it with "30-50%". Then select the word DAY, and replace it with the word "OFF". The new text should be in the correct position.

6. For the final frame, let's use a bitmap image of an American flag, adding to the feeling of Labor Day festivity. Duplicate Frame 3. In the Duplicate Frame dialog box, set the Number to 1, and click the radio button for After current frame (you could also click the radio button for At the end, since we are duplicating the last frame). Before adding the flag image, select the new Frame 4, and delete the three objects in the Content Area layer. Leave the Border layer locked. This clears the layer for the new content to follow.

7. Choose File>Import. In the Import dialog box, navigate to the **RF_Fireworks** folder and select **amer_flag.tif**. Click anywhere on the canvas to import the document. The first thing you notice is that the image is too large. It must be scaled down. We are also going to slightly rotate it. To ensure it fits in the confines of the border, resize it to a Width of 480 pixels.

8. With the image selected, choose Modify>Transform>Numeric Transform from the Main menu. In the Numeric Transform dialog box, choose Resize from the pop-up menu, and then enter a new Width of 480 pixels. Make sure the Scale Attributes and Constrain Proportions check boxes are clicked. The height is automatically changed to 326 pixels to preserve the proportions. Click OK.

Use Numeric Transform when you need to scale, resize, or rotate an object with precision.

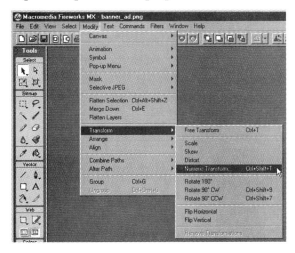

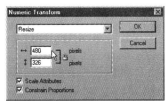

If you can no longer see the flag, it's because it's off the canvas. In the Properties panel, set the X and Y coordinates to 0 to make it visible again.

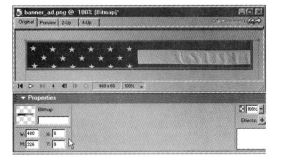

9. Now we can easily rotate and move the flag to create better composition. Select the Scale tool from the Tools panel.

Move the cursor close to a corner to allow you to rotate the image. Rotate and move the flag so it resembles the illustration below.

10. Before we add text to this frame, let's brighten up the flag. This is easily accomplished with Live Effects. From the Properties panel, select Effects>Adjust Color>Levels. The Levels dialog box appears, showing the histogram. The top sliders are the Input Levels. Move the far-right slider to the left. The entire flag gets brighter. Set the slider as shown below. Now move the center slider slightly to the left. This causes the blue in the flag to "pop". When you are happy with the effect, click OK. Since it's a Live Effect, you can edit the settings at any time.

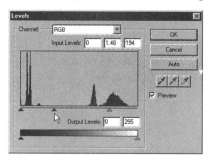

11. Next, let's boost the color saturation so it will get the viewer's attention. In the Properties panel, select Effect>Adjust Color>Hue/Saturation. In the Hue/Saturation dialog box, move the Saturation slider all the way to the right. If it looks too saturated on your monitor, back off slightly. Now move the Lightness slider slightly to the right. We applied a value of 10, which makes the blue of the flag resemble the #0000CC blue that appears in the other frames. When you are satisfied with the settings, click OK.

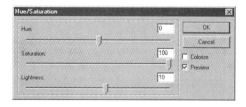

12. Finally, let's add some text. Select the Text tool from the Tools panel and click the left side of the flag. Keep the same Arial font (or sans-serif font of your choice) you used before, but choose Bold, Italic, and a smaller Size. We used a 40-pt. Size. Select White #FFFFFF as the Fill color. Enter the text, "This weekend only!"

When importing bitmap graphics, get in the habit of performing Live Effect color adjustments on them, even if only slightly. The chance of a bitmap graphic being perfect "out of the box" is slim.

Use Drop Shadow and Glow Live Effects to add contrast to text objects.

13. The white text gets lost where it runs over the white stripe in the flag. A drop shadow will fix this problem. From the Properties panel, choose Effect>Shadow and Glow>Drop Shadow. Set the Distance to 0, Color to Black #000000, Opacity to 100%, Softness to 7, and Angle to 315.

14. Save the file to your **Work_In_Progress** folder.

Export the Animated GIF

1. Before exporting, choose Frame 4 from the Frames panel. This is the frame with the greatest range of color. As we attempt to shave file size from the animated GIF, this will be our test frame. If this frame looks good, so will the others.

2. From the Main menu, choose File>Export Preview. In the Export Preview dialog box, there are three tabs. In the Options tab, set the Format to Animated GIF, and the Palette to WebSnap Adaptive. Dither should be unchecked. Set the Maximum number of colors to 32.

We can use this small number of colors without causing noticeable image degradation because we use a limited color palette of red, white, and blue, plus the darker shades used in the drop shadows and bevels. By selecting 32 colors, the file size is shaved to less than 15K. (Depending upon the font you used and placement of the flag, your file size may vary.) Such a low file size ensures fast download times.

3. Choose No Transparency from the Transparency field at the bottom of the Options tab.

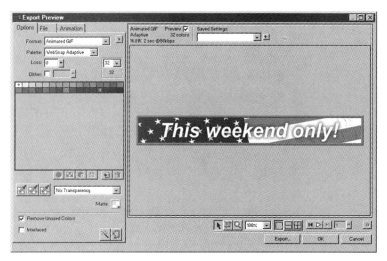

When exporting GIFs and animated GIFs, try to use the minimum possible number of colors that does not sacrifice too much image quality. You can often choose 64 or even fewer colors without noticeable degradation. Keep your audience happy with small file sizes.

4. Click the File tab. This tab is used for changing the size of the exported file. You designed the banner ad at the intended size, so no changes are necessary on this tab.

5. Click the Animation tab. You already set each frame to play for 2 seconds, so we can leave the top area alone. Under that, make sure the Loop icon is selected, and in the Number of times to repeat field, choose Forever. Make sure the Auto Crop and Auto Difference check boxes are clicked.

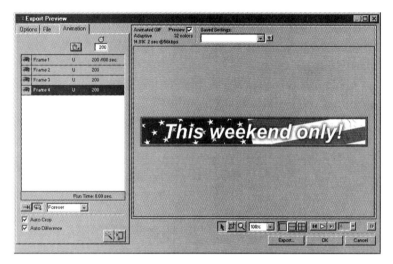

6. Finally, click the Export button. The file is automatically named **banner_ad.gif**, since your Fireworks file was named **banner_ad.png**. Set the Save as type field to Images Only. Click Save in the Export dialog box to finish the export. Save the Fireworks file to your **Work_In_Progress** folder. You can open and view this exported image in a browser.

The exported file size is under 15K. Let's suppose the file size limit for the job is 50K. You would certainly take advantage of that sort of luxury.

Upon export, Fireworks appends the new file extension to the original file name.

Let's add to the animation, pushing the final file size toward 50K. In the first part of the project, we kept our layers to a minimum. For an animation containing only 4 frames, that did not pose a problem. In this part of the project, we are going to start with Frame 4 and make two fast tweens. One will be a tween of the text, "This weekend only!" The other tween will be of the flag bitmap.

When you tween two objects, each must reside on its own layer. As it is now, the text block and flag are both on the same layer. To fix this, let's cut the text and paste it on a new layer.

Embellish the Animation with Tweening

1. With Frame 4 selected, select the Content Area layer, and click the New/Duplicate Layer icon at the bottom of the Layers panel. This adds a layer directly above the Content Area layer. Name the new layer "Text".

2. Use the Pointer tool to select "This weekend only!" on the Content Area layer. Cut it from the layer by choosing Edit>Cut from the Main menu, or pressing Command/Control-X. This places the content on the clipboard.

3. Select the new Text layer, and choose Edit>Paste, or press Command/Control-V to place "This weekend only!" on the new Text layer. With the text on its own layer, you are ready to tween it.

4. Let's add 4 more frames to the animation. The tween will start on Frame 4 and end on Frame 8, for a total of 5 frames. We want the border to be present, so we need to duplicate Frame 4. Select Frame 4. From the Frames panel Options menu, choose Duplicate Frame. In the Duplicate Frame dialog box, set the Number to 4, and check the radio button for At the end. Click OK.

5. Before we tween the text, we must remove it from the new frames. Starting with Frame 5, delete "This weekend only!" by selecting it with the Pointer tool, and then choosing Edit>Cut from the Main menu, or pressing the Delete/Backspace key. Repeat this process for Frames 6 through 8.

6. Before we can tween it, we must turn it into a symbol. After an object is converted to a symbol, Fireworks can perform some fairly sophisticated tweens with it. Select Frame 4, then select the text. To convert the text to a symbol, press the "F8" key on your keyboard, or choose Modify>Symbol>Convert to Symbol from the Main menu. In the Symbol Properties dialog box that appears, enter "text" for the Name, and click the Animation radio button. Click OK.

7. The Animate dialog box immediately appears. Fireworks will tween the symbol, but you must set the parameters for the tween. Let's start with a simple tween for the text — scale it smaller. In the Animate dialog box, set the Frames to 5, and Scale to 50. Leave the other settings at their defaults of 0 and 100. Click OK.

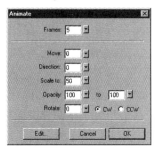

8. Select Frame 8 to test the settings. The text should be 50% smaller. Now look at Frames 5 through 7. Fireworks tweened the symbol for you, and saved you a lot of time and effort.

9. Before you tween the flag bitmap, let's lock the Text layer so you don't accidentally alter it in any way, and then hide it from view. Select Frame 4, and then click the pencil icon on the Text layer to lock it. You should see the padlock icon. Click the eyeball icon to hide the layer.

10. To prepare for tweening the flag, we must remove it from Frames 5 through 8 as we did with the text. Starting with Frame 5, select the bitmap graphic, and then delete it. Repeat in Frames 6 through 8.

11. Select Frame 4, then select the bitmap (flag) object. Press the "F8" key or choose Modify>Symbol>Convert to Symbol from the Main menu. The Symbol Properties dialog box appears. Name the symbol "flag" and click the Animation radio button. Click OK.

12. In the Animate dialog box, set the Frames to 5, Move to 20, Direction to 180, Scale to 200, Rotate to 30, and click the Clockwise (CW) button. Leave the Opacity setting at 100 to 100. Click OK.

Depending on the speed of your computer, this may take a few moments. Fireworks is making the calculations not only for the final result in Frame 8, which you specified, but also for Frames 5 through 7 to produce a smooth tween.

Remember that in order to tween something, it must reside on its own layer.

13. Look at the various frames of the tween, and notice how the flag scales, moves, and rotates. Return to Frame 4 and return the Text layer to view. You can now see both tweens happening at once. This was possible because you moved the text onto a layer of its own before you tweened it.

14. Before we export the file, we need to change the speed setting for Frames 5 through 8. On the Frames panel, change the Frame Delay for these frames to 10. Make sure the Include when Exporting check box is clicked. The frames will play in rapid succession, creating the illusion of motion — which is the whole point of tweening. Press the "F12" key or select File>Preview in Browser from the Main menu. Although you have not yet exported the file, you can view it in a browser window to see how it appears.

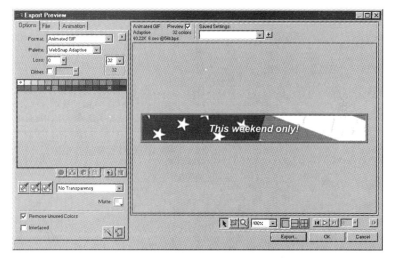

15. From the Main menu, select File>Export Preview. Since you already exported this file, Fireworks remembers the settings. Set the Export Preview Options to 32 colors and WebSnap Adaptive. This time, the file size is just over 40K, well within the proposed 50K limit. Name the file "banner_ad2.gif", and save it to your **Work_In_Progress** folder. Save the Fireworks document in the same folder in case you want to return to it later.

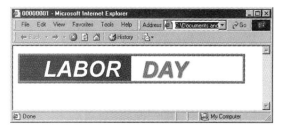

You completed a professional-quality animated GIF. There are many other uses for this file type than just making banner ads. Still, banner ads rely heavily upon the animated GIF, so your skills as an animated GIF artist should be in demand for some time to come.

Banner ad creation could be considered an art form — there are so many elements to consider. As you design, just ask yourself, "Would I want to click this banner?" Let that maxim be your guide.

With a monitor resolution of 1024 x 768 pixels, the minimum you should consider as a designer, you will still be able to see the entire document — with the rulers showing — at 100% magnification.

When designing for a minimum monitor resolution of 800 x 600 pixels, stay at 760 pixels or less for the width to avoid forcing the user to use the horizontal scroll bar to see the entire image. When viewing your Web pages, it's perfectly acceptable for the user to scroll up and down using the vertical scroll bars, but it is not considered acceptable to make them scroll horizontally.

In this project, you are setting the canvas at 700 pixels wide because you are going to use the rulers.

Project D: The Cable Store Web Site

Fireworks was designed primarily as a tool for creating imagery for Web pages. In this project, you are going to put the program to the test of designing a Web interface.

A Web page is composed of individual graphic elements, and the only way to see how the parts fit together as a functional unit is to design it in one piece. In this way, you can build the overall appearance of the page and the various navigation elements — in this case, the buttons.

Your assignment is to build a Web interface for a fictitious company called The Cable Store. They need your help to sell more computer cables. First, you will build the interface. Then, you will use the Button Editor to make the buttons for the products. Finally, you will slice the document, add interactivity, and export the document — including the requisite HTML.

Build the Interface

1. Open a new document, 700 × 420 pixels in Size, 72 Pixels/Inch Resolution, and White Canvas Color. Save the document as "web_interface1.png" in your **Work_In_Progress** folder.

2. Select View>Rulers from the Main menu to make the rulers visible, if they are not already visible on your screen. By default, the 0,0 point is the top-left corner of the canvas. Do not alter this default location. From the top ruler, drag down a horizontal guide to the 100-pixel mark. After you release the guide, you can still move it up or down if necessary. If you zoom in at 300% magnification, you can precisely position the guides.

3. Drag down a guide to the 80-pixel mark, and another to the 60-pixel mark.

4. Drag a vertical guide from the left ruler to the 200-pixel mark. You should have a total of 4 guides now. Lock the guides by selecting View>Guides>Lock Guides. You don't want to accidentally move them.

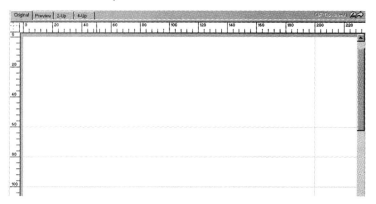

5. Choose File>Import, and navigate to your **RF_Fireworks** folder. Select **circuit_board.tif**, and then click on the canvas to import the file. Drag the graphic around the canvas until you arrive at an interesting composition that makes it clear this is a circuit board. In the Layers panel, name the layer "bg".

You will eventually create slices, and they will snap to these guides, saving time and effort. The graphics you will create can snap to these same guides, which is a further timesaver. Guides are more than just a convenience. Be sure to take advantage of them.

Habits such as locking guides should be developed early in your career as a Web designer. They will become especially useful when your projects begin to get more complex.

If you import an image that takes up the whole canvas, it's a good idea to keep it on its own layer so you can lock it when necessary. Otherwise, you might accidentally select it with any click on the canvas.

Remember that Inner shadow is a Live Effect, so you can change the settings at any time.

6. Use the Pointer tool to select the imported bitmap. In the Properties panel, select Effects>Adjust Color>Hue/Saturation. Set the Hue to 210, Saturation to 100, Lightness to 30, and click the Colorize and Preview check boxes. Click OK. This should create a bright blue color to offset the white navigation buttons. Click OK.

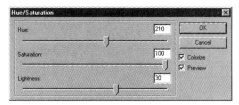

7. Lock the bg layer by clicking the pencil icon. Click the New/Duplicate Layer icon to make a new layer. Name the new layer "content area."

8. Select the Rectangle tool from the Tools panel, or press the "U" key on your keyboard. From the Properties panel, apply a White Fill and a Stroke of None. Draw a small rectangle from the intersection of the bottom-horizontal and right-vertical slices. Resize the rectangle in the Properties panel. Set the Width to 425, Height to 270, X to 200, Y to 100, Fill to White #FFFFFF, Edge to Anti-Alias, and Texture Amount to 0. Enter a Rectangle Roundness of 15. From the Effect menu, select Shadow and Glow>Inner Shadow and accept the default settings.

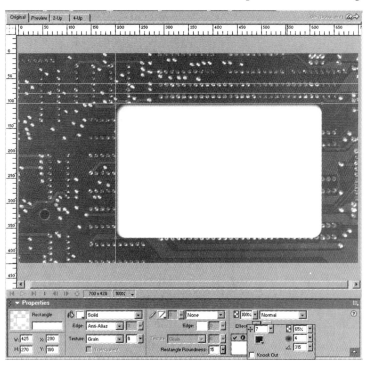

9. Above the content area layer, insert two new layers. Name the first new layer "top strip", and name the one below it "top tabbed buttons". You are going to draw a rounded rectangle and then duplicate it to make the tabbed buttons. The top strip layer will block out the tops of the tabbed rectangles for a realistic effect.

D-2 PROJECT D/THE CABLE STORE WEB SITE

10. Select the Rectangle tool from the Tools panel. With the top tabbed buttons layer selected, draw a small rectangle above the large rectangle in the top blue area. Set the Width to 90 and Height to 60. Apply a Rectangle Roundness setting of 30. Use the Pointer tool to drag the small rectangle so the bottom edge snaps to the horizontal guide that is placed at 80 pixels. In the Properties panel, select Effects>Bevel and Emboss>Inner Bevel. Set the Bevel Edge to Flat, Width to 2, Contrast to 75%, Softness to 3, Angle to 135, and Button preset to Raised.

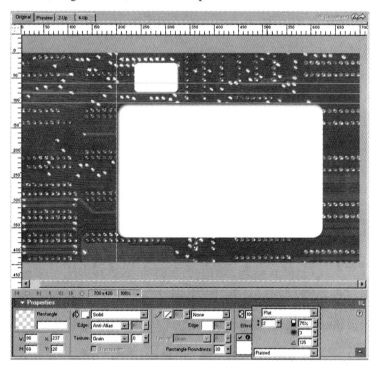

11. We are going to feature four tabs with accompanying text. Since you are going to duplicate the first tab, let's apply some text to it. When you make duplicate tabs, the text will also be duplicated. Use the Text tool to select a 15-pt. Arial Font, Black Color, and Bold and Italic Styles. With the top tabbed buttons layer selected, enter the word "Main". Center Main two pixels up from the bevel edge and directly below the 60-pixel horizontal guide. At increased magnification, your screen should resemble the illustration below.

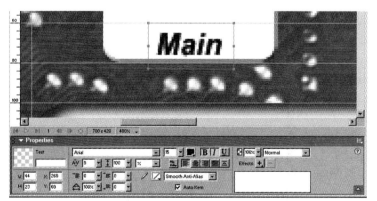

As you drag, you can also hold down the Shift key — but do not press the Shift key until after you have started to drag. This keeps the duplicate on the same horizontal or vertical axis as the original. Most graphics software applications utilize this convenient keyboard shortcut. You'll save a lot of time using this trick.

If you were to select multiple objects by Shift-clicking them, you would run the risk of moving them. Selecting objects using the Layers panel eliminates this risk.

The reason we made the rectangle extend past the edges of the canvas is because the drop-shadow would not extend all the way to the left edge if we made it the same width as the canvas. In general, it's best to have objects extend past the canvas edge whenever possible because nothing outside the canvas will export.

12. Let's duplicate the tab and its associated text. With all the other layers locked, select the top tabbed buttons layer (this selects both the smaller rounded rectangle and the word Main). Use the Pointer tool to drag the selections to the right. As soon as you initiate the drag, hold down the Option/Alt key. This allows you to create a duplicate rectangle, leaving the original in place. After the new tab is placed to the right of the first tab, release the mouse. Use the Left Arrow and Right Arrow keys to position the duplicate next to the first tab so they are perfectly aligned with no overlap and no blue background showing between them.

13. Return to the Layers panel and select the top tabbed buttons layer. This selects both tabs and both text blocks. With the four objects selected, repeat the previous Option/Alt-drag process, and move the two new tabs to the right of the two existing tabs. Use the Arrow keys to precisely position them.

14. Use the Text tool to replace the text in the second object with "About Us". Change the text in the third object to "FAQ". Change the text in the last object to "Warranty". Use the Pointer tool to select each new text block and center it with the Left and Right Arrow keys. When everything is in place, select the top tabbed buttons layer to select all tabs and text objects. Move them to the right or left with the Arrow keys until they are centered over the main content area.

15. These so-called "tabs" don't look very much like tabs at this point in development. You need to fix that. Lock the top tabbed buttons layer. Select the top strip layer, unlocking it first, if necessary. Use the Rectangle tool to draw a large rectangle that has a White Fill and a Stroke of None. Start to drag beyond the top-left corner of the canvas. Drag it to the right and down, well beyond the edge of the canvas, so the edge snaps to the 60-pixel horizontal guide. In the Properties panel, apply a Drop-Shadow with the settings shown below. Lock the top strip layer in the Layers panel.

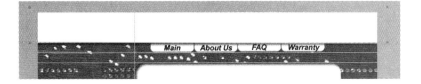

We used an Arial font because of its cross-platform compatibility, but you can use any font you prefer. It is a good idea, however, to use the same font throughout for consistency. Your font size/kerning settings might not produce the same result as ours, but try to create a design that is similar to ours.

Subtle drop shadows often accompany inner bevels. Use two or more Live Effects at once for more complex effects.

Feel free to alter these settings. Remember to err on the side of applying too little effect, rather than too much. Less is usually more.

16. It's time to put the header text on your top strip. Add a new layer named "logo" above the top strip layer. With the logo layer selected, choose the Text tool from the Tools panel. Apply Arial Font, 62 pt. Size, Fill of Blue #0066FF, Bold Style. Enter the words "The Cable Store" wherever you prefer on the top strip. The goal is to match the blue in The Cable Store with the blue in the circuit board. If the color of the circuit board does not match, return to the bg layer and tweak the Hue/Saturation Live Effect. Select the word "The" with the Text tool and change its Fill to Black. Select the Pointer tool. In the Properties panel, change the Kerning ("A|V" field) to a value of -5 to reduce the amount of space between the letters.

17. Use the Pointer tool to move the text so it's centered above the tabs and centered vertically in the top strip.

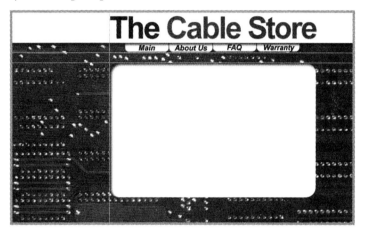

18. Let's add a subtle bevel and drop-shadow to the logo text. Use the Pointer tool to select the logo text object. In the Properties panel, apply an Inner Bevel using the settings shown below on the left, and then apply a Drop Shadow with the settings shown below on the right.

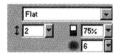 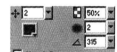

19. Lock all the layers except the logo layer, and then add a new layer. Place it directly above the bg layer. Name the new layer "big logo". Now copy (select Edit>Copy or press Command/Control-C) the logo you made earlier. Lock the logo layer. Select the new big logo layer and paste it (select Edit>Paste or press Command/Control-V) on this layer. You won't see anything change because the duplicate is on top of the original logo. Use the Pointer tool to drag the duplicate layer so it's under the white content area window.

Repetition is an important element of design. Look for ways to creatively add repetition to your designs.

20. Select the Scale tool from the Tools panel and drag out the top-right corner of the big logo to enlarge the object. (Dragging from a corner preserves the height/width ratio.) Enlarge the object and move it around until your result is similar to the image below.

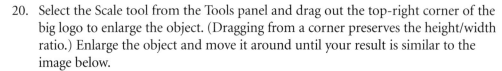

21. Select the enlarged logo. In the Properties panel, notice the Live Effects. When you duplicated the object, they were duplicated, too. Select the Inner Bevel effect and delete it by clicking the minus (-) sign. Select the Drop Shadow effect and edit it by clicking the small "i" in the blue circle. Change the settings to match those shown below.

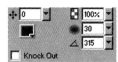

22. The result is a bit harsh. Select the big logo layer and lower its Opacity to 50.

Now the object resembles a watermark over the blue circuit board (bg) layer.

Adjust an object's opacity to create interesting effects.

23. Notice the white area to the left of the logo. Let's add a graphic to complete the header of the Web interface. Add a new layer above the logo layer. Name the new layer "top cable". Choose File>Import, and navigate to the **RF_Fireworks** folder. Select **cable_usb.tif**, and click anywhere on the canvas to place the image.

Numeric Transform offers the most precise way to transform an object.

24. Notice that the image is too large. From the Main menu, select Modify>Transform>Numeric Transform, and scale down the image to 30%. Click OK.

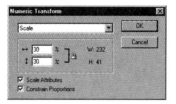

25. Let's turn the image around. From the Main menu, select Modify>Transform>Flip Horizontal. Position it in the top-left corner so the end of the cable is extending past the left edge of the canvas.

26. Select the object, and from the Properties panel, select Effects>Adjust Color>Invert. Apply a Drop Shadow with the settings shown below.

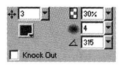

The majority of the interface is complete. Next, you will use the Button Editor to create buttons for the products; they will be placed on the left side of the interface.

Create Buttons with the Button Editor

If you are wondering why we did not use the Button Editor to create the tabs, it's because of the drop shadow above them. As you will see later, we can have any tab appear in front of the other tabs by showing that slice with the top strip's drop shadow hidden. Now we are going to make five buttons that will each point to a different product. The Button Editor is perfect for this task, and will save a lot of time.

1. Lock all of the layers in the Layers panel. Create a new layer and place it above the top cable layer. Name the new layer "buttons". Select the Rectangle tool from the Tools panel. Apply a White Fill and a Stroke of None. Draw a small rectangle anywhere on the left side of the canvas. In the Properties panel, set the Width to 150 and Height to 25. Set the Roundness to 50, or less, if you prefer. Don't worry about its position for now. In the Properties panel, apply an Inner Bevel with the settings shown below on the left, and a Drop Shadow with the settings shown below on the right.

2. Select the Text tool. Apply an Arial Font with a Size of 15 pt., Black Color, Bold and Italic Styles, and then enter the words "Sample Cable" over the button. Center the text on the button.

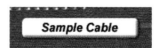

Usually, it is the Up and Over states that are required. Adding more states increases the file size of your Web page.

We are going to ignore the Down and Over While Down states. Most of the time, the file size they add is not worth their benefit.

You must reserve an area on your canvas for the buttons that is 200 pixels wide. Widening the buttons to the exact 200-pixel size results in simpler HTML and fewer exported graphics. With any size less than 200 pixels, the leftover pieces to the right and left of the buttons would have to be exported separately. The HTML to accommodate those extra pieces would be unnecessarily bloated. A good rule is to line up your buttons and slices whenever possible. The HTML will be less compli-cated, causing pages to load faster, with less chance for browser error.

3. Next, let's convert the image into a button symbol, allowing you to quickly and easily create the other buttons. Click the buttons layer to select both the button and the text. From the Main menu, select Modify>Symbol>Convert to Symbol, or press the "F8" key on your keyboard. The Symbol Properties dialog box appears. Keep the default button name "Symbol", and in the Type area, click the Button radio button. Click OK.

4. The button on the canvas assumes a different appearance. Double-click it to bring up the button as a symbol. Now you can create the different states of the button. Click the Over tab, and then click the Copy Up Graphic button to use the Up state as a starting point. Select the rounded rectangle, but do not select the text. In the Properties panel, edit the Inner Bevel effect as specified below.

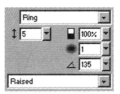

The only difference is that you changed the Inner Bevel from Smooth to Ring. This makes the button appear to depress when you mouse over it. Still in the Over state, select the text object. Use the Arrow keys to move it down one pixel, and then move it to the right one pixel. This completes the illusion of the button being depressed. To test it, click the Up tab, then click the Over tab. The effect is quite convincing.

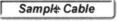

The crosshairs you see in the middle indicate the center point of the button symbol.

5. Next, you must define the active area of the button symbol. Click the Active Area tab. Select View>Rulers. Drag the right edge to the 100-pixel mark, and drag the left edge to the 100-pixel mark. You might have to zoom in to do this. It must be precise, with the total width of the button at 200 pixels.

Drag the top edge to the 20-pixel mark, and the bottom edge to the 20-pixel mark. Make sure the Set Active Area Automatically check box is not checked; otherwise, Fireworks will not acknowledge your changes. The final button should be 200 × 40 pixels in size. If you are not sure of the exact dimensions, select the active area and note its size in the Properties panel.

Look in the Library panel. Notice that the Button Symbol is there. You can edit a symbol from the Library, if you prefer.

The symbol is complete. Click the Done button in the lower-right area of the Button Editor.

6. Next, you need to position the button. Zoom in closely, and position the button so the left side is flush with the left edge of the canvas. (The right side will be flush with the vertical guide placed at the 200-pixel mark.) Move the button up so the top is flush with the horizontal guide at the 100-pixel mark. Be precise. If you are off by even one pixel, Fireworks will be forced to produce very complicated HTML. You might find it easier to see the edges of the button symbol if you hide the bg (circuit board) layer.

7. Drag in four more instances of the button symbol from the Library, and place each below the one before it. When everything is pixel-perfect, show the bg layer again.

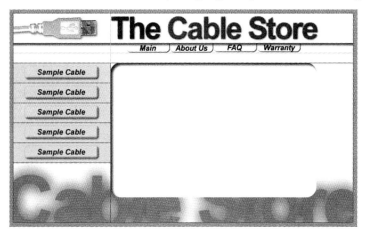

8. Next, set the text for each button. Select the topmost button, and in the Text field on the Properties panel, change the text to "RCA Cable". Change the text in the second button to "USB Cable", in the third button to "RJ45 Cable", in the fourth button to "Serial Cable", and the fifth button to "Crazy Cable". Save the file by pressing Command/Control-S on your keyboard. Select File>Preview in Browser, or press the "F12" key, and choose a browser from the list. The browser launches with your interface. Mouse over the buttons to test them. When you're finished, close the browser and save the Fireworks file in your **Work_In_Progress** folder.

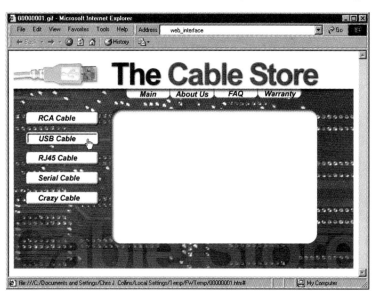

Create Slices and Apply Rollover Behaviors

1. Next, you are going to make slices over the four top tabs. You get more flexibility using slices (with frames) to specify the Up and Over states than you do using button symbols. Zoom in close to the leftmost top tab until it takes up most of your screen. Keep all layers locked except the Web Layer. Select the Slice tool from the Tools panel.

2. Drag a slice over the leftmost Main tab. When you make your first slice, you don't have to worry about its size.

The icon under the Slice tool is used to show the slices, and the one to the left is used to hide the slices. It's useful to hide slices when you are designing so they are not visually distracting.

Avoid using the Polygon Slice tool, if possible. It requires much more JavaScript, complicates the HTML to a fault, and slows browser performance.

As long as the Web Layer is unlocked, it's not important what layer you are on. A slice is just a certain area of the canvas. A slice is not affected by the graphics that reside under it. When you export a slice, you export the "snapshot" of whatever is within the boundaries of the slice.

Slices can be duplicated, copied, and pasted, similar to any other object.

You don't have to make an accurate slice with your initial cut. Instead, you can use the Properties panel to modify the slice.

The top and bottom edges snapped to the horizontal guides. Note that the width and positioning are off. To correct this, go to the Properties panel and view the information about the slice.

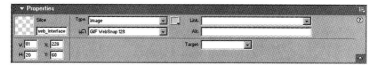

You can precisely set the width and positioning in the Properties panel. The width of the tab can be identified by unlocking the top tabbed buttons layer and selecting the actual object. Its Width is 90. Set the Width (W) to 90 in the Properties panel. Note that the slice is still too far to the left. Select it by holding down the Command/Control key to temporarily activate the Pointer tool. Drag the slice until it's positioned properly. You can also use the Left and Right Arrow keys to correct the positioning.

3. Select the first slice with the Pointer tool and drag it to the right. As soon as you begin the drag, hold down the Option/Alt key to produce a duplicate. The new slice snaps to the edge of the first slice. If necessary, use the Arrow keys or zoom in to ensure the slice's positioning is pixel-perfect. Repeat this process to make the other two slices.

4. Select the first slice. In the Properties panel, note the leftmost field above the Height/Width and Positioning fields. Change the first Name to "button_main". Repeat this process for the other slices. Name the second slice "button_about_us", the third slice "button_faq", and the fourth slice "button_warranty".

5. You need to name the buttons you made from the button symbol. Unlock the buttons layer, and use the technique from Step 4 to name the buttons in the Properties panel. Name button one "button_rca", name button two "button_usb", name button three "button_rj45", name button four "button_serial", and name button five "button_crazy".

6. You now need to make an Over state for the top tabbed buttons. To accomplish this, go to the Frames panel. Note that your document has only one frame, so Frame 1 is automatically selected. In the Frames panel Options menu, select Duplicate Frame. In the dialog box that appears, set the Number to 1, click the After current frame radio button, and then click OK.

You now see two frames in the Frames panel.

7. With Frame 2 selected, unlock the top strip layer. Select the object by selecting the layer itself, since it's the only object contained on this layer. In the Properties panel, note the Drop Shadow effect. Click the checkmark so it turns to a red "X". This hides the effect on Frame 2 only. (Frame 1 still shows the drop shadow.)

8. Lock the top strip layer again. Select Frame 1, then select Frame 2, and notice the change. Also, notice how the Over states for the buttons on the left are visible in Frame 2. Frame 1 is the Up state for all button symbol instances, while Frame 2 is the Down state. To get a better view, you can hide your slices by clicking the icon to the lower left of the Slice tool. When satisfied, show the slices again.

9. Now you need to tell Fireworks to assign the Over state to Frame 2, and produce the necessary JavaScript for a mouse rollover. Select Frame 1, and then select the button_main slice. You see a little white icon in the middle of the slice that resembles a target. Single-click the target. A menu appears. Select Add Simple Rollover Behavior. This causes Frame 2 to display on mouse rollover. Repeat this procedure for each of the remaining three slices.

You can test the result by previewing it in a browser by selecting File>Preview in Browser, or pressing the "F12" key. Close the browser when finished. Save the document to your **Work_In_Progress** folder.

Create the Main Content

1. You need to make slices to contain the actual content that will be displayed in the white content area. You want to keep the HTML simple and the file size low. To accomplish this, it would be best to remove the inner shadow from the content area in the slice — you want that inner shadow area to download only once. Begin by dragging some guides to the canvas so your slices can easily snap to them. Drag a horizontal guide to the bottom edge of the RCA Cable button (using existing edges keeps the HTML as simple as possible). Drag another horizontal guide to the bottom edge of the Crazy Cable button. Drag a third horizontal guide to the bottom edge of the white area where it meets the blue background.

2. Use the Slice tool to drag a slice so it snaps to these new guides. With the slice still selected, name it "content_slice_text" in the Properties panel.

3. Drag another slice under this one; apply the same width. Drag it so it snaps to the third guide you made. In the Properties panel, name the slice "content_slice_image."

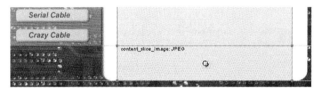

4. This slice will contain the product images. They will compress well as JPEGs. With the slice still selected, find the Slice Export Settings field in the Properties panel. Select JPEG - Better Quality from the pop-up menu. In the content_slice_image slice, this has already been done.

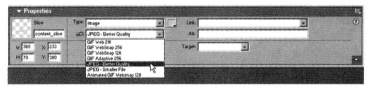

5. Now you are ready to create the actual content. You have nine buttons, so you need to make nine separate content areas. This requires nine additional frames. From the Frames panel Options menu, choose Add Frames. The Add Frames dialog box appears. Set the Number to 9, and click the At the end radio button. Click OK. You can now see a total of 11 frames in the Frames panel. The slices still show, however, so you can easily make your new content fit in the boundaries of the content_slices_text and content_slices_images slices.

6. With this many frames, it might be difficult to know which frame goes with which button. To clarify the process, let's name Frames 3 through 11, starting (from left to right) with the top tabs slices, then the Cable buttons (from the top to bottom). Start by double-clicking Frame 3, and name it "main". Name the next frame "about us". Continue with the rest of the frames, naming them "faq", "warranty", "rca", "usb", "rj45", "serial", and "crazy". When finished, your Frames panel should resemble the screen shot below.

7. Above the buttons layer, create a new layer and name it "main content". Lock all the other layers, including the Web Layer, but leave this new layer unlocked. Select Frame 1 and then choose the Text tool. Apply an Arial Font of 15 pt., Black Color, and Bold Style. Enter the following greeting: "Welcome to the Cable Store, your one-stop shop for computer cables." Push the text up and to the left as far as it can go while still remaining within the boundaries of the slice.

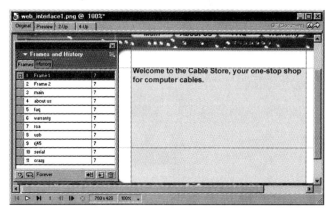

8. With the main content layer selected, you can create content for all of the buttons. Choose the appropriate frame, and then add text within the boundaries of the content_slice_text slice. For the products, you would put the images within the boundaries of the content_slice_image slices.

9. Images of the five different cables (appropriately named TIFF files) can be found in the **RF_Fireworks** folder. They need to be scaled down. You can copy these or add your own content. Be sure to add different text for each frame so you can see how the buttons swap the content. Put some images in the smaller slices reserved for them, resizing if necessary, so you can see the JPEG compression and the images as they change when a different product is selected.

As the mouse hovers over the buttons, the appropriate content appears for the button; but when a visitor first sees the site, some initial text should be presented. This text can be placed on Frame 1 with its own layer to hold the content.

Naming your frames makes it easier to apply rollovers and disjointed rollovers.

Below are examples of content areas for each slice. The content is complete. All that is left is to associate each relevant slice and button with its own content.

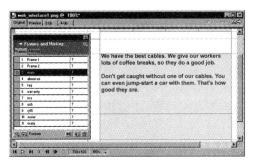

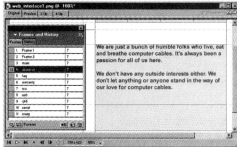

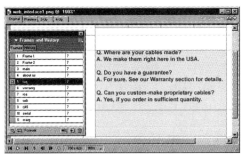

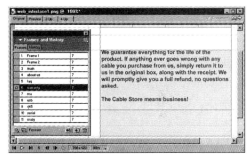

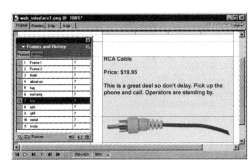

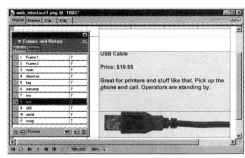

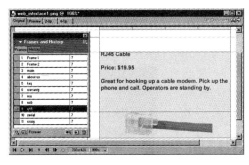

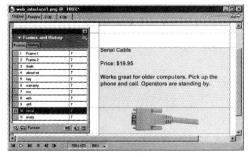

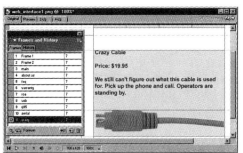

As you learned in Chapter 11, a disjointed rollover is a term used to describe a case where interacting with one graphic on a Web page causes another graphic on the Web page to change. This is what you must do now, so the slices and buttons display their proper content.

Notice the curved blue line that connects the slice to its target. This allows you to see the association that has been made.

Create Disjointed Rollovers to Display Content

1. Select Frame 1 and unlock the Web Layer so you can select the slices and attach the disjointed rollover behaviors to them. Start with the Main tab slice. When you mouse over it, you want the main frame's content area to show. Select the button_main slice and notice the icon that resembles a target. Do not click the target; drag it to the content_slice_text slice and release it. The Swap Image dialog box immediately appears, asking you which frame's image you want to display. Choose main (3) from the Swap Image From pop-up menu, and then click OK.

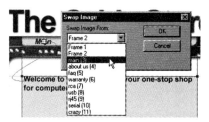

Since you only made text content for the top row of slices, you are done with the first slice. Before continuing, test it in a browser (File>Preview in Browser, or press the "F12" key). Each tab should have two behaviors attached to it — a rollover and a disjointed rollover. Close the browser.

2. Repeat this process with the remaining top row of slices, selecting their corresponding frames from the Swap Image dialog box.

3. Let's apply the disjointed rollover behavior to the column of Cable buttons. Unlock the buttons layer so you can select each button. Start with RCA Cable and drag the target icon to the same slice you used in Step 1. From the Swap Image pop-up menu, choose rca (7), and then click OK.

4. Next, you want to make the second association so the image slice (below the text slice) also swaps. Drag the target again, and drop it on the smaller content_slice_image slice. Again, select rca (7) from the Swap Image pop-up menu, and click OK. Now you see two blue curves extending from the button and connecting to each of the two slices.

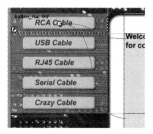

5. Repeat this two-step process for each of the remaining buttons. Test the results in the browser (File>Preview in Browser, or press the "F12" key) to see the completed Web interface in action. When satisfied with the results, close the browser. Lock the buttons layer. Save the document.

All that is left is to export your document.

Always export your images to a folder named "images" so they are separate from the HTML file. In a complex site, it would be confusing to have all the files in one folder.

The Copy to Clipboard option in the HTML field is used when you are working with an HTML editor, such as Dreamweaver. This option allows you to paste the HTML code into the editor.

*Notice a "Browse" button at the bottom of the Export dialog box. By default, Fireworks puts the **images** folder into the same folder as the HTML — in this case, your **Work_In_Progress** folder. If you were using Fireworks to work on a site with an unusual folder hierarchy, you would click this button to specify the folder you need. For this project however, ignore this button.*

Export the HTML and Images

1. From the Main menu, select File>Export. The Export dialog box appears.

2. Save the file into your **Work_In_Progress** folder.

3. In the File Name field, assign any name you prefer. A suitable name for a home page such as this would be "index.htm".

4. In the Save as type field, keep the default choice of HTML and Images. Both file types are needed for a functioning Web page.

5. In the HTML field, choose Export HTML File.

6. In the Slices field, choose Export Slices.

7. Make sure the Include Areas Without Slices and Put Images in Subfolder check boxes are clicked. You only sliced certain areas. You need Fireworks to slice the remaining areas for you.

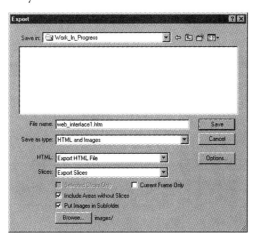

8. Click Save. As a test, open the HTML file directly from your **Work_In_Progress** folder. You should see the finished page with everything working properly. If something is not working, export the file again, and make sure the settings are entered as above.

In this project, you built a complete Web interface, using many of Fireworks' powerful features. You gained a lot of experience using the Live Effects panel and the Properties panel. With practice, you will soon be able to create sophisticated interfaces of your own in Fireworks.

Even though Fireworks is the most comprehensive Web design solution currently available, and is quite up to the task of building a complete Web site, it's still only part of the equation for a Web designer. You may have noticed that all of your text was in the form of graphics. For HTML text, it's best to use an HTML editor, such as Dreamweaver. In a more realistic scenario, you would be working with Fireworks and Dreamweaver open at the same time, toggling between the two programs.

There is a lot of overlap in functionality between these two applications. Dreamweaver, similar to Fireworks, can write its own JavaScript code for rollovers and disjointed rollovers. Due to this overlapping functionality, many Web designers use Fireworks to create the layout and export the image slices, but prefer to assemble the slices and add the HTML text in Dreamweaver (or another HTML editor). To use a cooking analogy, many designers prefer Fireworks to prepare and process the ingredients; then they rely on Dreamweaver to mix the ingredients and prepare the dish.

GLOSSARY

Achromatic

By definition, having no color; therefore, completely black or white or some shade of gray.

Acrobat

This program by Adobe Systems, Inc. allows the conversion (using Acrobat Distiller) of any document from any Macintosh or Windows application to PDF format, which retains the page layout, graphics, color, and typography of the original document. It is widely used for distributing documents online because it is independent of computer hardware. The only software needed is a copy of Acrobat Reader, which can be downloaded free.

Active Area

On a Web button, the area that when clicked, turns into a hand symbol and takes the user to a new Web page/site.

Adaptive Palette

A sampling of colors taken from an image, and used in a special compression process usually used to prepare images for the Web.

Algorithm

A specific sequence of mathematical steps to process data. A portion of a computer program that calculates a specific result.

Align

Line up objects according to Right, Left, Center, Bottom, Top, Horizontal, or Vertical positioning.

Alpha Channel

An 8-bit channel of data that provides additional graphic information, such as colors or masking. Alpha channels are found in some illustration or graphics programs, and are used in video production.

Animated GIF

File format used to create simple animations for the Web.

Anti-Aliasing

A graphics software feature that eliminates or softens the jaggedness of low-resolution curved edges.

ATM (Adobe Type Manager)

A utility that causes fonts to appear smooth on screen at any point size. It's also used to manage font libraries.

Auto Levels

Fireworks filter that makes the Levels adjustment decision for you.

Banding

A visible stair-stepping of shades in a gradient.

Behavior Handle

Part of a hotspot, the behavior handle allows you to assign attributes to the hotspot.

Bit (Binary Digit)

A computer's smallest unit of information. Bits can have only two values: 0 or 1. This can represent the black and white (1-bit) pixel values in a line-art image. In combination with other bits, it can represent 16 tones or colors (4-bit), 256 tones or colors (8-bit), 16.8 million colors (24-bit), or a billion colors (30-bit).

Bit Depth

This defines the total number of colors possible in an image. Common bit depths are 8-bit, 16-bit, 24-bit.

Bitmap Image

An image constructed from individual dots or pixels set to a grid-like mosaic. Each pixel can be represented by more than one bit. A 1-bit image is black and white because each bit can have only two values (for example, 0 for white and 1 for black). For 256 colors, each pixel needs eight bits (2^8). A 24-bit image refers to an image with 24 bits per pixel (2^{24}), so it may contain as many as 16,777,216 colors. Because the file must contain information about the color and position of each pixel, the disk space needed for bitmap images is usually quite significant. Most digital photographs and screen captures are bitmap images.

Bitmapped

Forming an image by a grid of pixels. when viewed carefully, curved edges in a bitmap image will often be seen to have discrete steps because of the approximation of the curve by a finite number of pixels.

Bitmap Tools

Fireworks tools used when editing bitmap images. Include the marquee tools, lasso tools, Magic Wand tool, Pencil tool, Pen tool, Brush tool, Eraser tool, Blur, Sharpen, Dodge, Burn, and Smudge tools, Rubber Stamp tool, Eyedropper tool, Paint Bucket/Gradient tools.

Blend

See *Gradient*.

Blending Modes

The different types of blends that can be applied to an object. Include Normal, Screen, Lighten, Darken, and many more. Each mode has a unique way of blending the base color and blend color to arrive at the result color.

Brightness/Contrast Filter

Adjusts the brightness and/or contrast of an image. It affects the entire tonal range of an image (or selected portion of an image), from highlight to shadow. The Brightness/Contrast filter is best used in situations that require only minor adjustments.

Burn

1. To expose an image onto a plate. 2. To make copies of ROM chips or CD-ROMs. 3. To darken a specific portion of an image.

Button

When created in Fireworks, a button on a Web page is actually an image that contains a link that is defined by HTML, and may often include associated JavaScript to handle Up, Over, and Over while Down states.

Button Editor

Very powerful Fireworks tool that allows you to generate complex Web buttons in a short period of time.

Button States

In a Web button, the Up, Over, Down, and Down While Over states define how the button will look when the user is not interacting with the button (Up state) hovers the mouse over the button (Over state), clicks the button (Down state), and hovers the mouse over the button while it is clicked (Down While Over state).

Byte

A unit of measure equal to eight bits (decimal 256) of digital information, sufficient to represent one text character. It is the standard unit measure of file size.

Canvas

The area of the Document window where development takes place. This is where you draw your objects using the Fireworks vector and bitmap tools.

Cloning

Duplication of pixels from one part of an image to another using the Rubber Stamp tool.

Closed Path

A path that is complete and allows for a fill to be applied.

Color Cast

The modification of a hue by the addition of a trace of another hue, such as yellowish green, or pinkish blue. Normally, an unwanted effect that can be corrected.

Color Look-Up Table

The palette of colors used in an image.

Color Model

A system for describing color, such as RGB, HLS, CIE L*a*b, or CMYK.

Color Palette

The colors that can be used in the document. For the Web, the most frequently used color palette is the Web-safe color palette, containing only those colors that will display accurately on both Macintosh and Windows systems.

Color Picker

A function within a graphics application that assists in selecting a color.

Color Tools

Settings used to change or modify the color in an image. Include the Stroke Color box, Fill Color box, Swap Stroke/Fill Color box, No Stroke/Fill, Set Default Stroke/Fill Color box.

Compression

A digital technique used to reduce the size of a file by analyzing occurrences of similar data. Compressed files occupy less physical space, and their use improves digital transmission speeds. Compression can sometimes result in a loss of image quality and/or resolution.

Contrast

The relationship between the dark and light areas of an image.

Copyright

Ownership of a work by the originator, such as an author, publisher, artist, or photographer. The right of copyright permits the originator of material to prevent its use without express permission or acknowledgment of the originator. Copyright may be sold, transferred, or given up contractually.

Curves Filter

Offers the most precise adjustment of any of the Fireworks bitmap filters. The Curves filter is similar to the Levels filter, with two distinct differences: Curves allows you to adjust any color along the entire color range; Curves offers more control than Levels.

Default

A specification for a mode of computer operation that operates if no other is selected. The default font size might be 12 point, or a default color for an object might be white with a black border.

Digital

The use of a series of discrete electronic pulses to represent data. In digital imaging systems, 256 steps (8 bits, or 1 byte) are normally used to characterize the gray scale or the properties of one color.

Digital Camera

A camera which produces images directly into an electronic file format for transfer to a computer.

Dingbat

A font character that displays a picture instead of a letter, number, or punctuation mark. There are entire font families of pictographic dingbats; the most commonly used dingbat font is Zapf Dingbats. There are dingbats for everything from the little airplanes used to represent airports on a map, to telephones, fish, stars, and balloons.

Disjointed Rollover

When one Web button is hovered over or clicked, another object changes its state.

Dithering

A technique used in images where a color is represented using dots of two different colors displayed or printed very close together. Dithering is often used to compress digital images, in special screening algorithms, and to produce higher quality output on low-end color printers.

Docking

A panel that is in a fixed position on the screen.

Document Window

Conveniently displays a variety of information about the document in use. Allows the user to see a preview of an image, as well as 2-Up and 4-Up views to compare optimization settings.

DPI (Dots Per Inch)

The measurement of resolution for page printers, phototypesetting machines, and graphics screens. Currently graphics screens use resolutions of 60 to 100 dpi, standard desktop laser printers work at 600 dpi, and imagesetters operate at more than 1,500 dpi.

Drag and Drop

One method of copying a file from one area (or application) to another. Simply select the object, and then use the cursor to drag it to the desired location, and drop it into place by releasing the cursor.

Draw Program

Applications that are used to create vector images.

Drop Shadow

A duplicate of a graphic element or type placed behind and slightly offset from it, giving the effect of a shadow.

EPS (Encapsulated PostScript)

Acronym for file format used to transfer PostScript data within compatible applications. An EPS file normally contains a small preview image that displays in position within a mechanical or used by another program. EPS files can contain text, vector artwork, and images.

Export

To save a file generated in one application in a format that is readable in another application.

Extension

A modular software program that extends or expands the functions of a larger program.

Fade In and Fade Out

In animation, a type of transition that slowly brings the action into view at the beginning of a scene, and then slowly dissolves the action from view until it is no longer visible at the end of a scene.

Faux

When creating type, Fireworks allows you to artificially make letters bold or italic. This is called "faux bold" and "faux italic." You should always use real bold and italic when they are available.

File Format

Methods of compression that also determine the bit depth of the image.

Fill

1. To add a tone or color to the area inside a closed object in a graphic illustration program. 2. The color of the inside area of a closed path.

Filter

In image-editing applications, a small program that creates a special effect or performs some other function within an image.

Flash

A popular Macromedia program that generates movies for viewing on the Web.

Flash Player

The "helper" program that is required to view Flash movies.

Flat Color

Color that lacks contrast or tonal variation. Also, flat tint.

Floating

A panel that is not docked, and can move freely about the screen.

Font

A font is the complete collection of all the characters (numbers, uppercase and lowercase letters and, in some cases, small caps and symbols) of a given typeface in a specific style; for example, Helvetica Bold.

Frame-By-Frame Animation

In animation, each frame is drawn separately, and is slightly different from the frame before it. When viewed at sufficient frame rate (speed), the illusion of motion is created. Without motion, there would be no animation; you would simply have a series of still images.

GASP

Acronym for Graphic Arts Service Provider, a firm that provides a range of services somewhere on the continuum from design to fulfillment.

Gigabyte (G)

One billion (1,073,741,824) bytes or 1,048,576 kilobytes.

Global Preferences

Preference settings which affect all newly created files within an application

Gradient

An area in which colors (or shades of gray, or the same color) are blended to create a gradual change from one to the other. Also known as blends, gradations, and graduated fills.

Graphics Interface File (GIF)

A CompuServe graphics file format that is used widely for graphic elements in Web pages.

Grayscale

1. An image composed in grays ranging from black to white, usually using 256 different tones of gray. 2. A tint ramp used to measure and control the accuracy of screen percentages on press. 3. An accessory used to define neutral density in a photographic image.

Greeking

1. A software technique where areas of gray are used to simulate lines of text below a certain point size. 2. Nonsense text use to define a layout before copy is available.

Grid

A division of a page by horizontal and vertical guides into areas where text or graphics may be accurately placed.

Group

To collect graphic elements so an operation may be simultaneously applied to all of them.

GUI

Acronym for Graphical User Interface, the basis of the Macintosh and Windows operating systems.

Guides

Guides are used for the layout and alignment of objects.

Hand Tool

A tool that allows you to pan around and view different areas of the document.

Highlights

The lightest areas in a photograph or illustration.

Histogram

Shows the distribution of the values of your image, ranging from black (left side) to white (right side).

Hotspots

In an image map or Web button, the areas that are linked to different Web pages.

Hue

The wavelength of light of a color in its purest state (without adding white or black).

Hue/Saturation Filter

Adjusts an image's hue (shade) and its saturation (intensity). It can also adjust the lightness and darkness of an image.

Hyperlink

An HTML tag directs the computer to a different Anchor or URL (Universal Resource Locator). The linked data may be on the same page, or on a computer anywhere in the world.

HyperText Markup Language (HTML)

The language, written in plain (ASCII) text using simple tags, that is used to create Web pages, and which Web browsers are designed to read and display. HTML focuses more on the logical structure of a page than its appearance.

Image Map

An element on a Web page that contains many links, each to a different Web page/site.

Image Slicing

Technique that allows the user to cut an image into pieces (slices). Each slice can be saved with its own unique settings to allow for quicker download time, to add text to a portion of an image, or to include rollover effects.

Import

To bring a file generated within one application into another application.

Index Transparency

Sets a particular color (usually white) to transparent.

Indexed Color Image

An image which uses a limited, predetermined number of colors; often used in Web images. See *GIF*.

Instance

Copy of a symbol. When a symbol is updated, every instance of the symbol in the document is also updated.

Intensity

Synonym for degree of color saturation.

Interlaced GIF

A file format that allows an image to download a little bit at a time, allowing the user to get a preview of the graphic before it is completed downloaded to the user's system.

Jaggies

Visible steps in the curved edge of a graphic or text character that result from enlarging a bitmapped image.

JPG or JPEG

A compression algorithm that reduces the file size of bitmapped images, named for the Joint Photographic Experts Group; JPEG is a "lossy" compression method, and image quality will be reduced in direct proportion to the amount of compression.

Kerning

Moving a pair of letters closer together or farther apart, to achieve a better fit or appearance.

Keyframe

The important frames in an animation, usually at the start and end of a scene of action.

Kilobyte (K, KB)

1,024 (210) bytes, the nearest binary equivalent to decimal 1,000 bytes. Abbreviated and referred to as K.

Layer

A function of graphics applications that allows elements to be isolated from each other, so a group of elements may be hidden from view, locked, reordered, or otherwise manipulated as a unit, without affecting other elements on the page.

Leading ("Ledding")

Space added between lines of type. Usually measured in points or fractions of points. Named after the strips of lead which used to be inserted between lines of metal type. In specifying type, lines of 12-pt. type separated by a 14-pt. space is abbreviated "12/14," or "twelve over fourteen."

Levels Filter

An excellent feature that allows you to adjust the tonal range of an image. With this filter, you can set the value of the highlights and shadows (an image's tonal range) without "throwing away" information, which can happen with the Brightness/Contrast filter. Use this filter to deepen the darkest shadows, and lighten the brightest highlights. Once these two extremes are set, you can adjust the midtones.

Library

In the computer world, a collection of files having a similar purpose or function.

Lightness

The property that distinguishes white from gray or black, and light from dark color tones on a surface.

Line Art

A drawing or piece of black-and-white artwork with no screens. Line art can be represented by a graphic file having only 1-bit resolution.

Link

A bit of Hypertext Markup Language (HTML) code that, when clicked, takes the viewer to a different Web location. Links are often found on image maps and Web buttons.

Live Effects

Effects that are applied to an object from the Fireworks Properties panel that can be changed at any time without negatively impacting the object.

Lossy

A data compression method characterized by the loss of some data (JPEG).

LPI

Lines per inch.

Macro

A set of keystrokes that is saved as a named computer file. When accessed, the keystrokes will be performed automatically. Macros are often used to perform repetitive tasks.

Masking

A technique that blocks an area of an image from view by hiding portions defined by a second image or shape.

Marching Ants

The dotted moving lines that surround a selection.

Matte Color

A color used during anti-aliasing that blends the foreground color to the background color, not to white.

Medium

A physical carrier of data such as a CD-ROM, video cassette, or floppy disk, or a carrier of electronic data such as fiber optic cable or electric wires.

Megabyte (M, MB)

A unit of measure of stored data equaling 1,024 kilobytes, or 1,048,576 bytes (1020).

Megahertz(mHz)

An analog signal frequency of one million cycles per second, or a data rate of one million bits per second. Used in specifying CPU speed.

Menu

A list of choices of functions, or of items such as fonts. In contemporary software design, there is often a fixed menu of basic functions at the top of the page that has pop-up menus associated with each of the fixed choices.

Metafile

A class of graphics that combines the characteristics of raster and vector graphics formats; not recommended for high-quality output.

Midtones or Middletones

The tonal range between highlights and shadows.

Monochrome

An image or computer monitor in which all information is represented in black and white, or with a range of grays.

Montage

A single image formed by assembling or compositing several images.

Mouse-Out Event

What happens to the Web button when the user moves the mouse away from/off of the button.

Mouse-Over Event

What happens to the Web button when the user hovers the mouse over the button.

Neutral

Absence of hue, such as white, gray, or black.

Noise

Unwanted signals or data that may reduce the quality of the output.

Object-Oriented Art

Vector-based artwork composed of separate elements or shapes described mathematically rather than by speci-fying the color and position of every point. This contrasts to bitmap images, composed of individual pixels.

Offset

In graphics manipulation, to move a copy or clone of an image slightly to the side and/or back; used for a drop-shadow effect.

Onion Skinning

Derived from traditional cel animation. Each frame was drawn on thin tracing paper, making it possible to see several frames of the animation at one time. This technique provided an excellent way to ensure proper timing of the movement in the animation.

Opacity

1. The degree to which paper will show print through it. 2. Settings in certain graphics applications that allow images or text below the object whose opacity has been adjusted, to show through.

Open Path

A path that is not closed. An open path cannot contain a fill; only closed paths can contain fill.

Optimize Panel

Part of the Fireworks interface where you can balance the quality and download settings to achieve a happy medium between quality and download speed.

Output Device

Any hardware equipment, such as a monitor, laser printer, or imagesetter, that depicts text or graphics created on a computer.

Overlay

1. A transparent sheet used in the preparation of multicolor mechanical artwork showing the color breakdown. 2. A blue or green overlay allows you to distinguish when you are editing a slice or a hotspot.

Paint Program

Applications that are used to create raster images.

Panel

A term that is used interchangeably with "palette." A panel allows you to set certain attributes for an image or document, depending on the panel in use. In Fireworks, panels include the History, Color, Info, Frames, Layers, Behavior, Optimize, Styles, URL, Library, Assets, Project Log, Answers, Properties panel, and more.

Path

The outer area of an image that is defined by a series of points and line segments.

PDF (Portable Document Format)

Developed by Adobe Systems, Inc. (and read by Adobe Acrobat Reader), this format has become a de facto standard for document transfer across platforms.

Perspective

The effect of distance in an image achieved by aligning the edges of elements with imaginary lines directed toward one to three "vanishing points" on the horizon.

PICT/PICT2

A common format for defining bitmapped images on the Macintosh. The more recent PICT2 format supports 24-bit color.

Pixel

Abbreviation for picture element, one of the tiny rectangular areas generated by a computer or output device to constitute images.

Pixelated

When a raster image is scaled up, a viewer can actually see the individual pixels that comprise the image. This is considered a negative effect. Also referred to as degradation of the quality of the image.

PNG

Fireworks' native file format. Stands for Portable Network Graphic.

Point Handle

A line appearing from a point that allows that point to be modified, and the curve of a line segment to be changed.

Pop-Up Menu

Standard on many Web sites, these menus offer additional options to menu items.

PostScript

1. A page description language developed by Adobe Systems, Inc. that describes type and/or images and their positional relationships on the page.
2. A computer programming language.

PPI

Pixels per inch; used to denote the resolution of an image. Also known as DPI or dots per inch.

Preload

When the button states are loaded before the rest of the page.

Primary Colors

Colors that can be used to generate secondary colors. For the additive system (i.e., a computer monitor), these colors are red, green, and blue. For the subtractive system (i.e., the printing process), these colors are yellow, magenta, and cyan.

Properties Panel

Also referred to as the Properties Inspector, this important panel allows the user to view many important aspects of the document, as well as change the document's settings at any time. This panel is usually open and accessible at all times during development.

RAM

Random Access Memory, the "working" memory of a computer, that holds files in process. Files in RAM are lost when the computer is turned off, whereas files stored on the hard drive or floppy disks remain intact and available.

Raster Graphic

A bitmapped representation of graphic data. A class of graphics created and organized in a rectangular array of bitmaps. Often created by paint software, fax machines, or scanners for display and printing.

Rasterize

The process of converting digital information into pixels at the resolution of the output device. For example, the process used by an imagesetter to translate PostScript files before they are imaged to film or paper.

Reflective Art

Artwork that is opaque, as opposed to transparent, that can be scanned for input to a computer.

Resolution

The density of graphic information expressed in dots per inch (dpi) or pixels per inch (ppi).

Retouching

Making selective manual or electronic corrections to images.

Reverse Out

To reproduce an object as white, or paper, within a solid background, such as white letters in a black rectangle.

RGB

Acronym for red, green, blue, the colors of projected light from a computer monitor that, when combined, simulate a subset of the visual spectrum. Also refers to the color model of most digital artwork.

Rollover Image

An image that changes its appearance when the user places the mouse over the image.

ROM

Read Only Memory, a semiconductor chip in the computer that retains startup information for use the next time the computer is turned on.

Roundtip

Ability to virtually use two applications at one time. You can select a Dreamweaver document from the Fireworks interface and edit it without having to launch Dreamweaver.

RTF

Rich Text Format, a text format that retains formatting information lost in pure ASCII text.

Rulers

Rulers measure your document, and measure objects that are placed on the document.

Saturation

The intensity or purity of a particular color; a color with no saturation is gray.

Scale

To reduce or enlarge the amount of space an image will occupy by multiplying the data by a scale factor. Scaling can be proportional or in one dimension only.

Scanner

A device that electronically digitizes images point-by-point through circuits that can correct color, manipulate tones, and enhance detail. Color scanners usually produce a minimum of 24 bits for each pixel, with 8 bits each for red, green, and blue.

Select Tools

Tools used to make general selections, including the Pointer tool, Subselection tool, Select Behind tool, Skew, Rotate, and Distort tools, and Crop and Export Area tools.

Shape Layer

A special vector layer is created whenever the special shape tools are used.

Shape Tools

These vector-based tools include the Rectangle, Rounded Rectangle, Ellipse, Polygon, Line, and Custom Shape tools. They allow you to create and edit vector shapes in Photoshop.

Sharpness

The subjective impression of the density difference between two tones at their boundary, interpreted as fineness of detail.

Silhouette

To remove part of the background of a photograph or illustration, leaving only the desired portion.

Slice Tool

Allows you to create and edit user-defined slices of an image for creation of Web graphics.

Smoothing

An export option that slightly blurs the image. Used to reduce file size.

Snap-To (Guides or Rulers)

A feature in page-layout programs that drives objects to line up with guides or margins if they are within a pixel range that can be set. This eliminates the need for precise, manual placement of an object with the mouse.

Spell Checker

Utility that automatically checks for spelling errors in your document. Suggests correct spelling for misspelled words.

Stacking Order

In the Layers panel, the order in which the layers appear. Layers at the top of the stacking order hide the layers below it. The layer at the bottom of the stacking order is below all other layers and objects in the document.

Static Navigation Bar

A group of Web buttons that do not have any special effects, such as rollovers, applied to them.

Stroke

The outer area of an image (the outline).

Styles

Preset effects that can be applied to any object or text element.

Symbol

A reusable element that is stored in the Library panel. Could be a graphic symbol, animation symbol, or button symbol.

Tagged Image File Format (TIFF)

A common format for use with scanned or computer-generated bitmapped images.

Text Editor Window

Fireworks tool that allows you to set the parameters for text elements in your document.

Tools Panel

This area reveals the tools available for use.

Tracking

Adjusting the spacing of letters in a line of text to achieve proper justification or general appearance.

Transparency

Ability to see through a color to other objects below it; 100% transparent cannot be seen (invisible on screen); 0% transparent is completely opaque (cannot see through it at all).

TrueType

An outline font format used in both Macintosh and Windows systems that can be used both on the screen and on a printer.

Tweening

In animation, the designer draws the important frames (See keyframes) in the animation at the start and finish of a scene, and Fireworks draws all of the other frames in between. This is an excellent time-saving feature for animation artists.

Type Family

A set of typefaces created from the same basic design but in different weights, such as bold, light, italic, book, and heavy.

Unsharp Masking

A digital technique performed after scanning that locates the edge between sections of differing lightness and alters the values of the adjoining pixels to exaggerate the difference across the edge, thereby increasing edge contrast.

Vector Graphic/Image

Graphics defined using coordinate points, and mathematically-drawn lines and curves, which may be freely scaled and rotated without image degradation in the final output. Fonts (such as PostScript and TrueType), and illustrations from drawing applications are common examples of vector objects.

Vector Tools

Tools used to manipulate vector graphics. Include the Line tool, Text tool, Knife tool, Rectangle/Rounded Rectangle tools, Ellipse tool, Freeform tool, and Path Scrubber tools.

Vignette

An illustration in which the background gradually fades into the paper; that is, without a definite edge or border.

Web Tools

Tools that are used to manipulate objects that are destined for use on the Web. Include the Rectangle/Circle/Polygon Hotspot tools, Slice/Polygon Slice tools, Show/Hide Hotspot and Slices tools.

White Space

Areas on the page which contain no images or type. Proper use of white space is critical to a well-balanced design.

Wizard

A utility attached to an application or operating system that aids you in setting up a piece of hardware, software, or document.

WYSIWYG

An acronym for "What You See Is What You Get," (pronounced "wizzywig") meaning that what you see on your computer screen bears a strong resemblance to what the finished job will look like.

XHTML

eXtensible HTML. The most recent release of HTML.

Zoom In/Zoom Out

To increase the magnification on a specific area of an image is called "zooming in." To decrease the magnification on an image is called "zooming out.

A

active area tab 250
adaptive color palette 20–22
add color 69
add color to transparency 70
adjusting color 166–171
  auto levels 171
  brightness/contrast 166–167, 170
  curves 167–168
  hue/saturation 168
  invert 169
  levels 170
Adobe GoLive 19, 232
Adobe Illustrator 8, 19
Adobe Photoshop 8, 19, 26, 146, 194
  exporting to 146
  importing 146
Alien Skin Eye Candy 4000 174–175
Alien Skin Splat LE 176
align panel 110
aligning shapes 110–113
  bottom 112
  center horizontal 112
  center vertical 111
  distribute heights 113–114
  distribute widths 112
  left align 110
  right 111
  top 111
altering paths 102–105
  anti-alias fill 105
  expand stroke 103
  feather fill 105
  hard fill 104
  inset path 104
  simplify 102–103
alternate text 225–227, 252
animated GIFs 16, 208–220
animation 208–210
animation symbols 32, 214
answers panel 33
anti-aliasing 10, 70, 104, 129–130, 155
  crisp anti-alias 129
  no anti-alias 129
  smooth anti-alias 130
  strong anti-alias 130
ASCII 119
attaching text to paths 136–140
  detaching 138
  direction 138
  orientation 137
  position 137

auto crop 219
auto difference 220
auto kern 123
auto levels 171
auto-sizing text blocks 128

B

base color 199
basic shapes 54–60
before and after 211
behavior handle 223
behaviors panel 31
bit depth 9, 13, 16, 67
bitmap mode 29
bitmap tools 36–37
  blur 36
  brush 36
  burn 36
  dodge 36
  eraser 36
  eyedropper 37
  gradient 37
  lasso 36
  magic wand 36
  marquee 36
  oval marquee 36
  paint bucket 37
  pencil 36
  polygon lasso 36
  rubber stamp 37
  sharpen 36
  smudge 36
bitmaps 144–164
blend color 130
blending modes 130–136, 198–199
blur 171–172
  blur more 171
  blur radius 172
  gaussian blur 172
blur tool 36, 177
brightness/contrast 166–167, 170
brush tool 36, 155
burn tool 36, 177
button editor 246–255
button symbols 32
buttons
  editing 254
  properties 249–252
  states 246, 248–251
  symbols 246–247, 252
  updating 254

C

check spelling 134
circle hotspot tool 38, 222
color 131, 199
color depth 13, 67–69
color look-up table 9, 13, 20
color mixer panel 30
color palettes 20–22, 30–31, 67
  adaptive 256 22
  custom 22
  web 216 21
  WebSnap 128 22
  WebSnap 256 21
color picker 79, 156
color tools 38
  fill color box 38
  no stroke or fill 38
  set default stroke/fill colors 38
  stroke color box 38
  swap stroke/fill 38
combining paths 98–102
  crop 100–101
  intersect 100
  join 99
  punch 100
  split 99
  union 99
commands menu 27
complex shapes 60–67
compression 160
constrain proportions 97
convert to alpha 172
convert to symbol 247
converting text to paths 135–136
creating a new document 17–19
crip anti-alias 129
crop path 100–101
crop tool 36, 152
curves 167–168
custom color palette 22

D

darken 131, 199
defalt stroke/fill color 38
DHTML 246
difference 131, 199
digital cameras 9
disjointed rollovers 255–256
distort tool 36
document specific tab 227
document window 27–29
dodge tool 36, 177

drawing tools   155
   brush   155
   eraser   155
   gradient   156
   paint bucket   156
   pencil   155

E

edit color   68
edit menu   27
effects   85–93
   bevel   87
   emboss   87
   glow   87
   shadow   87
   styles   88–89
ellipse tool   37, 56
end caps   103
erase   131, 199
eraser tool   36, 155
expand stroke   103
export area tool   36
export options   218
   animation tab   219
   file tab   218
   options tab   218
export preview   218
export settings   31
export window   20–21
export wizard   220
exporting   19–24, 252
   Dreamweaver library items   233
   GIF   67–72
   HTML   226–229
   to other applications   232
eyedropper tool   37, 79, 153

F

fade in   216
fade out   216
file formats   15–16
file menu   27
File Transfer Protocol
   See FTP
fill color box   38, 79
fill options   79–80, 82, 122, 156
fills   78–85
   gradients   81–82
   patterns   80
   solids   79
   textures   81
filters menu   27
find and replace panel   32

find duplicate words   133
find edges   173
fixed-width text block   128
Flash Player   16
frame delay   219
frame-by-frame   208–210
frames panel   30, 209–210
free transform   94–95
freeform tool   37, 105–106
FTP   230
full-screen mode   40
full-screen with menus mode   40

G

GIF   13, 15, 20, 67, 69, 118, 144
gradient tool   37, 156
graphic interchange format
   See GIF
graphic symbols   32, 208, 213–214
grids
   editing properties of   45
   showing   44
   snapping to   45
grouping   113–114
guides
   creating   42
   editing properties of   43
   locking   43
   manipulating   43
   snapping to   44
   viewing   43

H

hand tool   39, 48, 50
help menu   27
helper applications   15
hide slices and hotspots   235
histogram   170
history panel   30–31
hotspot tools   222
   circle   222
   polygon   222, 235
   rectangle   222
   square   222
hotspots   31, 222–225
   properties   225
HTML   19, 222, 226
   comments   226
   setup   226
   tables   227
   updating   241
hue   131, 199
hue/saturation   168

I

ignore words with numbers   133
image maps   222–244
image retouching   166–192
images   8–24
   types   8–15
importing bitmaps   144–147
   copy and paste   145
   drag and drop   144
   import   145
   scanning   145
index transparency   69
info panel   31
interface   26–40
interlaced GIFs   16
interlacing   71
internet service provider
   See ISP
intersect path   100
invert   131, 169, 199
ISP   230

J

jaggies   9
JavaScript   246
join path   99
joint photographic experts group
   See JPEG
JPEG   16, 20, 67, 118, 144, 160–163
   progressive   161
   quality   161
   smoothing   161

K

keyframes   213
knife tool   37, 108

L

lasso tool   36, 148, 188
layer properties   198–200
layers   194–206
   collapsing   197
   creating   194
   deleting   198
   duplicating   194–195
   expanding   197
   hiding   196
   locking   197–198
   naming   195
   organizing   196
   selecting   195
   viewing   196

layers panel 30, 130, 194–198, 235
levels 170
libraries 208
library panel 32, 208, 213
lighten 131, 199
line art 15
line tool 37, 60
live effects 166, 173
lock color 68
looping 219
lossless compression 15
lossy compression 15, 161
luminosity 131, 199

M

Macintosh 11, 21
Macromedia Director 19
Macromedia Dreamweaver 19, 26, 232, 252
Macromedia Flash 16–19, 26
Macromedia FreeHand 8, 19
magic wand tools 36, 152, 188
making selections 148
manipulating guides 43
manipulating shapes 93–109
marquee tool 36, 148, 188
matte color 70
Microsoft FrontPage 19, 232
miter limit 103–104
modify menu 27
modifying selections 154
mouse-over event 248
multi-frame editing 211
multi-layer editing 198
multiply 131, 199

N

navigation bars 246–266
no anti-alias 129

O

onion skinning 210–213
opacity 130, 200
open paths 61
optimize panel 20, 31, 67, 69, 160
optimize to size wizard 220
optimized 19
options 38–39
original 27
oval marquee tool 36, 148

P

page preview 29
paint bucket tool 37, 156
PaintShop Pro 8
panels 30–34
    customizing layout 34
    default layout 34–35
    docking 33
    floating 33
paragraph settings 126–128
    indent 126
    live effects 128
    space after 127
    space preceding 127
    styles 128
path scrubber tool 37, 107–110
paths 61
pencil tool 36, 155
pen tool 37, 61–62, 66
personal dictionary 133
pixels 8–10
plug-ins 15
PNG 15, 69, 118, 144
point handle 61
pointer tool 35, 74
polygon hotspot tool 38, 222, 235
polygon lasso tool 36, 148
polygon slice tool 38, 235
polygon tool 37, 56–62
pop-up menus 27, 246–266
    advanced tab 262–263
    appearance tab 261–262
    content tab 260
    position tab 263–264
portable network graphics
    See PNG
preview 27, 67
project log panel 32
properties panel 26, 34–35, 56, 75, 76, 77, 81, 86, 105, 107, 120, 123, 125, 129, 130, 138, 155, 156, 166, 250
PSD format 146
punch path 100

Q

quick export 19
QuickTime Player 15

R

range kerning 123
raster images 8–13, 54
rectangle hotspot tool 38, 222

rectangle tool 37, 55
redraw path tool 37, 66
remove color from transparency 70
reshape area tool 37, 106–107
resolution 9, 10–12, 17
result color 130, 199
reverse direction 139
rich text format
    See RTF
rollovers 234
rotate around path 137
rounded rectangle tool 37, 55–56
roundtrip feature 146
RTF 119
rubber stamp tool 37, 178
rulers
    viewing 41

S

saturation 131, 199
scale attributes 97
scale tool 36
scanners 9
screen 131, 199
screen resolution 11
select behind tool 35, 74–75
select menu 27
select tools 35–36
    crop 36
    distort 36
    export area 36
    pointer 35
    scale 36
    select behind 35
    skew 36
    subselection 36
select transparent color 70
set magnification 29
shape adjustment tools 105–107
sharpen 173–174
    sharpen more 174
    unsharp mask 174
sharpen tool 36, 177
show all frames 211
show/hide slices and hotspots 38
show next frame 211
single-layer editing 198
skew horizontal 137
skew tool 36
skew vertical 137
slice tools 38, 235

slices   31, 234–243
  options   238
  rollovers   240
smooth anti-alias   130
smudge tool   36, 177
spell checker   133–134
spelling setup   133
split path   99
square hotspot tool   222
stacking order   114–116, 196
  bring forward   115
  bring to front   114
  send backward   115
  send to back   115–116
standard screen mode   39
static navigation bar   222
stretch   137
stroke color box   38
stroke options   122
strokes   75–78
  categories   76–77
  edge   76
  position   77–78
  size   75–76
  texture   78
strong anti-alias   130
styles   88
  export   89
  import   89
  save as   88
styles panel   31
subselection tool   36, 75
swap stroke/fill   38
swatches panel   30
symbol properties   213

T

table tab   227
tables   227
target   225, 252
target area   196
target size   220
text block settings   128–129
  auto-sizing   128
  fixed-width   128
  height   129
  location   129
  width   129
text editor   118
tcxt mcnu   27

text offset   138
text properties   119–133
text tool   37, 118–119
thumbnail options   197
tint   131, 199
tools panel   35–39, 54
touch-up tools   177–191
  blur   177
  burn   177
  dodge   177
  rubber stamp   178
  sharpen   177
  smudge   177
touch-ups   176–188
transforming objects   94–98
  distort   96
  flip   98
  numeric   97
  rotate   97–98
  scale   96
  skew   96
transparency   69–70, 130, 172, 218
tweening   208, 213–218
typographic settings   122–126
  alignment   124–125
  fill   122
  font   119–120
  horizontal scale   126
  kerning   123
  leading   123–124
  orientation   125
  size   120–121
  stroke   122
  style   121

U

ungrouping   113
union   99
URL panel   32

V

vector images   14–15
vector mode   29
vector object manipulation   74–116
vector path tool   37, 65
vector shapes   54–72
vector tools   37
  ellipse   37, 56
  freeform   37, 105–106
  knife   37, 108

  line   37, 60
  path scrubber   37, 107–110
  pen   37, 61–62, 66
  polygon   37, 56–62
  rectangle   37, 55
  redraw path   37, 66
  reshape area   37, 106-107
  rounded rectangle   37, 55–56
  text   37, 118–119
  vector path   37, 65
vectors
  fills   78–85
  live effects   85–93
  organization   110–115
  selecting   74–75
  strokes   75–78
  styles   85–93
view menu   27
viewing a web page   230–231
views   38–39, 39–41
  full-screen mode   39
  full-screen with menus mode   39
  standard screen mode   38
vignettes   188

W

WBMP   144
web 216 color   21
web layer   200, 235
WebSnap 128 color palette   22
WebSnap 256 color palette   21
web tools   38
  circle hotspot   38
  polygon hotspot   38
  polygon slice   38
  rectangle hotspot   38
  show/hide slices and hotspots   38
  slice   38
web-safe color   68
window menu   27
Windows   11, 21
world wide web   15–20
World Wide Web Consortium   232
WYSIWYG   238

X

XHTML   233

Z

zoom tool   39, 48–52

NOTES